DASHER

THE ROOTS AND THE RISING OF JIMMY CARTER

JAMES WOOTEN

SUMMIT BOOKS

NEW YORK

LIBRARY OF CONGRESS CATALOGING IN PUBLICATION DATA

WOOTEN, JAMES T
 DASHER: THE ROOTS AND THE RISING OF JIMMY CARTER.

 1. CARTER, JIMMY, 1924– 2. PRESIDENTS—UNITED
STATES—BIOGRAPHY. 3. PRESIDENTS—UNITED STATES—
ELECTION—1976. 4. SOUTHERN STATES—POLITICS AND
GOVERNMENT—1951– I. TITLE.
E872.W66   973.926′092′4 [B]   77-25272

ISBN 0-671-40004-5

Permission to reprint material from the following is grate-
fully acknowledged:

Why Not the Best? by Jimmy Carter. Copyright © 1975 by
Broadman Press. All rights reserved. Reprinted by permission of Broadman Press, Nashville, Tennessee.

Let Us Now Praise Famous Men by James Agee and
Walker Evans. Copyright © renewed 1969 by Mia Fritsch
Agee. Reprinted by permission of Houghton Mifflin Com-
pany, Boston, Mass.

ACKNOWLEDGMENTS

The assistance, encouragement and support that accompanied this book from concept to completion came from various quarters, not all of them compatible. Numerous journalists—my colleagues assigned to Jimmy Carter's remarkable campaign, like Ed Bradley, Ed Rabel, Charles Mohr, Eleanor Randolph, Curtis Willkie and Judy Woodruff, and new and old journalistic friends in Washington—were enormously helpful. Many members of the Carter family, including his son Chip and several of his old neighbors and acquaintances, patiently contributed their time and memories. Similarly, there was considerable cooperation from people on President Carter's staff, both before and after the election. *The New York Times,* of which I am an employee, was amazingly tolerant of the considerable energies I devoted to this enterprise which might otherwise have been spent in the newspaper's behalf. To all those who provided information, explanation, access and opportunity, I am deeply thankful.

There are others, though, who should be more specifically noted, for their contributions were both singular and of quite special value: Jules Witcover, of the *Washington Star,* who treated me as an equal, one of the few times in his journalistic career his judgment should have been questioned; Russell Baker, of *The New York Times*, who prodded me merely by example to try to do something right for a change; Gloria Spann, President Carter's sister, who was extraordinarily candid and cordial, and her husband, Walter, a paragon of Southern warmth, gentleness and hospitality; Rosalynn Carter, who made arrangements during her busy campaign schedule to talk awhile; Jody Powell, Hamilton Jordan, Rex Granum, Betty Rainwater, Barry Jagoda, Maxie Wells, Jim King, Caroline Shields and Susan Clough, of the President's staff, who all spent considerable amounts of time helping me try to understand their boss. I owe them all a great deal, but I am particularly indebted to Greg Schneiders, also of Mr. Carter's campaign and White House staff, and his wife, Marie, for a growing friendship that has always included productive guidance and criticism.

Seven others, however, merit my special thanks. Lillian Carter, beleaguered by the demands of her son's success, nevertheless carved several rich hours from her schedule for interviews, lunches, dinners and plain old arguments. It would have been virtually impossible to have even considered such a book as this without her help. Charles and Camille Morgan, my good old friends from Atlanta who beat Jimmy Carter to Washington, D.C., by a couple of years, were always a continuing source of strength, insights, and at certain times in my life, of solace. And for Dixon Preston's friendship, felt over all those miles from Georgia, I am deeply grateful. I am also most thankful that, as the world happened to turn, my own life was enriched professionally and personally by James Silberman, a man whose love of both publishing and writing seems a rare and wonderful chemistry, and by Roberta Pryor, an agent of remarkable skill and integrity.

Finally, I am at a loss as to how to express my genuine gratitude to David Halberstam, who was my friend before I started this book and whose inestimable contributions during the course of its progress have earned him a place in my book even higher than Clayton P. Delaney, though slightly lower than Patience O'Connor.

JAMES WOOTEN

For J.R. and Clara Wooten,
loving parents,
constant friends,
damned good people

Early on one frosty morning back in January of 1976, a sleek little corporate jet paused hesitantly at the end of a runway on the outskirts of Oklahoma City, its wing lights pulsating in the gray darkness, its twin engines screaming a strident protest against the prairie's peaceful silence—and suddenly, with a thunderous acceleration, it lurched into its takeoff roll. Inside, John Chipps, a jovial but intensely conscientious agent of the United States Secret Service, began muttering into his two-way radio. "Uh, base. Come in, base. This is Dasher," he said. "Uh, Dasher to base. Come in, please. Over." The static from the receiver stuttered through the tiny cabin as the plane abruptly lifted its needle nose and climbed steeply into the dawn.

"Uh, roger, Dasher, this is base. Go ahead," came the reply.

"Uh, roger, base, this is Dasher. I read you," Chipps answered, rotating his wrist and squinting at his watch. "We have a wheels-up on Dasher at oh six hundred. Do you copy?"

Another burst of static was followed by the same disembodied, singsong voice, pronouncing a crackling benediction on the speeding plane and its occupants. "Uh, that's a roger, Dasher, we do copy—and a good morning to you all."

The plane banked sharply, turning into the east and the sunrise. Chipps adjusted the pistol in his shoulder holster so that it would not dig into his side, leaned back in his seat, closed his eyes and was almost asleep when the sandy-haired man sitting just behind him reached forward and touched his shoulder.

"Mr. Chipps," the fellow said sternly. "I'm not sure I like being called 'Dasher.' " The agent turned toward the man uncertainly, about to explain that code names for all presidential candidates were chosen rather arbitrarily by some faceless gnome back in the Treasury Department in Washington. "But," said Jimmy Carter, his face exploding into an enormous grin, "it's a darn sight better than 'Peanuts.' "

I am very fond of truth,
but not at all of martyrdom.
　　　　　　　　—Voltaire,
　　LETTER TO D'ALEMBERT

EARLY, very early, on a January morning, deep in the bitter winter of 1977, a long black sedan pulled carefully into a parking space on Northwest Twenty-third Street near the Lincoln Memorial in Washington, D.C., and an old man crawled arthritically from the dark warmth of the rear seat into the dark cold of the dawn. His square face, creased by the deep furrows of his years, was the color of faded chocolate and his breath was visible in the frigid air—little silvery puffs of life that vanished as quickly as he blew them—as he reached back into the innards of the car for a well-worn Bible. He tucked it beneath his arm, rubbed his gloved hands together vigorously, wrapped and slapped himself in a lusty embrace against the cold and walked toward a little knot of people waiting at the base of the floodlit memorial. They were sipping coffee from steaming Styrofoam cups, and while they all seemed quite happy to see him, the old man greeted them with only a perfunctory grunt and started up the long, broad stairs, climbing as though in pain, bent beneath some invisible burden. When he finally reached the top, he stood motionless before the giant statue, dwarfed by its size, silhouetted against the white, white lights of its chamber. Reverently, he removed his ebony homburg, revealing a close-cropped skullcap of steel-woolish hair. He held the hat in front of him and bowed his head as though in prayer, and when he turned away a few moments later, tears were glinting in his large eyes. He paused at the top of the steps and gazed down the long mall, eastward past the frozen pool—a black mirror reflecting only the blackness of the early morning—beyond the great granite obelisk needling its way into the dawn, to the hulking dome of the United States Capitol, glowing pink in the distance, bathed by its own battery of floodlights. Then, haltingly, still bearing his unseen load, the old man descended the stairs to the small group of friends still waiting below.

"Going to be a great day, Reverend," one of them suggested cheerfully.

"Yes, sir, Daddy, it's going to be one fine day," another added, nearly chirping.

But the old man merely shivered and glanced up at the dark sky. "If it ever gets here," he growled.

"Aw, come on now, Reverend, let's see a smile," another of them teased gently as laughter spread around their tiny circle, but he still remained solemn and silent.

"Right on," shouted another. "Let's see those teeth, Daddy. They're not as flashy as his, but let's see them anyway." The old man was unmoved, his face impassive.

"Now, Reverend, don't you be like that," a young woman scolded. "This is no time to be down in the mouth. We're going to have a party today, all day long, so you just better get yourself in a party mood."

Her companion joined the cause. "That's right, Daddy," he said, breaking into a brief little dance. "We're fixing to celebrate, and I mean celebrate." The old man nodded and, in mock compliance with their demands, fixed a sad smile on his lips. He knew what they were trying to do. He fully understood their motives and appreciated them. After all, they were gathered there that morning for a sunrise service of hymns and prayers and readings from the Bible that would soon attract several thousand other people of like mind. It would be a liturgy of hope, focused on the various promises of their God, their government and their society, occasioned by the inauguration later that cold day of a new President of the United States; but although the old man was to play a principal role in the worship, he was neither emotionally nor psychologically prepared. He could not overcome the deep depression that had settled on him the moment he had emerged from the car. He had lived with it for some time, he knew, but it was always deepest when he was forced to address himself directly—as he was that morning—to the subject of hope. It hacked at him like a dull sword. Not only was he unable to overcome the sadness and the uncertainty within him, he was caught in the grip of its accompanying guilt. He was, after all, not really supposed to feel that way. He was, after all, a Christian clergyman.

At the very core of his creed was the broad faith that, whatever had happened before, the good will of the Deity he worshiped still moved progressively toward the complete and ultimate triumph of right. He had preached that so often from his own pulpit and from others, this theology steeped in hope; but more and more, as he grew older, he found himself unable to conceive of hope without simultaneously registering in his mind a certain futility he had never quite defined. Actually, he had never really tried to define it. It simply existed there within him, perched on a ledge in his soul, waiting to spring on him without warning. He had reached a point in his life at which he seemed utterly incapable of separating faith from doubt, hope from despair, creed from question. He could no longer be reminded of all the good promises—there had been so many of them in the years he had lived—without being reminded also of the meanness and madness that often murdered them. And there had been that in the years he had lived as well. He was neither senile nor neurotic, and he was, above all, far from heretical. He had simply lived long enough to come to grips with some basic facts about the life expectancy of promises, and it was hard for him to hope, very hard, even on such a day as that morning in January and even among such well-meaning friends, none of whom was about to give up on their chosen task.

"Now, come on, Daddy, what do you say?" one of them continued, ignoring the darkness of his mood. "Ain't this the day we finally get ourselves a President?"

Still, he was solemn. He stared down the mall again at the glowing Capitol in the distance and, as though in a trance, moved his eyes once more up the steps to the statue of Lincoln. Slowly, dubiously, he shook his head from side to side.

"Well, we'll see about that," mumbled Martin Luther King, Sr. "We'll see."

Not far from the Lincoln Memorial, in a warm bedroom on the second floor of an old mansion across the street from the White House, the man who had won the right to make the traditional promises that day was sitting in a comfortable overstuffed chair, studying what he meant to say a few hours later. He had been invited to the sunrise worship that morning, and, although he had told the old man he would be there, he had no intention of going and never had. He had learned over the years that his purposes were better served by the subjunctive than the declarative, and so he had said "perhaps" to the old man, knowing all along the answer was really "no." Still, nothing would come of it. The old man, after all, was considered his friend, and if that was not precisely the case—the man in the big chair had very few friends—that too was quite irrelevant. The old man had believed in him, and had worked in his behalf and had been of inestimable help at some rather desperate moments. The old man would know that on that morning there would be other demands on his time and he would understand, and if he did not, at least he would not mention it. The seated man glanced down at the copy of his inaugural address, opened across his lap. Bound in a slim, blue loose-leaf folder, it was typed error-free in the oversized letters used by script-writers for television news, a far cry from the oratorical assistance to which he was accustomed. There had been days, not many years before, when he had used little index cards on which he printed the key words that served as reminders to him of the components and the direction of the remarks he wanted to make. It had not always worked. There had been times, in fact, when it had failed miserably, and he had found himself lost in a sea of ideas—key words—washing around in his brain, and he would ramble and backtrack and seethe inside, well aware of how badly it was going. He had never really enjoyed making speeches, even though he recognized their value.

He often remembered, for example, a deliciously warm summer's night in rural Georgia in the early 1930s when his parents had allowed him to postpone his regular bedtime so that he could hear one of Franklin Roosevelt's fireside chats on their battery-powered radio, and although the precise date was always vague in his mind, he saw himself as no older than nine or ten—a slightly built, almost fragile, child with hair the color of straw and a sunburned face full of Huck Finn freckles—and he recalled that for years after that hot, heavily humid evening, even after his stern and stolidly conservative father had summarily dismissed the talk as so much New Deal twaddle, the resonant tones of the President of the United States, slicing crisply through the static from faraway Washington, would remain and endure for him as an oral symbol of authority and strength and leadership and hope, a force in his life that somehow he would never quite escape or outgrow.

But on that morning so many years later, as he sat in the big chair in the bedroom across the street from the White House, he was painfully aware that among the hundred million or so Americans who would hear his own words that day, there would not be one, young or old, who would respond automatically to his voice as a symbol of authority and strength and leadership and hope. Public speaking was something he could not do well, and he hated doing it most of the time for that very reason. He despised his own inability to master the art. Years before, he had enlisted the aid of an announcer from a little radio station near the tiny village where he lived, but although there seemed to him to be a marked improvement, it had not really made a great deal of difference. His public-speaking techniques were pitifully weak. He still plodded heavily on his own best lines. His voice still dropped like a wounded bird at the end of his phrases, frequently fading into total inaudibility; and without intending to do so, he still crowded his words together in indistinguishable masses, like hogs into a slaughter chute. He had tried so diligently to become better. He was a great believer in self-improvement—speed-reading, physical fitness, cultural blitzes of museums and theaters and opera halls—but try as mightily as he had, he knew that cool morning as he sat in the big chair with his inaugural address in his lap that no one would remember him as a man of great oratorical presence or power, and it bothered him.

It had been on his mind from the instant he had been awakened a few minutes before by a telephone call from the Army's Signal Corps switchboard. He had answered on the first ring and heard a male voice provide him with the time—five-thirty—and the weather forecast—clear but awfully cold, with the temperature in the upper teens and a brisk, north wind—and then ask if there were any calls to be placed for him. No, none, he had answered, returning the receiver to its cradle and slipping quietly from the large bed, careful not to awaken his wife.

They had grown up together in the same early-rising milieu of rural Georgia, but somehow she had never quite adjusted to such habits or accepted them as either virtuous or logical. She saw little merit at all in rising with or before the sun, and she was constantly amazed that anyone, including her husband, could spring so instantly and fully awake at that hour of the morning. Not that she was an indolent woman. On the contrary, she was disciplined and energetic and, like him, almost compulsively industrious—but only after she had come face to face with the inevitability of the day. He could leap into it like a paratrooper if he chose; she much preferred to leave her sleep behind in tiny increments, step by infinitesimal step, and then, having reluctantly escaped its wonderful grasp, to loll awhile against her pillow before finally accepting her fate. Over the years of their marriage, he had learned to tolerate her preference and while he often joked about it with her, he took great pleasure in indulging her whenever it suited his purposes. That January morning, it did. She had worked as hard as he to be where they were, in that warm bedroom across the street from the White House, and she had willingly, if not gladly, sacrificed the most beloved luxury of her life in the process. He would not need her for a while. She could sleep.

He could not. The speech was on his mind. He wanted to read it again and again, as many times as possible in the time that remained. He wanted to practice it, to hone it, to change it if he deemed necessary, even at that final hour, to make it say precisely what he wanted it to say. He wanted it to be remembered, as others had been remembered, for its content, if not for the style of its utterance. Still, even if the speech had not been pressing on him that morning, he would have found it most difficult to sleep much past his wake-up call. He had been getting up so early for so long that he doubted if he would ever be able to sleep late again. He could not even recall the last time he had. Like so many other human beings who achieve far beyond their peers, his great stores of raw physical energy and his careful stewardship of them had been as essential to his ambitions as intelligence and creativity. His self-discipline was rigid, his self-motivation pervasive. For more than two years, he had devoted himself like an indentured servant to a grinding, grueling canvass of America. It had taken him into every state and more than a half-million miles, back and forth across the country—always up with the sun or ahead of it, his socks and underwear drying on the shower-curtain rod in the bathroom of some motel room, then on to his first appointment and his second and his third and on and on and on into the afternoon and into the evening and into another unpleasant motel cubicle in some other city or town, with telephone calls until midnight and, once again, the nocturnal ritual of washing socks and shorts in the little lavatory and hanging them on the shower-curtain rod to dry—day after day, keeping every engagement scribbled into his bulging pocket calendar, shaking every hand in sight (including, once, a department-store mannequin), from Fairbanks to Miami Beach, from Waikiki to Bangor, in the snow and through the rain, in rented cars and chartered airplanes and commercial jets, elated, depressed, buoyed, exhausted, scared, nervous, sick, tired, bone-weary at times, but always moving on, on to the next stop, running, running, running, relentlessly, feverishly, for almost two solid years with a tenacious, ferocious, single-minded passion that stifled any self-indulgence except, of course, the supreme self-indulgence, his campaign.

One of his sisters, concerned for his physical and mental health, had asked him to ease up a bit, slow down and give his mind and body a chance to catch up, to rest and recuperate. "Honey," he had responded, "I can will myself to sleep until ten-thirty and get my ass beat, or I can will myself to get up at six o'clock and become the President of the United States."

That was precisely what he had almost accomplished by the time the telephone jangled that morning in the warm bedroom across the street from the White House. He was the President-elect, but in a few more hours, that title would be shortened by a word and a hyphen and he would be transformed, as by some magic potion poured from the Constitution of the United States, into one of the most important and powerful human beings on earth. It was what he had worked for so slavishly for so long. He had wanted it so much, probably more than anyone who had sought it before, and the very intensity of his lust for the office had often sustained him during the precipitous slips, dips and slides of his marathon pursuit, and now that it was within his reach, he wanted it more than ever. He could practically smell it, and he could hardly wait to begin. His wife could sleep. Washington could sleep. The whole country could sleep. He was awake, enormously alive and eager for what was his due. There was not a single dead cell in the man nor a milligram of uncertainty. He looked down at the opening sentence of his inaugural address. It had been his own idea to include it, his alone. He knew it was very good.

Nearly a year before, on one of his earliest trips to New England to press his campaign, seen then by most as a fool's errand, a friendly young man he met had introduced him to his son and he had reached down and taken the little boy's hand and said, "Hi, Bobby, my name's Jimmy Carter and I'm going to be your next President—and I'm going to be a wonderful President." Some who heard the remark considered it pompous, but although he was as prone to self-important inflations and exaggerations as any other man seeking public office, what he had told the little boy was simply an expression of the sort of jubilant optimism that had permeated his candidacy from the very moment it had begun. "I don't intend to lose," he had said again and again, as though intoning a mantra (even after two months as President, the same words would pop from his mouth in public, out of time and place but not out of character), and it soon became clear that, although his repeated self-assurances of victory were psychological crutches for him, they were also more. He believed them, by God, believed them when no one could or would or should, believed them fervently and passionately and probably more deeply than anyone who had ever had the temerity to tell himself that he really ought to be President of the United States.

Admittedly, it had been awkward for him at first to speak

of such a grand office in such personal terms, but the more often he had, the easier it had become. He was always careful to note, of course, how the Presidency he would surely win was for him a sobering prospect, how it prompted in him as much humility as pride—although he had never been particularly adept at the former—and how he sincerely believed that it called for as much somber reflection as celebration; but not once, not a single time in all those long months of telling himself and others that he was going to be the President of the United States, had he even suggested or hinted that he entertained any doubt about his adequacy for the office. "I'll be good," he had predicted more than a year before that January morning, long before it seemed even remotely possible that he would get the chance to prove it. "You wait and see," he had said, smiling the smile that would become his trademark. "I'll be damned good."

He would soon get his chance to prove it and he could hardly wait to begin. It had been the first thing he thought of that morning as he left his sleeping wife and the big, warm bed and, wearing only the jockey shorts in which he had slept, padded barefoot across the rich carpet to a table by the window. He pulled the chain on a small antique lamp. Its light was soft and narrowly focused, falling only on the table itself where lay the copy of his inaugural address. He had dropped to his knees beside the big chair and bowed his head, and when he had finished his prayers he had moved toward the center of the room, away from the furniture, seated himself on the rug and begun his morning sit-ups, his hands clasped tightly behind his head, elbows protruding on either side of his face—up, down, up, down, up, down, silently, easily, forcefully, with no visible strain.

Through diet and such exercises, he had managed to keep his weight consistently at just above 160 pounds, and on his five-foot, seven-inch frame, it seemed appropriate; but it also fostered the mistaken notion that he was a fragile man. He was small, but he was not delicate. His legs and arms were sinewy, lean and hard. He had the thick chest of a welterweight and a firm, flat abdomen that betrayed only the slightest traces of middle age. He did not smoke, except for a rare after-dinner cigar which he did not really enjoy, and he drank only sparingly, carefully—a couple of beers, perhaps, after tennis, or a light Scotch, for instance, in the evenings. He was fifty-two years old, bothered from time to time by hemorrhoids and allergic to Swiss cheese.

He was not a particularly handsome man, though women had always found him attractive, and as his face had become more familiar across the country, it was often suggested that he looked like John F. Kennedy. It was a weak comparison, suggested more by a common sharpness of features than by a common countenance, and perhaps by the casual but careful styling of his hair—parted fairly high on the right side of his skull, as Kennedy's had been, then brushed roughly down and across to his left ear, partially concealing it as it did the other, long enough to be carelessly mussed by a brisk wind, short enough to fall quickly back into place, with a smattering of red and a fleck of brown and a highlight here and there of black and a basic underlay of gray. But he did not actually resemble Kennedy or anybody else for that matter, although a few irreverent wags had suggested that he was Eleanor Roosevelt's illegitimate son. That, of course, was the result of his smile, as gigantic a smile as ever exploded on the face of any public figure—a smile that revealed a marvelous collection of teeth, well-kept, with a high, healthy gum line, and set in a spacious mouth with lips that seemed, like a clown's, to reach beyond their actual dimensions. The cartoonists of the land had enjoyed themselves immensely with such pronounced characteristics, but none of them had ever drawn him as someone else. His face prompted images not of some other specific face, but of collective faces, stereotypes steeped in nondescript but instantly recognizable sincerity: the high-school instructor, the small-town parson, the kindly obstetrician or the pharmacist, or perhaps the television anchorman, who reads from scripts typed in oversized print.

His calisthenics concluded, he had moved easily to his feet, his breath and pulse normal, unaffected by the sit-ups, and returned to the table with the lovely antique lamp. He sat down in the big chair beside it and reached for the copy of his inaugural address. In the quiet room, just across the street from the White House, he could hear the sound of his wife's breathing as he read.

He did not know, of course, but had he known of the old man's doubts, depression and uncertainty that morning, the President-elect would not have been at all surprised. He was aware that for most of the two years he had spent chasing his dream, and even after his election, millions of Americans had not completely shared Jimmy Carter's ebullient faith in Jimmy Carter, including many like the old man, who had voted for him nevertheless. It nettled him occasionally, but it did not surprise him. He believed he understood its origins. It was generated, he thought, by three separate but related phenomena.

First, there was the speed at which he had risen from almost total obscurity to the very pinnacle of international prominence and power. He had come so far so fast that the national psyche had not yet had time to absorb him. In the beginning, his campaign had been utterly laughable, so patently absurd at the start that at its successful conclusion it had seemed all the more implausible, perhaps the most unbelievable political enterprise the country could remember. Because it was built of such amazing stuff, it was widely perceived as peculiar and therefore suspect. Not since Wendell Willkie, thirty-six years before, had someone so unknown captured the nomination of his party, and then, despite prodigious erosions of strength caused by a series of blunders, he had won, and it seemed so inexplicable.

At the beginning he had been such a flimsy candidate. He had taken whatever he could get, wherever he could get it, adding wispy membranes of support here and there—in some forgotten beauty salon in Des Moines, some rancid Legion hall in Fort Wayne, some crumbling factory in Manchester, some dim hotel for the elderly in St. Petersburg—gaining momentum and strength in the same minute almost imperceptible increments that measured his wife's preferred departure from sleep, until at the end, his victory seemed an absolute surprise. He had achieved what was once thought, with no small amount of logic, to be impossible, and he had moved so fast and so far that when the dust settled around his triumph, the winner was a stranger, and he knew all that and it did not surprise him that his presence on the national scene prompted doubts and uncertainties.

Moreover, he realized that he had taken an unusual track in his surprising ascension, moving far outside the normal political matrix that Americans so often curse but generally find quite comfortable. He had presented himself to the country as a private citizen, never having held a Federal office before. He had served once as a governor, but that was not the sort of job experience most voters expect to find in the résumé of a presidential candidate, accustomed as most of them were to names and faces familiar enough to venerate or blame, or both. There was a rather deeply held notion that presidential candidates should serve some sort of Washington apprenticeship, and Carter had none. He was neither Senator nor Representative. He was, instead, a farmer—a gentleman farmer, perhaps, or more accurately a patrician planter and agribusinessman, but a farmer, nevertheless. He talked about it as though he was proud of it. He inserted it generously into his campaign literature and posed for publicity photographs and films in the middle of a field, with dirt trickling through his soiled fingers. There were early jokes about his real goal—to be Secretary of Agriculture—but he shrugged them off. "I'm a farmer," he would say—and the instant he opened his mouth, those who heard him speak had something else to wonder about. He was unmistakably from the Deep South. He drawled. "Ahmuh fahmuh and ahmuh Suthnuh," he would say, and somehow it just didn't sound quite right within the context of an American presidential campaign, neither the words nor the voice. There were no measured tones from him, only a twangy singsong, high-pitched to some ears, almost effeminate to others.

A farmer and a Southerner: it was beyond the ken of most voters, except Southern farmers, of course, a voting bloc never appraised as formidable. There had not been a President from the Deep South in more than a century, and no serious Southern candidates had emerged in years and years, except for George C. Wallace, and he was not really serious about winning, only running. It was an understandable absence. In a tragic cycle, the American South had almost compulsively produced politicians tainted by their region's racial recalcitrance—men who came to power by manipulating the racial fears and instincts of the Southern electorate and remained in power in the same manner, paying homage to the sanctity of a society built on the bones of slavery and preserved in an atmosphere of apartheid that had generated meanness and madness and murder. Now comes Jimmy Carter from that same soil. Although he seemed neither malevolent nor malicious, he was still a white Southern farmer, and that in itself was enough to place him outside the ring of acceptable candidates. Not that the rest of the country was exemplary in its record on race, but because the South was so obvious about it for so many years, it came to serve as a marvelous fount for the collective guilt of the nation. It was easy, simple and psychologically refreshing to reject the Southern candidate summarily, and that was a part of Carter's problem, not only in the campaign but even after his election.

It was exacerbated too by his rather simplistic religiosity. He seemed so comfortable with it, discussed it so easily. He had been "born again," he would say. Jesus had "come into" his "heart and cleansed it," he would explain. He would speak of the "Holy Ghost" and "justification by faith,

not works" and "eternal salvation" and "everlasting life"
and of the need for Christians to "witness for the Lord
daily" and of how he often taught a Sunday-school class
back in the little village where he lived and of how he had
once worked as a missionary for his church, spreading its
gospel in Boston and Pennsylvania, and it was all so—so different, different enough to be odd, and odd enough, perhaps, to be downright peculiar. It was the sort of thing one
expected to find on Sunday mornings on little Southern radio stations, this fundamentalistic, "Brother, are you
saved?" piety and zeal, but not from a man seeking such an
office as he. Yet, there he was, every day, all day: a "born
again," white Southern farmer who had spent no time in
either the House or the Senate and very little time at all in
Washington, D.C., who was actually presenting himself as a
candidate for President of the United States. There were
those who thought that was all very refreshing, a real-life
version of *Mr. Smith Goes to Washington;* but there were so
many, many more who found it somehow disconcerting, and
although that bothered him from time to time, it did not dis-
courage him nor surprise him, before or after he had won.

He was aware, after all, that almost anyone who had run
that year would have had problems with the voters. Given
his rather queer credentials and origins, he had also chosen
to participate in a very queer arena. He had diagnosed long
before he definitely decided to run that the country was suf-
fering from a malaise of uncertainty. It would express itself
toward any candidate. Through bitter experience, many
Americans had discovered that there were fewer things in
which they could implicitly believe. Institutions had failed
them too many times. Ideas long held were shredded or in-
verted. Too much had happened to too many on too many
yesterdays, and it was hard, very hard, for many Americans
to hope. After all, they had seen four Presidents in less than
thirteen years. One had been murdered, one had made a
grisly war, one had quit rather than be impeached and one
had not been elected.

Carter fully agreed with those who moaned about the poison in the well. He knew the doubts about everyone who stood for public office and he knew that the doubts about him, before and after his election, were symptoms of the country's trauma. He had aspired to leadership in an era of distrust, when cynicism had turned in on itself; he had reached for power at a moment when power was suspect, tainted by chronic abuse; he was about to assume the Presidency in the afterthroes of its lowest disgrace, while it still swirled in scandalous eddy. The malaise of uncertainty was deeply frozen. He would have been more surprised if there had been no doubts about him. He understood them, appreciated them and accommodated himself to them as inexorable facts of his presence at that moment in the politics of America.

Still, the doubts rankled him occasionally. Like all public figures, however exotic their roots or unorthodox their rise, Carter liked to be loved. He would describe himself as a very private person who enjoyed small groups more than large, but just like all the rest of them, his pale blue eyes would sparkle with excitement at the sight of a big, exuberant crowd. He loved it—loved the applause, loved the screaming, the outstretched hands, the cries of affection ("We love you, Jimmy! God bless you, Jimmy!"), loved all the trappings of celebrity, and the more there were, the more he wanted. Like others, he would listen with mock sincerity as someone asked how large a victory might please him, and like the others, he would smile benevolently and say that nothing would make him happier than all the votes—and there was as much truth as humor in his answer. He was the sort of politician who could be truly disappointed with a twelve-to-one majority. He was also the sort of politician who could be irritated eventually by doubts and uncertainties about his candidacy. "Ah, screw it," he had once said when his aides had brought him a copy of a poll that showed, only a few days before the election, that nearly a third of those who indicated they would support him were also dubious of him.

But generally he just accepted it. He had tried, he insisted, to deal with the suspicions. "People say they don't know me," he had said after his election. "Well, I understand that. I really do, but I don't know how else to explain. I've tried, and I've tried hard. I've spent two years now trying to let people get to know me. I don't know what else I can do. I guess it's just one of those things. If they don't know me by now—well, I don't know, I just don't know." He had done the best he could with the problem, he said. That was his creed. It had been his campaign slogan and the theme of his campaign autobiography. It was what he had always suggested to his wife and children when they came to him for advice. Do the best you can, he would say. There is no guarantee that everything will always be ideal, he would warn, so you simply do the best you can with what you have.

"And what if that doesn't work?" his eldest son had asked him once.

"Well, Jack," he had replied, "that probably means you haven't done your best."

As the President-elect closed the copy of his inaugural speech, ready for his shower and shave, light was beginning to filter through the lace curtains on the window near the chair, and at the Lincoln Memorial more than three thousand worshipers were beginning their early liturgy. First, they prayed for him. "Always, O Lord," they intoned in unison, their breaths visible in the frigid air, "may his eyes see the light of wisdom, his ears hear the voice of conscience, his lips speak words of truth, his heart beat in unison with justice, his spirit rise in pursuit of the best." They were bundled awkwardly in heavy coats and fur hats and mufflers, and despite their numbers, they seemed somber and subdued. Perhaps it was the cold or perhaps it was the early hour or, perhaps, like the old man who had arrived before them, there were other things on their minds. He was sitting behind a large pulpit on a platform raised above the crowd and his dark face was taut with grief, the grief of remembering what he always remembered when he addressed himself to the subject of hope. The Bible he had taken from the car was in his lap, and when he was introduced midway through the service for his sermon, he trudged slowly to the pulpit, opened it to the Gospel of John and, in a halting, breaking voice, read his text: "And Jesus said, 'Lovest thou me?' And Peter said, 'Lord, thou knowest I do.' Then said Jesus, 'Feed my sheep.' " He glanced up from the page and looked out on the crowd through eyes again brimming with tears. He was known for the fire and brimstone in his sermons, for the rhythmic cadence of his delivery, for the zest and enthusiasm he invested in his preaching, but that morning, as he began, his voice was strangely soft, nearly conversational. "I stand here with a bit of reluctance and timidity," he said, explaining the change in style, "because it was fourteen years ago that my son stood here and delivered his great speech."

That was it. That was what had been on his mind from the moment he had arrived, wasn't it? His son, his namesake, had been dead—murdered in Memphis in 1968—nearly nine years, a victim of the meanness and madness that had dogged his career as a dreamer, as a man of hope, and the old man had dreaded the moment that morning when he would appear at the same spot where his son had electrified an enormous audience in 1963 with the words of his vision. The old man was saddened to be there, not because he felt himself to be less of a man or less of a preacher than his dead son, but because he knew there would be a terrible rush of memories on him, memories of his son's death, of course, but also the memories of that sweltering August day when he had been so proud of him.

The crowd had swelled to nearly four hundred thousand by some estimates when his son was introduced, and when he began to speak, his sharp voice magnified by scores of loudspeakers scattered through the huge throng, a quick and heavy excitement caught the mass of people. It had been a brilliant summer's day, alive with its own heat, and it had attacked the city at dawn with a rush—just the sort of day for promises and hope. The old man's son had sensed that and risen to the occasion.

"This afternoon, I have a dream," he had begun, and before he had finished, he had crystallized the vision of black Americans for America and couched it in the language of those who want so desperately to move out of the past and into the society's possibilities.

The old man could hear the son's words in his mind again that January day as he looked out on the smaller crowd and sensed that they too were remembering. It was understandable, he knew, for even though it was a raw day, it was that special sort of Washington day on which promises and hopes were in order, an inauguration day providing a chemistry that challenged the elements; but the old man could not overcome his original thoughts of the day and, with a subdued voice, he focused on the essence of the text he had chosen from John's Gospel; yet, in so doing, he found himself dealing with a blatantly social gospel and raising the unfulfilled dream of his son, sketching an accurate if roughly drawn portrait of a society in which that dream had been crudely aborted. Things had changed, he knew, and tiny facets of the dream were struggling for life, but it had not come true. There was no "table of brotherhood" in the land, as his son had suggested there would be.

The old man paused in his sermon, wanting to stop, tired of talking. He glanced around him quickly, as though searching for a face. "I don't know if the President-elect is here or not," he said, turning back to the crowd, and for the first time that morning, his voice began to take on some of its old, familiar resonance. "He said he might be here, but I don't know if he is, so let me just say to him anyway, wherever he is, the sheep must be fed." By then, he was thundering. "That's what it's all about! The sheep must be fed!" He seemed finished and turned from the pulpit. Applause was already starting to build. Suddenly, as an afterthought, he turned back to the clump of microphones on the pulpit. "Martin Luther King gave his life that the least of them never be forgotten," he shouted, and turned away again. The applause was swelling. Still, he was not finished. Abruptly he approached the pulpit again, one more postscript in his mind, "That's what the President-elect is all about," he growled softly.

It was amazing. Even in his depression, the old man had finally issued a hint of hope about Jimmy Carter. With all that uncertainty bubbling in his heart, he simply could not leave that forum without, once again—as he had done so many times before—offering an utterance of faith in the man. It was a magnificent tribute to Carter's campaign, and it reflected the essence of his victory. There were small arguments about it, but it was perfectly clear to most election analysts that his triumph had been principally the product of his appeal to the hopes of those for whom hope was a scarce commodity, especially black Americans, and particularly those black Americans for whom the American dream was of little more substance than a breath exhaled on a January day in Washington, a silvery puff that quickly vanishes in the chill. Carter had reached out to them—pointedly, specifically—and they had responded in force at the polls.

In the dead center of Harlem, for example, in the last month of his campaign, he had gathered hundreds of them around him and called on them to trust him and place their hopes in him and had asked them, as he was leaving, how many would respond—and instantly, from the mass of men and women before him, scores of black hands were raised into the fouled air of New York City, straining, almost lifting the bodies beneath them, reaching not toward him, not for him, but upward, upward in the direction of their own dreams, not his, and there was not a fist in the lot of them. It was a moving scene that suggested just how skillfully he had styled his appeal to them and how willingly they would respond at the polls. It often seemed that they were desperately determined to believe affirmatively in his undefined possibilities—this white Southerner who was descended from slaveowners, this farmer who still paid black men less than white for the same work on his property, this presidential candidate who had failed even to notice until he was nearly forty years old that, in his tiny village, white children rode buses to school while black children walked, this pious man who had been a pillar for years in a church that refused membership to black people, this artful politician who had taken a stand as a presidential candidate for what he called "ethnic purity" against "black intrusion"—and the response of black Americans at the polls had more than compensated for the uncertainties about him elsewhere within the electorate. It had spread, by the time of the election, like kudzu.

In the mind of much of America, he was the Lon Chaney of 1976, the man of a thousand faces, and although he complained that such perceptions of him were false, he systematically, almost compulsively contributed to them himself. After presenting himself as an impeccably honest man, he frequently described himself in public as a "nuclear physicist," a designation totally inappropriate to the level of scientific skills he had acquired during his military service. It was a small point, he insisted. To raise it was to quibble. It was merely a matter of semantics, he claimed, but he knew it was just not accurate. Still, he often repeated it in his public appearances, even after conceding privately that it was probably not precisely so. He was prone, it seemed, to exaggeration, a common enough trait among politicians, but a tendency that clashed with his affirmations that he was not like other politicians. He talked often, for example, about his address "to" the United Nations, but he knew he was referring only to a speech he had made before an international energy conference that had nothing to do with the

United Nations other than that it happened to be meeting there. "Oh, did I say 'to,' " he would say to questions about the reference. "Well, I meant to say 'at.' " Then, the next day, on some other platform in some other city, he would say "to" again.

It was so damned hard to bracket the man. He offered himself to the country as a devout Southern Baptist, a denominational affiliation that normally implies a rigidly conservative Christian for whom alcoholic abstinence and a certain purity of language are cardinal virtues. Yet, in some circles—carefully measured by him, of course—he presented himself as a man who found great wisdom and truth in the neoorthodox writings of Reinhold Niebuhr and Sören Kierkegaard, philosopher-theologians who were regarded in most Southern Baptist congregations as alien if not downright heretical and bound for hell. While he did not abuse himself with liquor (as some presidential candidates he said he had observed), he was not an absolute teetotaler, carefully selecting, however, those with whom he drank, just as he did those with whom he discussed his more exotic theological readings. Similarly, he was not a vulgar man, nor given to deep profanities; but he was not above certain affiliation for the language of the street. To an aide who had relayed a local politician's request for a favor, he replied bluntly, "He can kiss my ass, and you tell him I said so"; and after explaining his compassion for the fallen Richard Nixon, he amplified his words by saying, "I despise the bastard, but I pray that he will find peace."

He was a quicksilver bubble, a living, breathing, grinning paradox, maddening for those who tried to define him. He was so resolute in his opposition to abortion and firm in his stand against the use of government funds for it. It was a moral question, he said, and he could take no other position, no matter what the political consequences might be. Yet, he invariably shaded his opposition so delicately with just a touch of disclaimer that many who supported legal abortion thought he agreed with them.

He had something for everyone, it seemed, and in such an election year and in such a country—so diverse in its ideologies—he was a genuine miracle worker. There would be no amnesty for those who had resisted the war in Vietnam, he said, but there would be a pardon, he added immediately—and when he was questioned about the difference between the two concepts, he bristled and said he would define the terms as he pleased. There were those who listened to his tax-reform pronouncements and came away believing that he had committed himself to the elimination of the income-tax credit for interest paid on home mortgages; but there were also those who heard the same pronouncements and believed just as firmly that he had not done any such thing. Some were sure they had heard him accuse an opponent of racism, but others who heard the same remarks were just not sure—and he, of course, insisted he had suggested nothing of the kind. In his famous interview with *Playboy* magazine, he had blurted out his belief that, like Nixon, Lyndon Johnson had been a liar when he was the President; yet when asked about that down in Texas, he had posed a carefully worded response that seemed to suggest that he had never said that at all, that it had simply been the interpretation of the magazine. Confronted with the evidence of his Johnson diatribe and the conflict in his explanation, he explained that what he had actually meant to say was that it was his own unfortunate interpretation, not the magazine's.

It was no wonder then that there were jokes about him. One comic tersely summarized his ambiguous image by predicting that, even if he should become President, he would never be enshrined on Mount Rushmore because there was not enough room for two more faces. Another recreated the imaginary moment in Carter's boyhood when his father asked if he had cut down the cherry tree. "That's an interesting question," the young Carter hedged. It was no wonder then that, even after his election, there was still a substantial uncertainty about him, and he knew it that icy

January morning as he sat in that warm bedroom across the
street from the White House, and he understood it in a way
no one else could. He knew better than anyone that there
was more to the doubts about him than simply his quick rise
to power or his role as an outsider or the peculiarities of the
year in which he had run.

There had been about him from the moment he had announced his candidacy—to the laughter of most, the wonderment of a few—a sense of purposeful, skillful enigma. He
preferred it that way. It suited his purposes perfectly. He
believed that the candidate who took clear positions on
every issue was not long for the political world. There
would be only one issue on which a successful candidate
would be judged that year, the amorphous, ethereal concept
of integrity, honesty, trustworthiness, credibility. There
might be a passing interest in others, but that would be the
underlying, permanent focal point of the voters, even if they
could not articulate it. Abortion, capital punishment, right-
to-work laws (he said he favored their abolition but would
not actively oppose them), welfare, taxes, the economy, foreign policy—all would crop up in the campaign, of course,
and all would be pertinent to one degree or another, of
course, but the crux of the election of 1976, he believed,
would be the legacy of the war and the scandals that had so
thoroughly poisoned the political well and traumatized the
electorate. To step outside that small ring would be fatal, he
believed. To answer every question on every topic defini-
tively would be suicidal, he believed. To compete by emphasizing one's governmental experience would be counterproductive, he believed—and so he believed that despite
the traditional wisdom that labeled him a long shot, his credentials, or really the lack of them, made him the favorite
right from the start.

Being unknown was his most valuable asset. He would be
precisely the sort of candidate millions of uncertain Americans might be looking for, even if they did not realize it.
They could live with their doubts about his views on abor-

tion or capital punishment or right-to-work laws ("I don't give a damn about any of them," he once said), as long as they felt relatively comfortable with his honesty and integrity and trustworthiness and credibility. Whatever else might be important to them, they would not be nearly so interested in or fascinated by what they already believed or knew or understood; millions of them would be ready and perhaps eager for something quite apart from their past experience as American voters—ready, perhaps, for a stranger. That was Carter's thesis as he began his campaign and from its genesis he worked diligently to remain forever new, forever fresh, and always as enigmatic as possible.

He was magnificently gifted for such a pursuit. He had a quick, eclectic mind and a finely tuned sense of the language. Using both, he was able to wade through all those long months of selling himself all over the country without revealing much of his merchandise. He was so often criticized for failing to take positions that after a while he simply declined to argue about it anymore; but the fact was that he took positions on several questions and issues—and the fact was that he stated such positions so carefully that he managed to maintain nonpositions on most of them. He paid close attention to nuance and shading and tints and hues of language. He rarely altered the specific expression of a particular view once it seemed to be rhetorically effective, that is, obfuscatory. Each noun, each verb, each qualifier was carefully selected over weeks and weeks of preparation, then tested here and tested there—like some new mouthwash commercial—in the days when no one was listening, and honed and tuned and turned and changed and crafted and etched into his mind, right down to the minute inflections and pauses. A Carter speech was a Carter speech, in the snow of New England, the cornfields of Iowa, the core of Harlem or the sunshine of Florida. In Maryland, in the spring of the election year, a reporter had complained to him in a crowded press conference that his answer had not been clear. Irritated, Carter had asked curtly if he wished him to repeat his answer, and when the reporter nodded, he did—word for word, comma for comma, gesture for gesture.

Still, there were special occasions on which he would change his style and the form of his public address. Before black audiences, for instance, or those predisposed toward the name of the old man's dead son, he would invoke the memory of Martin Luther King, Jr., including him in a passionately—for him—recited list of his American heroes; but before white crowds he thought to be less receptive to such a reference, he omitted the name. When he was challenged on the technique, he simply removed the litany of heroes from his speech altogether. Before certain audiences, for example, he ardently espoused the gradual withdrawal of American troops from South Korea; but before others, he ardently opposed it, he said, "except on a phased, gradual basis."

And so it was that Jimmy Carter found friends and foes on both sides of America's ideological aisle. When the votes were analyzed, he was found to have been least acceptable among Northern liberals and Southern conservatives. It was the secret of his strength, the very juice of his success, and the clearest truth about his campaign. He was not an ideologue. He was a pure pragmatist who had raised utilitarian politics to a new American art form. He had promised never to lie and never to mislead and if his credibility was eventually questioned, he had nevertheless therefore cornered the market on honesty early in the race. But he had never promised to rid the world of enigma. If his public image was clouded, his conscience was clear. He had always been a devout believer in little mysteries. In such a year, they were the very core of his political creed.

By noon that day, his patience with the pace of the time wore thin. He waited just inside the great doors of the Capitol with his wife, listening to the martial music from the inaugural stand just outside, the speech still on his mind. It had been there all morning—through his shower, through his modest breakfast, through his worship with his family and the members of his Cabinet at the First Baptist Church—and he was anxious to begin, to deliver it and let the country deal with it as it would. He had done the best he could with it, he thought, and if there were those who found it less than others had been, then there was nothing he could do about it. There had been so many, over the past two years, who had scoffed at him, jested about his apparent lack of the political skills necessary for such an enterprise, laughed behind his back at his drawl and his twang and his farm and his family and his teeth and his grin—but he had won. If not by much, still he had won. Whatever it was that he had lacked apparently had been unimportant, and whatever it was that he had worked with had apparently been sufficient, and he knew there were scores of men waiting just outside the door on the inaugural platform who would have traded almost anything for the prize he had won, however he had won it. He was right.

Even Walter F. Mondale, the man who was about to become the new Vice President—the first to hold the job by virtue of his election to it in more than three years—had marveled at Carter's success and his willingness to pay its price. He had himself entertained similar thoughts in the previous two years and had begun his own unofficial, unannounced campaign, flying off to this fund-raising banquet in New Hampshire or that party occasion in Indiana, testing the waters, making friends. He was still the senior Senator from Minnesota, for instance, in the late autumn of 1974 when he showed up in Johnstown, Pennsylvania, to campaign for a Democratic Congressional candidate there, and he had been splendid that evening at a grubby labor hall— ever ebullient, gregarious, often articulate, sometimes simply glib, but always emitting an aura of happy confidence about himself and the Democratic party and the country and

the local candidate and even Johnstown, a grim, gray cemetery of a town; and afterward, in the suite of the best motel,
his demeanor remained cheery, optimistic, evoking images
of Hubert H. Humphrey, his friend and mentor and fellow
Minnesotan. As the night wore on, however, Mondale
slumped back into a couch of ghastly floral print, watching
the blue smoke from his good cigar waft toward the ceiling,
not hearing the talk, talk, talk around him. His eyes were
surrounded by circles by then and his shoulders sagged beneath the weight of the day he was finishing. He noticed
that someone had noticed, sighed and smiled wanly. "Hell
of a way to make a living, isn't it?" he asked.

Not long after that, he would fold the campaign that had
never been officially launched, explaining that he simply
did not have the determination that would compensate for
all those miles and all those motel rooms. Of all those who
had dreamed the same dream as Carter, waiting outside for
him that January day, Walter Mondale understood its dimensions as thoroughly as anyone, and when he had been
asked to join the Georgian on the Democratic slate, he had
done so with visions of motel rooms dancing in his head. He
had agreed because he had known it would last for only two
or three months. Carter had lasted nearly two years, he
knew. It awed Mondale. He had never met anyone so determined, so single-minded. He called him "Iron Ass Jimmy,"
but not to his face, of course.

The two men had liked each other almost instinctively,
and much of their affinity was based on a common sense of
how the Presidency could be won in 1976. If Mondale had
not possessed the stamina for the pursuit, he at least owned
the philosophical credentials for membership in the Carter
entourage. Even as early as that trip to Johnstown, the future Vice President was talking about a one-issue election
two years hence, an election that would focus on integrity as
no American election had in generations. But Mondale
owned a significant weakness as a candidate in that, unlike
Carter, he tended to speak from a party platform. He had

several friends who often speculated how interesting it would have been if Mondale and Carter had opposed each other during the primaries, but it seemed clear in retrospect that it would not have been. Mondale would have pitched his campaign on the premise that as a Democrat he was a worthy candidate, and Carter would have beaten him on that point alone. Unlike Mondale, Carter was no child of the party, and while Mondale might have recognized that the party was no longer as significant as it had once been, it would have been difficult for him to change. He had always run on his identity as a part of the party. It was ingrained in him by Humphrey and by experience, both as a candidate and as a member of the Senate.

Carter's great asset was his lack of great loyalty to the party. Like George Wallace, he would offer himself in the early campaign as a man with only the most innocent links to it, focusing more on the individuality of his candidacy, not its relationship to some historic image or pattern, and it seems likely that he would have dealt with Mondale as effectively in the primaries as he did with most everyone else. That was something few of his opponents understood—his uncanny ability to adapt himself to change, to move with it, and at times a bit ahead of it—not too far ahead, but enough to negate weaknesses from the past. Carter used change as some men use money. Mondale might have understood the fact of change around him or even its dimensions, but like most of the others who either thought about running in 1976 or actually did, he was a victim of his habits. He would have insisted on presenting himself as the liberal he was, as the liberal Democrat he was, as the liberal Democratic Senator with all those years of experience in the Federal government, as the friend and confidant of Humphrey—and Carter would have beaten him and probably quite badly, except perhaps in Wisconsin.

It was a moot question, of course, by that day in January as Carter waited just inside the Capitol for the realization of his all-consuming dream. He heard the Marine Corps band strike up "Ruffles and Flourishes" and took a quick step forward, toward the inaugural stand, but he stopped abruptly. It was not for him, but rather for the man he had beaten, the fourth American President in thirteen years and the first ever to hold the office without having first been elected to the executive branch of the U.S. government.

Gerald R. Ford walked to the front of the platform and waved and listened to the cheering and waved again and smiled and pointed to someone he knew and mouthed an unspoken greeting and waved again and smiled again, a loser's smile, and as the applause swelled, he turned back to the enormous crowd gathered on the east plaza of the Capitol and waved again, first with one hand, then with two stretching far above his head, and when he turned again to take his seat, there were tears in his eyes. He knew what the applause meant. He appreciated it. After all, they were all gathered there beneath the chalky dome of the Capitol to affirm ritualistically that the adjustments had been duly made to the American system. He believed in that; it was simply hard for him to accept the incontrovertible fact that he had never been and never would be the adjustment duly made—and so the tears came. During the campaign, Carter had frequently called him a good and decent man. He was probably that. There was that sense about him, but Carter had also attacked him for a life-style and a circle of acquaintances that suggested a certain distance from the people he had been elected to represent. There was something to that, as well. Ford's life had been the labyrinthine pursuit of the traditional Capitol Hill power-seeker, and through an unprecedented series of warps in history, he had achieved more power than he had ever expected.

In the course of his pursuit, however, the good and decent man had somehow desensitized himself to the very sources of that power. Like most other human beings, Jerry Ford was a man who would not consciously do that which he judged to be wrong. He was a deeply religious man and perceived himself to be of stern moral fiber; but, like most human beings, Ford was an unconscious student of situation ethics, a man capable of skillful definitions. He was a mirror of the United States Congress. The friends he had made were those friends whose interests he eventually came to believe were common to the interests of the country and his constituency. There was nothing wrong with the system that could not be quickly repaired with an amendment here or a rider there or a little compromising or a little back-patting or a little arm-squeezing. There was, for instance, nothing wrong with enjoyable weekends of golf subsidized for him by the big business interests in whose behalf he would speak and vote and persuade. Like so many of his colleagues on Capitol Hill, his ganglia had been filed by the grating of his ambitions. He had fewer synapses than the people he supposedly represented. His moral and ethical boundaries had been enlarged by the constant stretching of conscience, the single most common calisthenic on Capitol Hill.

Still, he had become the President of the United States, and if some insisted on calling it a bastard Presidency, it was still a Presidency—something only thirty-seven men had experienced before, and it was still of comfort to him that cold day in January. He had that to prize and to remember, even if he would never enjoy such a moment as was about to be Carter's—to join that long line of grave men, their breath visible in the frigid air, speaking their visions of tomorrow, with the dome of the Capitol and American history rising behind them. Ford had come so close, so very damned close. The barometers of public opinion had at first given him no chance at all, so powerful was Carter's strange appeal; but he had moved steadily, narrowing the gap between them as measured in the polls, until finally some of those who twirled and splayed the calipers on the map of the American mind predicted that he would win. When he had not, there were those who had busied themselves with those tiny milligrams of history premised on what might have been.

What might have been the results, for example, if, as
Charles Mohr of *The New York Times* said but did not write,
Ford had not "picked up Poland and carried it toward the
wrong goal line" in his second debate with Carter? There
were other speculations—many others—as well, but none of
them dealt with the principal weakness in Jerry Ford's candidacy. He could never escape it. He was the extension of
trauma that gave Carter his strength. He evoked in the
American mind—even among those who voted for him—the
continuing uncertainty born of war and scandal. He was
Richard Nixon's good and decent surrogate. From the very
beginning of his pursuit, he was a loser.

Consider, for example, a moment in his life in August
1974. He had been President for three days and one hour
when he emerged from a little Episcopal church in Alexan-
dria, Virginia, just across the Potomac from Washington. He
squinted into the brilliant, summer Sabbath sun. For the
first time in his life, he had listened as a man of the cloth
had prayed specifically for him ("Me, Gerald Ford, the President," as he would identify himself during his campaign)
and for his welfare as "the leader of free men everywhere,"
and like the others who had worshiped there that morning,
he had lowered himself to the velvet-cushioned kneeling
rail in his pew, clasped his hands and heard the priest
mournfully beseech aid and comfort for one Richard Nixon
"in his moment of trial." The very mention of that name
seemed to deepen the hush of the worship. Breaths were
caught and held, inner ears cocked for some sign of the Deity's attitude on such a delicate matter. There was none, and
with the recessional ringing, the new President moved with
his handsome, all-American family and all the other worshipers out through the tiny narthex and onto the steps,
smiling and waving at the rather sizable crowd. He was tentative in his gestures, rather awkward, perhaps, but he was
sincere. He may have seemed a plebe just learning the sem-
aphore system, but he was the President. There was no mis-
taking that. It might have taken some people a bit more time

than others to accustom themselves to that fact, but on that bright day at that pleasant place in northern Virginia, there was no doubt that Gerald Rudolph Ford was the President.

At the foot of the church stairs, the long black fortress of a limousine sat waiting, its regal flags hanging limp in the heavy air. Flitting all about him were those lean, sturdy young men commissioned to protect him, the ones examining every molecule of air from behind their aviator sunglasses. All eyes except theirs were on him. Necks were craned for a better glimpse. There were sighs and even a shriek or two and finally a burst of applause when he stepped to the running board of the giant car and raised himself above the crowd, showing himself, smiling and waving. Then, abruptly, discordantly, like a clinker in a piano concert, there were boos. There were not many and they were not particularly strident, but they were there, rising timidly from a small knot of well-dressed adults standing behind a security rope on the far side of the limousine. So sudden, though, was the sound of their protest—so absolutely alien to the moment—that those who were applauding stopped, and the presence of the little group of dissenters was greatly exaggerated.

He had been President of the United States for a little more than seventy-three hours and he was already being booed—and right in front of his own church at that, and by people in suits and ties and respectable dresses, not the unwashed children of the just-passing era. His face changed. He seemed puzzled, confused, bewildered. He waved in the direction of the protest, his smile gone. Suddenly, he ducked into the womb of the enormous car, leaned back into armored darkness and disappeared down the curving drive, headed back to the White House, to his new home behind the tall iron fence.

"What did you think of the boos at church, Mr. President?" he was asked on Monday morning.

"Boos? What boos?" responded Jerry Ford. "I didn't hear any boos."

There were no boos for him that day, though, and none for
Jimmy Carter either as the President-elect finally took his
cue and walked through the big doors onto the inaugural
stand. He had finally reached that moment he had worked
for so hard, so long. He wore no overcoat and no hat. He had
dictated that the ritual would take place without the formal
garb traditional to it. He had chosen a dark blue suit with a
vest. He smiled at the dignitaries gathered around him,
waved at the crowd of some hundred thousand below,
glanced over at his ancient mother and grinned broadly. It
was a winner's grin, perhaps the most famous American grin
since Teddy Roosevelt's. The wind caught his hair briefly,
lifted it and mussed it. He touched it briefly and, magically,
it returned to its original shape. He sat down and waited for
the beginning of his new dream.

Around him spread the panoply of the government of the
United States, the government he had for two years used as
a target for his campaign—the government whose weaknesses he had presented to the American voters as the absolute antithesis of what it could be and should be and would
be under his leadership, the government he had said again
and again ought to be as good and kind and decent and honest and wise and compassionate and competent as the people of the country, the same people presumably who in their
infinite goodness and kindness and decency and honesty
and wisdom and compassion and competence had, only four
years before, given Richard Nixon one of the most overwhelming majorities in the history of presidential elections.

The Supreme Court was there—four of whose nine members had been appointed by the President whom Carter despised but prayed for—including Chief Justice Warren E.
Burger, a vain and pompous man with a strikingly handsome, patrician's face and a carefully kept mound of lovely
white hair. Burger looked like a Supreme Court Justice, and
although Carter did not much care for him personally, he
had always treated him with respect, both in his presence
and out of it, perhaps because the Court itself was gradually

moving toward his own stated position on the use of busing for school desegregation (he was against it, he said, because it just didn't work; he had not stated his position on those instances when it had worked), or perhaps because any campaign commentary on the Court would have necessarily involved him in some either-or position—precisely what he had tried to avoid in the long months of his pursuit.

Only four years before, as a governor, he had vigorously championed an antibusing amendment to the Constitution as a means of removing the question from the hands of the Court; but during his presidential campaign the year before he had taken a fairly definitive stand against an antiabortion constitutional amendment, even though abortion was, he said, a moral question for him and presumably of deeper ethical consequence than busing. There was just nothing to be done, he had said, meaning that there was absolutely no way he was going to step into a constitutional argument during a presidential campaign.

The Chief Justice, somberly gowned and regally coiffed, seated himself in one of the high-backed leather chairs placed in a semicircle behind the lectern and waited for his own moment. He was becoming quite adept at such ceremonies. He had been on the Court less than six years and he had already administered the oath of office to two Presidents and two Vice Presidents. He was about to enrich his hand from two pairs. Carter would give him a full house.

Stretched out on either side of the inaugural stand were the members of the Congress—the House of Representatives to the south, the Senate to the north—a body Carter had said was incapable of national leadership. It was no reflection on its members, he said, it was simply that 535 different people could not serve as a monolithic symbol of or force for authority and hope. The Founding Fathers of the country just had not intended it to be that way, he said. What they had foreseen in building the philosophical framework of the new government was one person, the President, speaking with a clear voice to the people, setting a standard

of ethics and morality and excellence and greatness and calling on the American people to make sacrifices for the
greater good and answering difficult questions and propos-
ing and executing new, bold programs and intelligent foreign policies and secure defense postures. The Congress
just couldn't do any of that, Carter had always argued. It just
was not within its power or its capability. It had to be one
man, the President, and at that point in American history, it
had to be Jimmy Carter. If there was to be a national leader,
he would have to reside in the White House, not on Capitol
Hill, and if there was no leadership in the White House,
there was simply no leadership at all, he had said.

That had been the approach he had taken in his campaign
against Ford, sitting that January day just a few feet away,
waiting out the dwindling moments of a Presidency Carter
had once called "pitiful." Ford, he had said, was just not a
leader. "Anything you don't like about Washington, you can
blame on Jerry Ford," he had told a group of Texans the
year before, and later he had suggested that the President,
never widely perceived as an intellectual titan, had been
"brainwashed"—that marvelous, double-edged code word
for stupidity—into his statements about the lack of Soviet
domination in Eastern Europe. All of that was over now.
The armistice was signed. Political peace had come to the
Capitol, and the two of them sat there that day, smiling cor-
dially in each other's direction, as though neither had ever
questioned the other's decency, sanity, honesty or ancestry.

Vice President Nelson Rockefeller had escaped all that in
the previous year, and he seemed sanguine enough about
missing it that day as he sat nearby, laughing and waving
and throwing an occasional kiss to dignitaries on the platform. He was, if anything, a gregarious man, so gregarious in
fact that on one of his several presidential campaigns he had
opened the door of his hotel room late one evening and
spied a young woman he knew passing in the corridor.
Would she like to join him for a drink? he asked. No, she
had said. Surprised, Rockefeller had asked if he could borrow a quarter from her. The woman was surprised and hesi-

tant. It was for the "magic fingers" in his bed, he explained. She fished in her purse for the coin, gave it to him and left hurriedly. Twelve years later, as he sat there on the inaugural stand that January day, he had not yet paid her back.

Perhaps he had forgotten, just as he had probably forgotten that sunny afternoon in 1972 when he and Senator Robert Dole, then the chairman of the Republican National Committee, had chosen to walk rather than ride from Rockefeller's offices in midtown Manhattan to the formal opening of a nearby Nixon for President storefront headquarters, an event that would feature Tricia Nixon and the late Ambassador Kenneth Keating. The limousine was waiting just at the curb for them, but Rockefeller, then the governor of New York, gave it a wave of his hand and he and Dole set out on foot. Passersby gasped, and Rockefeller greeted them happily. "Hiyuh, felluh," he rasped again and again, reaching for the outstretched hands, winking, waving, looking for the next surprised face. At the corner of Forty-ninth Street and Park Avenue the light was red, and so they waited at the curb, a bit impatient but enjoying the spectacle they were creating. Suddenly, Rockefeller spied two women standing nearby, chewing gum as though it were the last nourishment on earth. They were hookers, appropriately booted, skirted and bewigged, but the governor of New York did not discriminate. "Hiyuh, girls," he said, flashing his smile.

"Hi, yourself," said one of the women. "Whatcha doin' this afternoon?" She moved toward him immediately, but her face went blank when he offered her his hand.

"What about your buddy?" the other woman asked, glancing past the governor at Dole, still waiting at the corner on the curb.

"Oh, that's Bob," Rockefeller said. He turned toward the Senator. "Bob, Bob," he yelled, "come over here and meet these ladies." The light changed and Dole ignored the summons. Rockefeller noticed he was being left behind in his own parade and moved away from the women, back toward the corner.

"Hey, whereya goin'?" the girls shouted together.

"Oh, I've got a date with Tricia Nixon," he shouted. "Why don't you come along?" Then he was gone, and the two women, still gnawing frantically at their gum, stared at each other, a bit bewildered.

"Who the hell was that?" one of them asked.

"I don't know," said the other, "but I sort of liked the looks of Bob."

So had Jerry Ford, who had picked Dole as his running mate the previous year. Rockefeller, appointed by Ford, had removed himself voluntarily from consideration at Ford's insistence, and Ford, after discarding Senator Howard Baker and William Ruckelshaus and William Scranton, had inexplicably settled on Dole. It was, in the view of some, an act much akin to suicide. There were those who strongly believed that if someone other than Dole had been Ford's choice—anyone other than Dole, as a matter of fact—it would have been Ford, not Carter, taking the oath of office that January day. But he had not, and he was not. In a few more minutes, he would be a member of one of the most exclusive fraternities in the world. A former President with only one other living counterpart, he would be put out to pasture on what Carter had called "those plush green fairways of special privilege," and Rockefeller, having so mightily coveted the Presidency, would walk away knowing he had gone as far as he could go and never been elected to boot. He had once spent a million and a half dollars just to woo the support of the Ohio delegation to the Republican National Convention.

"I, Jimmy Carter," he began, his right hand raised, palm toward the elegant Burger, his left hand on a Bible given him by his mother, "do solemnly swear—" and a silence captured the moment and the place as his treble drawl was amplified through the scores of loudspeakers scattered about the Capitol plaza. The thousands of faces in the crowd below turned upward in one movement, as though it had been choreographed, all eyes on this Southern farmer in the act of achieving the impossible, including the eyes of those men of his own party he had beaten the previous year—the men who had never quite grasped the essence of the year as he had and whose inability to adapt to the rapidly changing political climate had doomed their campaigns from the start: Henry Jackson, the pedantic hawk who might have been the ideal candidate for 1976 except for the fact that he had to ruin everything by actually running; Morris Udall, the affable liberal who never quite understood that the country is essentially illiberal; Lloyd Bentsen, the Texas padrone who found it difficult to campaign in the life-style to which he was accustomed, since braceros were inappropriate on the hustings; Frank Church, the chubby dove who went after the Central Intelligence Agency before he went after any votes and discovered that nobody really gave a damn that he had done either; Birch Bayh, the handsome Hoosier, who found out that very few people who vote in the Democratic primary elections of New Hampshire and Massachusetts have ever belonged to a college fraternity; Milton Shapp, formerly Milton Shapiro, the garrulous Pennsylvania governor who finished behind "no preference" in Florida—and there were others, too, who had tried their hand and failed, including Sargent Shriver and Fred Harris.

A notable exception was Edmund G. Brown, Jr., the Zen Jesuit governor of California who entered six primaries and won six primaries—a lean young man who might have played a better Jimmy Carter than Jimmy Carter but who dawdled too long over the beads and entrails before deciding to seek the nomination. By that time, Carter all but had it in his pocket. There was another exception there, too, that day. George Wallace, the veteran of three previous campaigns, one of which had cost him the use of his legs, sat morosely in his electric-blue and chrome-plated wheelchair, a tragic, pitiful figure—gaunt, hollow-eyed, his marriage in shreds, most of the meanness and madness drained from him, facing an uncertain future and haunted by a campaign in which he had been humiliated by Carter's dominance. He was an exception to all the others because he had not simply failed in 1976, he had been utterly reduced to the whinings and mewlings of a man without a constituency. And there was Hubert Humphrey sitting nearby, almost as shocking to see as Wallace—an aging, ailing Hamlet, wrapped almost comically in a huge fur coat, looking much like the affluent ghost of elections past. That had been precisely his role in 1976. At least Mondale's move into the Vice Presidency had elevated Humphrey once again to the status of senior Senator from Minnesota. There was some comfort in that.

There was little comfort at all, though, for the tall, handsome Senator sitting nearby. Edward M. Kennedy stared blankly toward Burger and Carter, the men at the center of the scene. He had watched the farmer's rise through unbelieving eyes. He had heard the feverish calls for him to challenge Carter, to rekindle whatever was left of that old flame. "Christ, Teddy," one old friend had told him, "you can take that cracker just by saying you haven't quite decided not to run," and on alternate days he believed that was true. He was, after all, the exiled prince of the party. The other days, though, he realized that too much had happened to too many people on too many yesterdays. It would have been hard for him, very hard. In 1984, he would be Carter's age.

"So help me, God," Burger intoned.

"So help me, God," said Jimmy Carter. It was done. What had begun more than four years before when he had come home from the Democratic National Convention in Miami Beach convinced that even he would have been a better candidate than George McGovern had ended there beneath the Capitol dome. The hardest thing he had done, he had once said, was actually tell people he was running for President. He had been embarrassed by it and he had postponed the date of his announcement repeatedly simply because, as one old friend remembers, he thought it was "high-heeled" of him to "just raise up and say it," say that he was a candidate for President. Once he had made the leap, however, he had never looked back. He had taken their measure, every one of them, and the system's too, and in the process he had endured all the jokes and the laughter and the derision and the blank stares when he introduced himself as a presidential candidate and all those insolent journalists who had nothing in their minds except traps and snares for him and all that talk about his duplicity and all those doubts and uncertainties about who he really was—and now it was over. He lowered his right hand and removed his left one from the Bible his mother had given him, kissed his wife, shook hands with Burger and Ford, and turned to the applauding crowd as the Marine Band struck up "Ruffles and Flourishes."

This time it was for him. He breathed deeply, nearly a gulp, and then he grinned that grin. At last he had been identified. Finally, everybody knew who he was. He was the President of the United States.

When the ovation faded, he began. "For myself and for our nation," he said, "I want to thank my predecessor for all he has done to heal our land." It was a simple, direct and perhaps a rather obvious thing to do, yet it caught by surprise most of those who heard the words and saw what happened next. He moved away from the lectern, took a single step to his right and extended his hand to Gerald Ford. The applause swelled again, this time to as great a peak as it would reach during the inaugural ceremonies—and Ford was moved to tears again and wiped them clumsily from just beneath his eyes with the knuckles of his hand. It was the first symbol of what would become a symbol-minded Presi-

dency, and it had been carefully crafted to reflect two concepts Carter believed were of signal significance. First, the
gesture showed him to be a man of compassion and grace in
whom the principal Christian virtues resided. It was his day
and everyone knew it. The ceremonies for the next twelve
hours and beyond were designed to honor him and his ascension to the power vested in the office. There was no
mandate on him to share it with anyone else and particularly
none that would have directed him to focus attention on
Ford and whatever he had or had not done during the two
and a half years since his own oath-taking. Still, Carter had
presented himself again and again as a politician unlike all
the others, as a man who would not be changed by the
power he would surely win, a gracious, courtly man with a
new sense of elegance in human relationships, and the
twenty words in the opening sentence of his inaugural address would establish that in the minds of the people firmly.

Moreover, the words would reflect the end of an era that
had set the country's teeth on edge. He simply pronounced
a final benediction on Watergate and Vietnam. By doing so,
he hoped to provide the country with the impression that it
was so—that it was over, once and for all. That had also
been a principal thrust of his campaign. He had given the
American people to believe that, if he became the President, it would be an act of cleansing for the American soul, a
regeneration of its fouled spirit, the salvation it sought from
the devils of its recent past. It was all a very simple process,
he had suggested again and again. He did not have all the
answers, he had said, and he had a lot to learn, he had insisted, but of one thing he was certain: he could mark with
great finality the closing of that period—and his gesture that
morning was meant to accomplish that delineation.

It was a brilliant piece of politics. It had nothing to do
with substance and everything to do with style. Carter had
merely followed the advice of Vermont's venerable Senator,
George Aiken who, in the midst of the Vietnam War, had
suggested that the government of the United States simply

declare itself the winner and come home, and in retrospect, Aiken had probably offered as sage a piece of advice as anyone else who struggled to find solutions to the war. It probably would have provided a satisfactory solution, even though it had nothing to do with the facts. The American memory, collectively, was childishly abbreviated, Aiken realized, and Carter knew that too, and so that frigid morning, as the first act of his Presidency, he declared that all yesterdays were canceled or at least irrelevant and unimportant in the context of the day and the days to come.

Still, perhaps the new President did not grasp the depths of yesterday's wounds. There were moments in his campaign, in conversation and in rhetoric when their extent appeared to dawn on him, but even then he could not bring himself to admit it. He believed, strategically, that the less said about the Watergate scandals, the better, and he operated on that track consistently. For a while he painted his target as "the Nixon-Ford Administration" but quickly dismissed that approach, sensing that perhaps it served no purpose other than to raise an uncomfortable specter in the electoral mind. To compensate, he used his ability with the language merely to suggest the same picture, leaving the final brushstrokes to those who wanted to complete it; but generally, he and all the others who sought the office in 1976 were like the parties in a divorce who would not admit, other than in a broad obeisance to honesty, that each of them had mutually helped to murder the marriage. It had simply happened, and it happened yesterday and it had nothing to do with anyone in particular and it had nothing to do with today and tomorrow.

Guilt was a commodity Carter banned from his campaign. Yes, in a sense we were all responsible for Vietnam and Watergate, and therefore the enormous guilt was to be borne by an enormous goat. The people, collectively, would share in tiny allotments the blame for what had happened to the people, and with such small dollops to deal with, the whole matter could be dealt with quickly. By declaring it to be finished, it would be finished—and the people would sigh in unison, good riddance. Perhaps Carter was uncomfortable with the idea of guilt, except the sort of guilt that could be dealt with neatly by a theological equation that could dump "the sins of mankind" on the back of a savior in whose death would occur the collective compensation for mankind's sins—a transaction that mystically became a reality simply by saying it was so. For months, Carter had dwelt on the rosy theme that nothing had really damaged the country. Its system of government had not been injured, the economy was still healthy and the American spirit had emerged unscathed. The war and the scandals had really registered no impact at all on the society, and if there was guilt to be placed at all, it was merely an attitude that was to be blamed, the attitude that suggested that the American people weren't really good enough to be trusted. But see, said Carter, I trust the American people; ergo, our long national nightmare is over. The twenty words and the handshake with Ford would suffice. The new President was also a devout devotee of symbols. They had served him well throughout his career. He was not about to change.

All that each person is and experiences, and shall never experience, in body and in mind, all these things are differing expressions of himself and of one root, and are identical: and not one of these things nor one of these persons is ever quite to be duplicated, nor replaced, nor has it ever quite had precedent.

—James Agee,
LET US NOW PRAISE FAMOUS MEN

SOMEWHERE UP OVER AMERICA, perhaps between Pittsburgh and Memphis or between Boston and Tampa or maybe between Dallas and Los Angeles or between Billings and Chicago—somewhere up there at twenty-five thousand feet and six hundred miles per hour—he was eating his lunch one afternoon in the spring of his long campaign, forking up neat little portions of a lobster casserole from a plastic tray perched on a pillow in his lap and talking, once again, about how he did not intend to lose and about a government that ought to be as good as the people and about how much he loved the little village where he had grown up and to which he had returned after leaving for a while. A less than eloquent man, he was at his most eloquent when he addressed himself to the subject of home and hearth and the fields he loved to tramp, searching for arrowheads with his dark-haired wife.

"There's some sort of strength there for me," he said. "I know what it is, I think, but it's hard to articulate. It's just there—maybe it's in the air or the water, but of course, it isn't—and, you know, I've really made an effort to define what it is that happens to me when I go home, because I think it's important to understand that process if I'm going to completely understand myself. We talked once about using it as a part of my campaign—you know, the way I feel about the place and all—and that's when I tried to write it down or talk it into a tape recorder, but it was so miserable, what I said, I mean, and it didn't make much sense to anybody except me and we just decided to forget it, except to point out to people that I really love my home and my roots; but, I'll say this, it's something I wouldn't ever surrender even if I can't explain it. I can be so tired that I don't think I can go another step, or maybe depressed a little if things haven't gone too well, and when I get home and change my clothes, it's like I'm a completely new man. I sleep better, I eat better, I feel better, I think better—my whole perspective on the world is improved just by being there. If you haven't experienced that sort of thing firsthand, I don't think it can be explained to you."

But, of course, there was no need for him to explain. What was required was merely that he do it—go back as often as he could within the context of a campaign that might take him in any given week into nine or ten states and find him on Friday afternoon a thousand miles away—and Jimmy Carter, for most of the long months that he pursued his dream, met that requirement. George McGovern, four years earlier, had had the right idea and Carter knew it. "Come home, America," he had urged—but at every break in his campaign schedule, McGovern would head straight back to Washington. In stark contrast, Carter actually went home— home to Georgia, home to Plains, the dusty, dreary little village that had, at various moments in his life, been both a boon and a bane for him. He did love it, though. There was no doubting the depths of his feelings for the place. When he had stayed away too long, chasing votes from Houston to Seattle, a certain restlessness would emerge in his otherwise placid personality. The place itself would begin to creep into his speeches more often the longer he stayed away from it.

Late one evening in Iowa, more than a year before his inauguration, he bolted from a bowling alley ahead of his scheduled time of departure and left behind a clutch of chattering women, all fond of him, fawning over him, pledging him their loyalty, love and support. "We're going home," he told the agent in charge of his Secret Service detail, and off he and his little entourage rushed to the nearest airport where a chartered jet was waiting. The agents hustled to keep up with the candidate. They were airborne in a rush, but midway in the flight, the pilot reported that the airport at Americus, only about a fifteen-minute drive from his home, would probably be closed by the time they arrived by a weather front moving toward it. They would have to land at the airport in Albany, Georgia, about an hour's drive away. Carter would not hear of it. He asked the plane's airspeed, made a few calculations on a pad and ordered the pilot to lay on the coal. They could make it to Americus with time to spare, he said. The agent in charge of the detail frowned, but Carter was insistent. "We're going home," he said, "the fastest way. Now, you go tell the pilot to get his ass in gear." They landed at the Americus airport a few minutes before it was closed by the weather.

As he picked at the remains of his casserole that day a couple of months later, he remembered that night. "They were really worried," he said, "but I wasn't—except that I was concerned about getting home as quickly as possible and spending as much time there as possible before I had to leave again. Mother wasn't feeling too well, you know, and I wanted to see her, and there were things to be done around the house—and besides, I knew Rosalynn was going to be there, too. I hadn't seen her in about three weeks as I recall and, well, I just had a real need to be there with them, you know." He drank long and deep from his glass of milk and left a thin, chalky mustache across his upper lip. "I think that's probably the hardest part of running for President," he said, "and people don't believe me when I tell them that. They don't believe me because they don't know how much I love that place and those people, and maybe they don't believe me because they don't have a place to love like I do. Maybe that's one of the real problems in this country these days: the lack of roots, the mobile society, the constant moving from here to there—and, you know, the absence of anything that lasts in people's lives. Everything is so—so damned disposable nowadays. I know it's probably foolish, but I'd like to see everybody in the country get to know his family tree, to study it, to find out about their own people— who they were, where they came from, how they lived, when they died, where they're buried. I think that might make a lot of difference about the way people think about themselves and other people around them."

It was a pursuit in which he had invested considerable time and some money himself, this probing for the people and the places in his background. He had spent long hours with his aging uncle—Alton, his father's older brother—visiting the old homesteads where his ancestors had lived and loved and died, sprucing up the ramshackle cemeteries, and just sitting and talking about the history of their family. "That Jimmy, he sure loves to wonder back over everything I know and everything I ever heard," his uncle had cackled one morning down in Plains. "I bet he knows more about the Carters now than anybody alive, including me. We've traipsed up and down all over this part of the country, looking for deeds and records and such stuff as that, and I recollect that once he brought one of those tape-recorder gadgets in here and we just sat around and talked for hours about the family. I reckon he wanted to get it all down before I die."

Carter had begun his search for his lineage years before the thought of running for President had entered his mind, and when he actually took to the road as a candidate, it became an important part of his soft-spoken, intimately presented spiel. "My family's lived in Georgia over two hundred years," he would say—and that afternoon on the jet plane cruising somewhere up there over America, he traced some of the family's roots, offering detailed biographical sketches of his ancestors several generations back, providing years of birth and dates of death, building a quite masterful narrative that prompted what seemed at the moment to have been a reasonable question.

Did any of his ancesters own slaves? he was asked.

His face changed abruptly. He had been relaxed, coasting pleasantly along on the flow of his tales from the past, enjoying himself immensely and knowing that he was entertaining his companion in the next seat. Did any of his people ever have any slaves? His translucent eyes turned to frost. He handed his tray and pillow to a passing stewardess and busied himself with his napkin, brushing crumbs from his lap and the sleeves of his coat. Had any of the Carters owned slaves? He finally responded without looking in the direction of the question. The conversation, it seemed, was over. "No, no, I don't think so," he said briskly. "Well, actually, I don't know," he added. "I just don't know about that. I never really went into it in much detail, so I—I just don't know. I'll have to check on that when I get back home."

He never mentioned it again.

About twenty miles north of the Carters' spacious brick home on a tree-lined street in Plains stand the remnants of a two-story house where no one has lived for years and years. The interior is void of anything save the ghostly outline of a staircase against a crumbling wall, the staircase that Sarah Carter must have climbed a hundred times back in 1858 to minister to her ailing father-in-law, James. He had come to visit his son, Wiley, and Sarah and their children a few weeks before, and when he had become ill, wracked by a fever, there had not been much hope that he would recover. He was, after all, almost eighty years old. He was seventy-seven, in fact, seven years beyond Biblical life expectancy as recorded by some Old Testament actuary, and the fever was cruel and deep in his frail form. It seemed there was nothing to be done for the old man except to make him as comfortable as possible. Neighbors dropped by frequently to inquire about his condition, and the talk in the comfortable parlor just inside the door was soft and subdued. His death was a blessing, they said when it came.

James Carter was buried in a metal coffin that cost $50, wearing a three-piece suit, shirt, underwear, socks and shoes purchased for $17.60. He owned more than three hundred acres of good land that were sold the next year for $1200. He also owned six slaves, including a mother and a child. The four black men were sold for a total of $4467—Green brought $1106, Solomon went for $1261, Frank, an even $1200, and Titus, $900—while Mary, the mother, and Joe, her baby, were purchased together for $1225. It was a more than respectable estate built over the many years since he had come to Georgia from eastern North Carolina with his father, Kindred Carter, and his mother and his younger brother, Jesse. Their possessions were in an ox-drawn cart and they had turned their backs on American roots already more than a century deep, planted near the James River in Virginia in 1637 by Thomas Carter, who had come as a colonist from England and whose great-great-great-great-great-great-great-grandson would become the thirty-ninth President of the United States.

It was sometime in the mid-1780s when Kindred, his wife, James and Jesse straggled into McDuffie County, Georgia, and began to carve a place for themselves in their new home. Kindred found what he had been told he would find—good rich land, thickly forested, and waiting to be cleared and broken and planted and tilled, ready to yield itself to the man who would take it. It would not be easy, he knew, and he was grateful for a wife who could produce sons. The work would be hard and the days would be long, and there were the Indians—the Cherokees and the Creeks. Both were most unreliable, though the Cherokees seemed much more civilized, and neither tribe could be trusted to any great extent. It was as though they judged the land to be theirs. There were sporadic raids on isolated houses in the forest and several attacks on larger settlements, and Kindred and James, the men of the family—like most other men of their time—were never far from their weapons. Still, they survived there and prospered on the land they claimed hard by a little creek. In 1798, James, who was then twenty-five years old, married a young woman named Eleanor Duckworth, the daughter of a prosperous and generous man who gave the new couple more than a hundred acres of virgin land in nearby Warren County, a little farther to the west.

Kindred died in 1800 when he was about fifty years old, leaving his family a comfortable estate of more than three hundred acres, most of it used for growing cotton and wheat, and a sizable collection of livestock—horses, cattle, mules and swine. Together, the two brothers—James and Jesse— worked the land for several years after their father's death, and James expanded his interests by opening the land his father-in-law had given him. It was new ground, never planted before, and it was, as usual for the Carters, hard work. In 1815, he decided to move to Warren County to be closer to his enterprise, taking with him his wife, Ellie, and his son, Wiley, who was in his midteens by then, much the same age James had been when Kindred had brought him across the mountains from North Carolina and down into Georgia. James decided to concentrate on cotton as his chief money crop on the new land, and as his father had prospered, so did he. His holdings grew to more than five hundred acres of prime land. Meanwhile, sometime after 1825—the year the Creeks signed away their right to nearly five million acres in southwest Georgia—Jesse moved from his father's land in McDuffie County down to Talbot County, a part of the land the Creeks had traded for a home west of the Mississippi. Jesse bought a sizable parcel and began his career as a cotton planter, and in 1835 James decided to join him, leaving his son, Wiley, back in Warren County to look after his interests there. In 1850, when James was 69 years old, the local census noted that he was still farming.

But by then, Wiley's first wife, Ann, was dead, and he had

married Sarah. He had not had an altogether pleasant life since his father had left. For one thing, he had tangled with a man named Usry over the ownership of a certain slave. Wiley held title, he said, and moreover, the slave was in his possession, and when Usry came to claim him, there were shots. The Warren County sheriff testified at Wiley's trial that both men had raised their guns simultaneously, but that Wiley had fired first, hitting Usry in the shoulder and mortally wounding him. Wiley was acquitted, but it was an event the community would not soon forget, and so Wiley moved.

As his father, James, had left him behind when he joined his brother, Jesse, so Wiley left behind in Warren County his nineteen-year-old son, Littleberry Walker Carter. The year was 1851. Wiley's route of exodus was south and west, and he finally settled in a tiny community called Quebec in Sumter County, about twenty miles from a prosperous little town known as the Plain of Dura, a collection of houses and stores and a sure sign of the march of civilization, a post office that had been operating for more than thirteen years when Wiley encamped nearby. All around Quebec were acres and acres of rich, productive land, planted mainly in cotton but supplemented with sugarcane and rye and wheat and corn. The dense forests were teeming with game, the streams were full of fish, and Wiley and Sarah went to work on their new life. By 1858, when his aging father came to visit, they owned one of the largest plantations in the area— more than twenty-two hundred acres, and, of course, the two-story house where James would spend his last days.

Two years later, in 1860, Wiley's son, Littleberry, who had been living with his in-laws in Warren County, brought his wife, Mary Ann, down to Sumter County to be near his parents and his two younger brothers. The tension between the two principal regions in the country was growing, and less than a year after Littleberry and Mary Ann arrived, a Rebel artillery unit attacked a government fort in the harbor at Charleston, South Carolina, and the war that had long been expected was a reality. In Americus, the seat of Sumter

County, a merchant named A. S. Cutts, who was a veteran of the Mexican War, immediately reactivated his old outfit, a unit called the Sumter Flying Artillery. It became Company A of the 11th Battalion of the Georgia Volunteers, and when Cutts was given permission by the Confederacy to increase his complement from a company to a battalion, his first volunteers were Wiley Carter's three sons, including Littleberry. Off they went to Virginia, resplendent in their new gray uniforms, and from the spring of 1862, when they enlisted, until the end of the war three years later, they did not see their home again. Their unit was in the thick of the war in the north—from Boonsboro to the Wilderness to the Spotsylvania Courthouse to Hanover Junction and Petersburg—but all three survived. Littleberry showed no indication of an urge for upward mobility. He joined as a private. He came back to Sumter County with the same rank.

What he and his brothers found on their homecoming was what defeated Confederate survivors were finding all over the region—a society and an economy on the brink of total disintegration. The good life was gone for those who had enjoyed it before, and for poor whites it was an even deeper poverty. Littleberry struggled to make ends meet for Mary Ann and their son, William Archibald. He continued to farm and he began to diversify as best he could, entering into a partnership with another Sumter Countian that produced a homemade merry-go-round, a popular form of entertainment called a "flying jennie." The partnership soured, as much had soured in the South since the war, and in 1874, Littleberry died. He was only forty-two years old. Some accounts indicate that he and Mary Ann died of diphtheria on successive days, but another narrative from that time suggests that, like his father, Wiley, Littleberry was involved in the violence that was common to the region and the era. In that version, he was killed by his partner in a dispute over the proceeds from the homemade merry-go-round. His murderer fled to South America and was never apprehended or prosecuted.

The records for Littleberry's son, William Archibald, are

clearer. When he married Nina Pratt in 1885, he moved with
her to the little community of Arlington, in Calhoun County,
near the Early County line. Three years later, Alton Carter
was born there, and some years later, after his parents had
formally moved into Early County, where his father was already farming and getting started in the sawmill business,
another son, James Earl, was born. The year was 1894. William, who came to be known as Billy, was doing quite well.
He had nursed his finances and managed to purchase some
of the best land available, and through hard work and scrap-
ing along, he bought a few buildings here and there in the
county, including an old store he rented in 1902 to a man
named Will Taliaferro.

The next September, the renter moved out and opened up
his own business in Rowena, a little community in the eastern section of Early County, taking with him a desk from the
store he had rented from Billy. Alton, the older son, then
fifteen years old, was commissioned by his father to retrieve
the desk from Taliaferro. "I went after the blamed thing,"
Alton remembered in the summer of 1976, "but this fellow
said he'd bought it from my daddy. So I went on back home
and when Daddy came in that night, I told him the man
claimed he had bought the desk. Well, Daddy—he said he
didn't know anything about that and he said he'd just go
over there to Rowena in the morning and get it himself,
since I hadn't done the job."

The next morning, Alton accompanied his father on the
short trip. Billy walked into Taliaferro's new store and demanded the desk. "It was a mighty rough scene," Alton recalled. "They got into a terrible argument—screaming and
shouting at each other—and then they got to scuffling and
wrestling around and there were some blows exchanged and
they were both bleeding by then and all of a sudden that
fellow came up with a gun, a little pistol. It wasn't there one
minute and then, all of a sudden, there it was. I wasn't no
more than fifteen or twenty feet away when he shot Daddy.
Shot Daddy in the head, the back of the head. There wasn't

much I could do. I cried, of course, and ran to help him and tried to take care of him, but there wasn't much I could do. Daddy was in bad shape." Two days later, on September 3, 1903, the *Early County Times* reported that Billy was "barely alive," and in the next week's edition, the newspaper recorded his death.

In three successive generations, the Carters had killed and been killed over what they considered to be their property—a human being, a merry-go-round and a desk.

Billy's brother, Calvin, who had remained in Sumter County and moved from Quebec to Americus, was named the administrator of the estate, and after making several trips down to Early County to help his dead brother's family, he suggested that it might be much better for everyone concerned if they moved closer to him. So, sixteen-year-old Alton, by then the man of the Carter family, organized the move that would take him, his mother, his three sisters and his ten-year-old brother, James Earl, to the tiny village about eight miles west of Americus that was to be their permanent home. It had been named for a wilderness locale mentioned in the Old Testament as the spot where Nebuchadnezzar, the Babylonian ruler, had raised a golden idol that Shadrach, Meshach and Abednego declined to worship, a refusal that, according to the story, brought them to a trial by fire inside a blazing furnace. The Plain of Dura the place was called in the Bible—but by the time the Carters arrived in 1904, the town was known simply as Plains, Georgia. With funds from their father's estate, a house and a store were purchased, and although Alton continued to go to school for the rest of that term. he quit the next autumn and took over the business. His younger brother, however, continued his education, graduated and in 1916, when he was twenty-two years old, enlisted in the U.S. Army as a private. He came back home to Plains following World War One as a lieutenant, and in 1923 married a small but strong-willed young woman named Bessie Lillian Gordy.

Earl's new wife was the great-great-granddaughter of Peter Gordy who had settled in Baldwin County, Georgia, soon after the turn of the nineteenth century. His son, Wilson, born in 1801, followed the same instincts that had led many of the Carters to southwest Georgia following the treaty that moved the Creeks out of the state, and sometime in the 1820s, he settled in Muscogee County, packing his household goods in a huge hogshead—a large cask with an axle and shafts, commonly used to take tobacco to market—and, seated on a perch above the crude vehicle, whipped the mules all the way to his new home. He married a daughter of Irish descendants, Mary Scott, and among his several sons was James Thomas Gordy, born in 1828. In 1864, James, then thirty-six years old, enlisted in Company B, 6th Georgia State Militia, and was assigned to the duties of a wagonmaster. Two months later, in July 1864, during the Battle of Atlanta, his unit was overrun by Union forces at Conyers Station and scores of prisoners were taken, including many from Company B. Private Gordy escaped somehow and came home the next year to become a farmer and a tax collector.

One of his sons, Francis Marion Gordy, became a physician, and was later elected to several terms as the ordinary, or clerk, of Chattahoochee County before he won a seat in the Georgia Senate in 1907. When Dr. Gordy moved to Columbus, he was elected again to a different seat for the 1909–1910 term. He returned to Chattahoochee County the next year and was promptly returned to the office as ordinary. He seems to have had a natural bent for getting elected. Dr. Gordy was the great-uncle of the thirty-ninth President.

His brother, James Jackson Gordy—named for Stonewall not Andrew—was born the year before their father, James, went away to war. He became a well-read man whose passion was politics—a familiar face around the golden-domed state capitol up in Atlanta, about 120 miles north of his home in Richland. Invariably, when the legislature was in session, Jim Jack, as he came to be known, wound up with a patronage job, living in an Atlanta boardinghouse but calling the capitol his home. He had never held elective office, unlike his brother, the doctor, but he had held several jobs—postmaster at Richland, Federal revenue agent and deputy Federal marshal—that went to those whose political alliances were with those in power, and somehow, Jim Jack always made the right moves at the right time. He practically worshiped Eugene Talmadge—the uproarious sham populist whose machine dominated the state for many years and whose gubernatorial campaigns often focused on his claim that the people had just three friends they could consistently rely on: God, Sears, Roebuck and Ol' Gene.

Jim Jack was also enamored of the strange, acerbic agrarian radical, Thomas Watson—a Congressman and twice the presidential candidate of the Populist party. Watson's defeats apparently worked some evil contortion on his soul and he changed almost overnight from a passionate zealot trying to merge the political and voting support of Southern blacks and whites outside the economic system—which was the bulk of the population—to a vehement racist and anti-Semite. He was, nevertheless, Jim Jack's hero, and in 1906, eight years after his daughter, Lillian, was born at Richland, he named his youngest son Tom Watson Gordy. He wrote his son's namesake to tell him of the blessed event and enclosed a dollar for his subscription to Watson's new political journal, the *Jeffersonian Magazine*.

Alton Carter remembers Jim Jack as a completely political animal, a man who was never so happy as when he was "up to his hips" in the intrigues, the plots, the electioneering, the raucous give-and-take that characterized the political life of the South. "Lordy, Lordy! Jim Jack Gordy!" the local populace would come to say about his zeal and his zest for politics. He worked for Congressional candidates and for county candidates and he knew how to get the job done. Alton would remember years later that there had not been a single election in all the years he knew Mr. Gordy—or knew about him—in which he had not played a prominent role. He never ran for office himself, but he manipulated the fortunes of those in the area who did.

Understandably, he was not altogether pleased when Lillian came home to Richland one day from Plains and announced that she planned to marry Earl Carter. Her father had heard of him, of course—heard of him from Lillian and from people with whom he had consulted about his daughter's swain—and what he had heard he had liked. Earl Carter, they had told him, was a man who could be trusted. He worked hard, had a good business sense about him and came from a respected family whose reputation was sound and unquestioned, despite his father's fatal involvement with Taliaferro. Still, Earl did not seem the sort of fellow who would be of much help in a campaign, and Mr. Gordy just could not envision him as an actual candidate. He liked Earl, but he liked a man with an interest in politics better. That was the sort of son-in-law he had in mind, but Lillian seemed determined, and he knew there was probably nothing he could do short of shipping her off to school somewhere else.

The courtship had been traditional for those days. The young couple had met in 1920, soon after Earl had returned from his military duty and while Lillian was a nursing student at the Plains Hospital. Her supervisor, Dr. Samuel Wise, introduced them after making an energetic pitch on Earl's behalf, describing him as a much better prospect than Lillian's former suitor. This Earl, the doctor had said, would really amount to something someday. He had more ambition than anybody he'd ever seen, he added. Lillian was skeptical. She very much enjoyed the company of George Tanner, and she had no intention of alienating him and taking up with this Carter fellow, no matter what the doctor said.

When she met him, though, she found a courtly, soft-spoken young man who thoroughly enjoyed a good time, treated her and others he met with an honest gentleness and seemed almost totally void of ego and selfishness. "I liked him right off," she remembered years later. They went to

Americus on their first date to see *The Merchant of Venice*, and they dated each other steadily after that night. For the first couple of months of their relationship, they limited their physical contact to hand-holding. Then she allowed him to kiss her. "That's how it was then," she recalled. Earl had bought a sizable farm about two miles west of Plains and they often drove there on their dates to walk in the fields or picnic in the forests. After two years, he asked her to marry him. She agreed, but stipulated that their wedding would have to wait until she returned from Atlanta with her nursing degree. A year later, on September 27, 1923, they were married. Her father, still an imposing figure at sixty years old—he was over six feet tall, weighed nearly two hundred pounds, had pale blue, almost translucent eyes and wore a cavalryman's mustache over his broad, infectious smile—gave the bride away.

Earl and Lillian moved into a rented house on the main street of Plains, just across from the Methodist church, and they began a marriage that would last for thirty years—last until his death. Dr. Wise had been right about him. He was every bit as ambitious, hardworking, imaginative in his business dealings and shrewd as he had said. Like the Carters before him, he would begin his career with a respectable legacy from his family and he would focus his energies on the gathering of land and cash. He wanted a large family and he wanted to provide amply for it, and Lillian was a willing partner, even though she puzzled him with her zealous interest in a variety of matters he deemed irrelevant. For one thing, she read almost constantly. It had been a part of her life so long, a gift from her father whose large library was available to her from her earliest days as a little girl, and she found no reason to give up her books simply because she had become a wife. Earl was also uneasy about her irreverence. Unlike his mother and his sisters, she was less than devout and more than willing to question theological premises he had always accepted as gospel truth. Once she told him she was not all that sure there was life after death and, at any rate, it was of no concern to her. He shook his head and declined to pursue the subject. But Earl loved Lillian, and deeply so, and the gentleness she had noticed in him on their first meeting became a strength of their marriage.

She became pregnant in January 1924, went to Dr. Wise in February to confirm her suspicions and informed Earl sometime in March. "I'd never seen him more excited," she remembered a half century later. "He danced a little jig around the living room, and when he finally stopped he came over and hugged me and kissed me and said if it was a girl he wanted to name it after his mother, Nina. And then he asked me what we ought to name it if it was a boy. I know he thought that since his father was dead and mine was still living that I'd want to name it for my daddy. But I said, 'Earl, if it's a boy, there's just one name for him.' And he said, 'What's that, Lily?' and I said, 'Well, can't you guess?' and he just stood there and looked at me until I said, 'James Earl Carter, Junior.' "

It was 1924, an interesting year, if not a particularly exciting one. Woodrow Wilson had died in February after four years of paralysis and a memory that had failed so badly that he could not remember his name. In 1921, he had been succeeded by Warren Harding, the Ohio editor whose skill with the language allowed him in his campaign to avoid a position on the U.S. entrance into the League of Nations, the primary issue in the race with the Democrats' James M. Cox, also of Ohio, and a young New Yorker named Franklin Roosevelt. Harding had chosen the taciturn Calvin Coolidge as his running mate and had run a "front-porch" campaign designed to assure the American voters that, after the years of war, he was just the man who could lead the country back to the old virtues, back to normalcy. He opposed the League of Nations, he said, but he supported something he called "an association of nations," and managed to avoid definite pronouncements on all the rest of the questions put to him: what specifically would he do to solve the growing problem of unemployment caused by the transition from a wartime economy to peace? and what was his thinking on the Versailles treaty, still hanging in the Senate? and what were his views on future American relationships with Europe in the postwar era? He obfuscated brilliantly, though he was not a particularly brilliant man, and won easily, taking with him to Washington and the White House an entourage of pals and cronies that came to be known as the "Ohio gang."

By 1922, Harding's popularity had waned to the degree that Republican losses in the Congressional elections were enormous. He had fashioned as nefarious an administration as Washington, a city somewhat accustomed to graft, had ever seen, and an agricultural depression—reflected in the failure of Earl Carter's potato crop and the loss of Lillian's honeymoon—made his reelection doubtful. So he left on a cross-country tour, intent on shoring up his popularity, although it would have no effect whatsoever on the young couple in Plains. Earl, voting in his first presidential election in 1916, had cast his first ballot for Wilson, the Democrat, and in 1920 had chosen Cox and Roosevelt, also Democrats. He was not certain just what being a Democrat meant, but he knew he was one, and Harding would have a devil of a time ever persuading Earl Carter that he or any other Republican was worth his time or his vote. Lillian felt much the same way, and on frequent visits to her parents in nearby Richland, her still active father, Jim Jack, was energetically supportive of their political loyalties.

Harding, of course, was never put to the test of a reelection attempt. In June 1923, three months before Earl and Lillian were married, the papers were full of the news that the Senate was investigating allegations, later proved, that Harding's Secretary of the Interior, Albert B. Fall, had taken a bribe in exchange for leasing government oil reserves to private concerns. The Attorney General, Harry M. Daugherty, an old friend and his political mentor from Ohio, was implicated in scandal also, and Jesse W. Smith, one of Daugherty's aides, had committed suicide after it was disclosed that he had made some Justice Department deals with those who were being swept up in the Teapot Dome affair—a scandal of Watergate proportions. There were cries for Harding's resignation. There was talk of impeachment. Neither came to pass. Instead, Harding died—died in San Francisco in early August, about six weeks before Earl and Lillian were married, and Coolidge, who believed the business of America was business—Earl thought that was just fine, even though Coolidge was a Republican—moved into the White House. The Democrats were as happy as the young newlyweds. After the scandals, 1924 would almost certainly be a Democratic year.

In the spring, Earl and Lillian bought a radio. Like the vast majority of Southerners, they had no electricity in their rented house, and the radio—it was the first in Plains—was powered by a battery. A few weeks later, Earl bought a Model A Ford for $350. It cost $60 more than the standard model because it had a self-starter, a convenience Earl wanted so that he could teach Lillian to drive. Mass production was having an impact on consumer prices. The original Model T had sold for nearly $1000. With the new car parked in the yard, the Carters would often sit on their front porch in the evenings, their new radio linked to the big battery, listening to music from Atlanta, with Lillian humming happily along to the latest tunes. The music of the country was changing, reflecting the nation's urge to be different. George Gershwin had just finished something he called *Rhapsody in Blue*, a blending of Tin Pan Alley idioms and syncopations into a classic form and orchestration; and operettas, such as Sigmund Romberg's *The Student Prince* and Rudolf Friml's *Rose Marie*, were as big or bigger on Broadway than the farces and the follies that had been its longtime mainstay. The Carters seldom attended such performances though and were content to take their music on their front porch in the evenings, tolerant of the crackling static that occasionally all but obliterated such songs as "Big Butter and Egg Man," "Lady, Be Good," "I'll See You in My Dreams," "Indian Love Call," and "Yes, Sir, That's My Baby." Lillian's favorite was a snappy little number called "Sweet Georgia Brown," but Earl liked all the music.

Sometimes, they would move into the living room and dance together, just the two of them and their new radio. Earl loved dancing, although he was not certain how proper it was for an emerging pillar of the Plains Baptist Church, the largest congregation in town, to be dancing with his pregnant wife in their living room. They were already talking at the church about what a fine deacon Earl would be in a few years, and he was cautious about his public image. The gossips could hurt him, he knew, but Lillian was undeterred. "I just laughed at him when he'd pull the curtains," she recalled, and if her husband grew tired of dancing, she would dance by herself, swirling around the room, riding the crest of her happiness.

Almost everything made her happy, including little debates with Earl on the theory of man's origins. She liked the Darwinian approach. Earl argued for a while and then gave up. He knew it wasn't what the church accepted. Such a theory had already been officially judged to be completely heretical by the Presbyterians that spring, and he felt sure the Baptists would make a similar pronunciation at their next national convention. He spoke to Lillian once—only once—about her interest in such matters, and she very curtly informed him it was none of his business. He backed off. It was her nurse's training, no doubt. She had known a lot about birth control when they were married, and he had known very little, and it was she who had spent one evening out on the porch patiently explaining to him the growth of the fetus inside her body—the stages of development, the processes taking place—and he enjoyed it thoroughly after shedding an initial embarrassment. Earl was neither dull nor dense. He had a good, quick mind. "But he wasn't all that curious," his wife remembered many years later. What he lacked of that instinct, she more than compensated for.

Blessed with an indefatigability that astonished the neighbors, Lillian went at her days as though each was to be the last. She was not averse to the domestic tasks traditionally assigned to the wife—she cooked and washed and sewed and cleaned the house and kept a little garden and canned vegetables—but she seemed always to have time for pursuits that seemed entirely out of place there in that tiny hamlet in southwest Georgia. She spent a great deal of time with the women in the black families in the community. She translated her familiarity with simple health and hygiene measures into the everyday language and experience of their poverty, including her knowledge of birth control and its advantages. Although none of the black men ever said anything to her about it, she knew that some of them thought she was overstepping the carefully drawn lines of their society, and she suspected that their pique was based on their belief that the more children in the family, the more work could be done. Earl said nothing about it. She wondered if he even knew, and doubted that he did.

She sensed that her behavior did not always please him, but she was determined to avoid the stagnancies that she felt were so easily absorbed by her contemporaries. At almost all of their meals, except when there were guests, she brought a book to the table and read while she ate. That spring she enjoyed a novel called *The Able McLaughlins* by Margaret Wilson, and *New Hampshire: A Poem with Notes and Grace Notes*, by Robert Frost. Both won Pulitzer Prizes that year. Earl preferred the newspapers—the weekly from nearby Americus, the daily from Columbus—and he seemed preoccupied with the real-estate advertisements. Like the Carters before him, he seemed instinctively drawn to property—to the ownership of land. He had no real sense of larger trends in the national economy, but he knew what was happening around him. Farms were being sold, and with cash in hand, it was a buyer's market. Earl saved his money. Lillian grew chubby.

In early summer, as the days grew longer and hotter and heavier with the dampness and the mosquitoes generated by the nearby swamps of the Chattahoochee River, Lillian's energy began to wane a bit and she spent less and less time away from the shaded retreat of their home and more and more time with her reading. She took great interest in news accounts of the storm raised in New York by the opening of Eugene O'Neill's play, *All God's Chillun Got Wings*. There were protests and pickets, the newspaper stories reported, and while the drama was reviewed positively by the New York critics, the controversy had destroyed its potential for financial success. It starred Paul Robeson, a black football star from Rutgers University, as Jim Harris, a poor American who seeks to climb out of his poverty and the disadvantages of a segregated exclusion from opportunity by courting and marrying Ella Downey. Miss Downey happens to be white. Lillian did not read or see the play, but she wondered about its plot line. It was untenable, she thought. There was much about her society that bothered her and much she would have preferred to be different—but not the taboo of miscegenation. That, she believed, was just as it ought to be. As a young student nurse, she had been less protected from the gossip and tales of the community than other young women, and she knew that it was not uncommon for some of the white men around to besport themselves with black women—and she thought that wrong. She believed in sexual purity before marriage and she held the vows of marriage to be sacredly inviolate, but she also added an additional layer to her objections.

It was wrong, she thought, for people of one color to be sexually involved with people of another color—and it seemed especially unthinkable for a white woman to be sexually involved with a black man. It was—well, it just wasn't right, and it was something she simply did not believe ought to be discussed. She thought, perhaps, that if she were in New York, she probably would have picketed the theater too. She had lived with black Southerners all her life. She was as gentle and as compassionate and as fair-minded a woman as her society could have possibly produced—but there were some things that were just not meant to be.

Why, if a black man ever looked at her sideways and Earl found out, as even-tempered as he was, he'd be bound to deal with it—bound by that code she could not bring herself to disapprove, the code that governed their society and managed their lives and colored their thinking and shaped their souls. Earl just might go after his shotgun, she knew, and then go after the black man who dared to suggest that the line could be crossed. He did not mistreat anyone, including black people. "Never abuse a nigger," she would hear him say so often over their years together—but she knew that he would probably respond with anger and perhaps violence if he found any Jim Harrises around Plains, casting their eyes about in search of an innocent Ella Downey. Earl subscribed to the universal Southern notion that white women, after all, were born to be protected, especially from the savageries of black men's sex which, as almost any white man with half sense and one eye could tell you, was different.

As almost any white male in the South knew, black men were much better endowed sexually than whites. It was, as almost everyone knew, an animalistic trait. Not that it could ever be discussed openly—this basic racial difference—but the facts could easily be disseminated in rousing jokes and bawdy stories. And white men mildly disturbed by nature's inequity could always take comfort in the fact that not only could they collectively ensure that few white women would ever come to realize the difference, it was they who were superior after all. Whatever else was true about black men, it was evident that white men were better men—smarter, more decent, more honest and much more capable of protecting their women against black men than black men were capable of protecting black women against white men. It was a prima facie case of superiority, as almost everyone knew—and Lillian, while she felt that it did not quite make sense, had lived with it much too long to give much thought to why it did not. Her life and Earl's, together and individually, moved in those days at a steady, predictable pace, within immutable boundaries beyond which neither considered going. There were only two kinds of white people, Earl would often say, those who will "abuse a nigger" and those who won't. It was a special sort of morality that was practiced in the white South with deep fervor, and the verb "to abuse" was as loosely defined as the noun "freedom."

Georgia's origins were libertarian and religious—so much so that in 1735, long before Kindred Carter brought his family down from North Carolina, the trustees of the sprawling colony officially banned both rum and slaves within its jurisdiction. The prohibition on both lasted fourteen years, and by 1750, Savannah was challenging Charleston as the major slave market on America's southern coast. The land was being opened up by leaps and bounds. Settlers were moving westward in droves, pushing the Creeks and Cherokees before them, forcing treaties down their tribal throats. The new land was vast and rich, and profits could explode with cheap labor. Free labor was even more profitable—the labor of mules and oxen, and, of course, the labor of slaves. It was distasteful, this trade in human chattel, but it was necessary to survival. The priests, products of the Church of England, and the ministers of the fledgling Methodist Church clucked at first, then held their pious tongues and, in the end, a few of them went to the market and purchased some human flesh themselves. Ultimately, there was no one to object, except the slaves. Their argument seemed feeble to those who owned them. "Solomon owned slaves," one eighteenth-century preacher cleverly rebutted, "and if the Lord Jesus had chosen an earthly trade more profitable than carpentry, there is no doubt that he too would have owned them—and we, like our Lord, are bound to treat the slave with decency and compassion." Earl Carter's humanistic creed was older than he knew.

Still, owning a slave was an expensive proposition, especially in terms of initial outlay, and by 1858, when Kindred's
son, James, died in the two-story house that his son, Wiley,
owned a few miles north of Plains, there were twice as
many white families in Georgia who did not own slaves as
there were those who did. Nevertheless, those without them
found the institution quite acceptable, and many families
worked diligently and saved so as to be able someday to
afford at least one or two. The black human being, in the
white human being's mind, served a special function, and it
was not to be spoiled by pampering. The education of black
people, both slave and free, was legally banned in Georgia.
Anyone caught teaching a black person to read was liable to
prosecution. It was a law that merely extended an earlier
statute against teaching Indians to read. White missionaries
working among the Cherokees had been arrested and jailed
for just such a crime, and over the years, several arrests were
made and similar punishment accorded those who showed
an interest in educating blacks.

Still, some of the black Georgians, slave and free, did acquire some reading skills surreptitiously. They could not be
displayed before the whites, of course, and those who could
read were careful to conceal the fact. While most slaves
were agricultural laborers—chiefly in cotton and rice—some
gained skill in ironworking, wagonmaking, masonry and carpentry. A few bought their freedom through such work; but
whites involved in the same trades objected, arguing that
the pursuit of such occupations tended to make black people
restless and unhappy. The state legislature was more than
happy to accommodate them and in 1845 passed a law
which forbade black people, slave or free, to enter into any
monetary contract for their work.

The logic was impeccable. Black people were subhuman
creatures, fashioned by the hand of God to be agricultural
laborers in the fields of white people whose responsibility it
was—divinely ordained, of course—to provide the necessities of life. To allow a black person to pursue any course

other than that was against nature and God's laws. It was to their own benefit to keep black people away from books and private enterprise. Such adventures would only spoil God's designs, and by adhering strictly to such designs, the white South, including Georgia, built its economy to a magnificent peak in the two decades before the Civil War, an economy based plainly and simply on slavery, nothing more, nothing less.

It seems clear that although many Southern historians have explained the war in more sophisticated economic terms—tariffs, taxes, etc.—the root cause was slavery, and the election of Lincoln in 1860 posed a clear and certain threat to the continuance of the institution. Without slaves, the Southern economy would be hamstrung. Cotton could not possibly be grown as cheaply if laborers were to be paid. It was an untenable position for the South. It meant war, a war that somehow seemed never to end. A week after Lee handed over his sword at Appomattox, Federal troops stormed across the Chattahoochee River at Columbus, only forty-five miles from the Plain of Dura, and even as long as a month after the Confederate surrender, they were still burying Federal prisoners at Andersonville, a few miles to the northeast.

The Southern society was sundered. The slaves became free citizens with no means of livelihood who simply returned to the plantations and the fields as day laborers and tenants, dominated by their former masters. As the economy faded, the sprawling properties were subdivided, and many black families who continued to work the land paid for its use and the hovels in which they lived by returning a share of the crops they raised to the white owners. These tenants included many poor whites, as well, but black or white, few of them ever had the cash to finance early planting and cultivation or pay for the necessities of life for their families while the crops were growing. The landlords generously advanced supplies and cash against the expected yield of the crops. Some of the landlords opened little stores to make shopping more convenient for their tenants. Of course, to allow for the risk involved and the credit extended, they charged much higher prices for the goods they sold than ordinary stores.

There were three distinct classes of tenants. There were those who rented acreage for cash or its crop value, those who supplied their own agricultural implements and paid in return for the land a quarter or third of the crop yield and those who had absolutely nothing to invest except their labor. Such families—and that included most tenants in the years after the war—were provided with land, a house, implements, work animals, seed, fertilizer, stovewood and, in many cases, food by the benevolent landlord. When the crops were harvested and sold, the money was divided equally between the landlord and the sharecropper, but since the landlord kept the records of his contributions to the tenant's well-being, few tenants finished the year in the black or even. The debts were held over to the next year and the next and the next. The cycle was unbreakable, and after years of work, the sharecropper had no more share in the land he tilled than he had when he began. His family's life was lived at levels below subsistence. Hope and dreams were murdered by the meanness and madness of the arrangement. A new South had been born. By 1890, nearly half the population in the states of the old Confederacy was black and more than 90 percent of the blacks in the South were illiterate. Less than 3 percent owned any land.

By the summer of 1924, as Lillian grew plump and tired, little had changed. Less than 2 percent of Georgia's black farmers owned the land they worked. There were schools for their children by then. The new state constitution of 1877 had provided separate educational institutions "for the white and colored races," and by that summer, illiteracy had been pared to only 40 percent among black Georgians. The black schools were not only separate in the summer of 1924, they were distinctly different. The state of Georgia, like every other Southern state, was most careful in the distribution of its educational funds. In the previous school year, it had spent just over $30 for the education of each white child in its system and slightly under $5 for each black child. The old thesis still operated: The black people should be protected against restlessness and unhappiness generated by too much education. It was devastatingly effective.

By the summer of Lillian's pregnancy, with a total black population in Georgia of more than a million, there were less than 1800 retail establishments owned by black people. By that summer, of that number of black Georgians, there were fewer than 150 black physicians, 50 black dentists and 40 black college professors in the state. Out of a million black people in Georgia in 1924, there were precisely 3 black engineers and exactly 417 black nurses. There were no hospital facilities for black Georgians except in the larger cities, and they were pitifully inadequate. Black doctors could not practice in white hospitals. The black death rate in the state in 1924 was nearly three times higher than the white death rate, and infant mortality was 2000 percent greater among black babies than whites.

Lillian did not have the statistics in hand, but she knew the basic realities they reflected, and it bothered her a great deal. If Earl was concerned about that, he said nothing, but in fact, he subsidized her interest in the poverty and the hunger and the lack of civilized opportunity she found in the surrounding area's black families. "I don't think any of our nigras ever went without food," she remembered many years later. She was a local CARE package administering to the immediate needs of her neighbors, a one-woman Red Cross flinging herself into the food emergency. Its roots and its continuing cause were never considered. "I was never much of a philosopher or a politician," she would explain in 1976. "I just saw what needed to be done and I did it. That's all." Later, after she had had her children, she would become a midwife to the community. "None of my birth-control talk ever helped," she would recall later. "If babies were money, then our nigras would have been wealthy."

There was never a doubt about her charity. It was deeply felt and passionately extended. Yet, Lillian—this wonderfully bright young woman, whose sensitivities were not only beyond her stolid husband but a matter of local wonder as well, this skilled, perceptive reader of books and whatever else her fragile hands could find—was caught in the same iron-jawed trap as her Southern contemporaries of like mind and similar instinct. There was a point beyond which she could not extend herself. It was not a question of whether she would. It was simply a matter of a single human being inevitably becoming the product of all that she had seen and heard and felt and experienced—a human being who was incapable of going beyond a certain boundary drawn for her by her society. She would through the years challenge that framework and she would not always enjoy the popularity that a daughter of James Jackson Gordy might have warranted. She would march right up to the edge of the limits— but she would never cross, and even fifty-two years later, the pressures of her life in Plains with Earl Carter would show themselves in her language.

A week before her son was elected President, an erratic black preacher from a nearby city tried to worship in the Plains Baptist Church. He was rejected, rather forcefully, though not bodily. The door was literally shut in his face. It was instant news around the country—big news. It might have cost her son the White House. Several weeks later, after he had won, she remembered the incident at the church.

"Somebody," she snarled, "should have shot that nigger before he came on the lawn."

Her labor began on the last day of September. She was alone in the house, and when Earl came in that evening from his work on the farm outside of town, there was no supper waiting. It was the first time she had failed to cook for him in the year since their marriage. As dusk fell, her

labor turned harsh, as in most first pregnancies. Dr. Wise
arrived, and Earl was shooed from the room. She was taken
to the Plains Hospital. Lillian knew what she was doing,
knew what was happening, but she could not help but cry
out. She had helped other women deliver their babies and
nothing in her own experience surprised her. "Except the
pain," she remembered years later. "Like everybody else, I
thought I was going to die. I prayed that I would not die.
Later, I prayed that I would die." Around noon on October
1, 1924, James Earl Carter, Jr., was born. "I felt I had just
become queen of the universe," his mother recalled so
many years afterward. "Not that he was anything to look at,
of course. He was as ugly as any newborn—but I'd always
been afraid that maybe I couldn't really do what all those
women I'd watched do. After I had, it made me proud. I felt
as though I was the queen. I didn't care about seeing Earl. I
didn't care about seeing anybody. All I cared about was that
the baby was all right and I had done it. I had done it. I had
had a baby. Lillian Gordy—uh, Lillian Carter was a
mother."

Earl, she remembered, was ecstatic. "His eyebrows were
dancing," she recalled. "That was the best way to know if
he was happy or not—when his eyebrows began to twitch.
That was the signal. 'Course, he had a wonderful smile and
he was smiling, of course, but the main thing was that Earl's
eyebrows were doing the St. Vitus's dance. He was so happy
that I forgot that I was the hero of the whole thing—which I
was, of course. He just went on and on about how pretty the
baby was. He wasn't, of course, but he was oohing and aah-
ing so much that you'd have thought the baby was Jesus
Christ. I knew he wasn't of course because I knew I wasn't a
virgin."

Lillian, wrinkled and far past the Biblical actuary's estimates, loved her joke so many years later, loved it and
laughed, and for a millisecond or two was as lovely as the
day she first became a mother. "It was a great day," she said.
"I was just as excited as Earl, but I couldn't seem to stay

awake. Once, when I finally woke up after a long, long nap, Earl was about to go to pieces. The baby was screaming his head off, really carrying on. The little thing was just hungry, but there was nothing his daddy could do because I was breast-feeding him. Earl was afraid to wake me up, but he couldn't handle a hungry baby either, so he was just about a nervous wreck by the time I came to. He wouldn't let the nigra woman take the baby. It was strange, as I remember it. She'd been around our house for quite a while, but Earl, he wouldn't let her have the baby. He said he was scared to trust such a little thing like that with somebody else. He sure loved that boy, but then, almost everybody did."

Southern summers linger long past Labor Day, sometimes reaching well into late October, giving autumn little chance to mark the transition of the seasons, and Earl and Lillian knew that and spent as many evenings as they could out on their front porch, poking at their new baby, examining him, enjoying what was left of summer's warmth, watching the trees change color and shape in the fading light, listening to their radio. Sometimes, after the baby was asleep, they would turn the kerosene lamps low in the living room and dance late into the night.

They were good times for them. He was thirty years old and she was twenty-six, and except for his poor eyesight— one of the reasons he took no interest in books—they were in good health. Lillian quickly regained the energy that was her hallmark and adjusted easily to her new role as a mother and soon returned to her former pursuits—her reading and her regular circuits around the community, checking on the health of its black residents. They called her "Miz Carter" and said "yes, ma'am" and "no, ma'am" to her and spoke well of her in their own circles.

By 1926 she was pregnant again, and when her first daughter was born that year, she was named Gloria. The little house in Plains was not big enough for the four of them, Earl complained, but Lillian said it was just fine. Still, he seemed uncomfortable there. He talked often of moving and finally in 1928, after resisting the idea so long, she relented, and they moved to a larger house on the farm Earl had bought before their marriage just outside of Plains on the fringe of a black community called Archery. Jimmy was four years old, and although Lillian had already taught him to read at a level far beyond his age, he was not quite ready for the gift he received from his godmother soon after they moved. It was the complete works of Guy de Maupassant. Lillian put it away, after reading the entire set herself.

Earl decided to open a store on the lot just east of their new house. "He asked me if I thought it was a good idea," Lillian remembered, "and I said it was completely up to him, just as long as he didn't expect me to work in it. I had no intention of becoming Earl Carter's clerk. I think I made that clear to him and he accepted it." He stocked his new business with the stuff of rural life—kerosene and lamp wicks, overalls and brogan shoes, tobacco and snuff, rattraps and castor oil, soap and sugar and flour and feed and seed, and it was an instant success. Alton, his older brother, who had been the dominant male figure in the Carter family for over twenty years by then and had become a storekeeper himself in Plains, was quite impressed with Earl's business acumen.

"You know, you see folks that work, work, work all their lives—I mean, just work like niggers from sunup to sundown—and never seem to have a thing to show for it, just barely scrimping along, making a living, not much more," Alton mused in the summer of 1976. "Then, you see folks like Earl. I think he was some sort of a wizard, maybe a genius or something like that. I don't mean he didn't work hard. He really did. He wasn't afraid of a hard day's work and he didn't mind getting his hands a little dirty—but the thing about Earl was that just about everything he touched turned to money for him. I don't think he ever made a mistake in his life when it came to money. That was the sort of fellow Earl was. Now, he was honest as the day is long, but he could sure find out where the dollars in town were, and he sure knew how to get his hands on them—and I'll tell you this, he knew how to use a dollar once he got his hands on it. Yes, sir, I believe my brother Earl was a sort of wizard when it came to money." Lillian agreed. She had come from a family that had everything it needed and she had married a man who was determined to go one step beyond. She and the children would have everything they needed—and more.

"We weren't rich," she remembered, "but we weren't poor. We lived very, very well in terms of having what we needed—and a little bit more. You take the radio, for instance, and the car. They cost a lot of money for those days, but Earl thought they were important for us to have and so he just bought them. It was always that way for us." Still, it was not an easy life. There was no plumbing in the house. An outdoor privy stood a few yards beyond the back door. The clapboard home was well shaded by a veritable forest of trees—pecans, magnolias, figs, mulberries and chinaberries—and in the summers it remained cool and comfortable inside. In the winters, though, the two fireplaces and the cooking stove in the large kitchen were insufficient to heat it well. In Jimmy's bedroom on the back side of the house, there was no source of heat at all, and he often went to sleep in the wintertime snuggled against the heat of bricks that had been warmed on the stove and placed in his bed. Water for household use was pumped by hand from the well in the backyard. Wood for the stove and the fireplaces was chopped and sawed. Each morning, the kitchen-stove fire had to be rekindled and each night the kerosene lamps were filled. The yard around the house had to be swept. There was no grass, only white sand. In Lillian's kitchen was an icebox in which she kept food from spoiling—sometimes. The ice was delivered a few times a month by an itinerant iceman.

Earl's land sprawled for hundreds of acres around the

house. More than two hundred black people lived on it in tiny, ramshackle structures he provided rent free. The men who worked for him were paid a dollar a day. Women received seventy-five cents and children got a quarter. The days were long, beginning well before sunrise with the clanging of a huge bell in the Carters' yard. In the big barn, the mules would be roused and hitched to wagons in the lantern light. The wagons were loaded with implements and seed or fertilizer or the appropriate supplies for the day's work and then driven to whatever portion of Earl's land was to be dealt with. There were rest periods scattered through the day for meals and to allow the mules a breather, but it would not end until sundown when the process would be reversed. The mules would be unhitched from the implements, put to the wagons and driven back to the barn. Water was pumped for them and they were fed—and then, only then, did Earl and his tenants, usually exhausted, head to their homes for their own supper.

His major crops were cotton, peanuts, corn, watermelons, Irish potatoes and sweet potatoes—and the requirements for each consumed the entire year in steady seasons of planting, cultivating and harvesting. There was always work to be done, and slack times were few. Soon after Christmas, regardless of the cold, the land was broken, a torturously slow task performed by mules and plows. Then, the land was harrowed, using discs and sharp-toothed implements, and then plowed again as a final step for planting. Guano distributors spread the fertilizer up and down the plowed rows in preparation for the seed. Corn planting began in March, then came the cotton, then the peanuts and then the other crops—and as soon as the seeds sprouted, cultivation began and continued until there was no further need for it or until the plants were mature enough to make it impossible. By early June, the crops were "laid by," left to nature, that is, until harvest time—but June was a time for cutting, shocking and thrashing grain and harvesting the watermelon crop and hauling it into Plains for shipment to the North.

By mid-July, the major crops were ready for harvest. The

cotton was picked by hand, the peanuts—which grow beneath the ground—were pulled, and later, after the corn
leaves had been plucked from the stalks for fodder, the ears
were picked by hand, and taken by the wagonload to the big
barn. The peanut vines were baled for livestock feed—and
suddenly, the summer would be gone again, and with the
abrupt arrival of winter, it would be the season for hog
slaughtering and meat curing and cane cutting in the fields.
It was also the time for making sure there was fuel for the
stoves and fireplaces. Dozens of trees were felled. Oaks and
hickories were cut into logs for the fireplaces and stacked
into neat cords near the house. Pine was split in smaller
chunks for use in the cooking stove, and the cycle would
have come around again to Christmas and breaking the land
that had yielded itself to the Carters in the previous year.

Still, there was time for the fun that Earl and Lillian enjoyed. They made time for it. They invited friends and relatives to the house. There were parties and dancing and
laughter, and one night Jimmy emerged from his bedroom
in the back, angry with all the adults in the house and the
merriment that was keeping him awake, walked out into the
yard with a blanket over his shoulder and climbed into his
tree house to spend the night. When the guests departed,
his father called for him to come down and come in. He did
not answer. Earl whipped him soundly the next morning
with a switch he pulled from a peach tree. When he called,
he wanted his son to answer. It didn't happen again.

In 1929, another daughter arrived for the Carters. She was
named Ruth and she was born just about the time her big
brother entered the world of private enterprise. Encouraged
by his father (Lillian remembers that Earl practically ordered him), Jimmy became a peanut salesman. For thirty-
eight of the next forty-eight years in his life, peanuts would
remain his major source of income. "I remember how he
looked," his mother said in the summer of his presidential
campaign. "Barefoot and no shirt. He'd pull that little wagon
of his out to the peanut fields and he wasn't any bigger than

a peanut himself." He would pull the peanuts out of the ground, shake the dirt from the vines and pile them on his wagon. Back in the yard near the house, he would pull the nuts from the vines and wash them carefully, leaving them to soak overnight. Early in the morning, as his father went off to the barn to begin his day, Jimmy would build a small fire in the yard beneath a black pot and boil the peanuts in salt water. He would put about half a pound in each of twenty brown paper bags from his father's store and after breakfast walk the two or three miles down the railroad tracks into Plains where he would sell the bags for a nickel apiece. He would return home in the afternoon, his wagon empty, place his dollar in the top drawer of his chest and head to the peanut field again to repeat the process.

He had a few regular customers, including the Plains cobbler who was a two-bag man, but most of his merchandise he hawked where he could, at Uncle Alton's general store and mule stable or the service station down the street from the house where he had been born only five years before. Sometimes the men he approached with his peanuts teased him and played pranks on him, and although his parents and his Uncle Alton remember him as a shy, quiet little boy, he was always back the next day, pulling his wagon, selling his wares. On Saturdays, when the farmers and their families traditionally gathered in Plains to shop and see each other, Jimmy often sold as many as a hundred bags—and, as always, the money went into the top drawer of his chest. He was his father's child. "He always knew to the penny how much he had," his mother recalled. "He didn't spend much time counting it or anything, but he always knew, right to the penny."

But there was time enough for him to play, too, and as the years of his boyhood passed, he lived a Tom Sawyer life of adventure and mischief. Most of his playmates were the children of the black tenants on his father's farm and the other black families who lived in Archery. It was hardly a town at all—just a collection of about twenty-five old houses

where the black families lived, an African Methodist Episcopal Church and school and a store or two, including
Earl's. Only one other white family lived in the area—the
Watsons—but their children were all older than Jimmy, and
he spent most of his time with black children. They swam
together and ran together and built tree houses together and
stayed in them overnight and often for entire weekends.
They rode horses and mules together and fished together
and hunted together and did chores together—fixing fences,
feeding chickens, milking cows, grinding sugarcane, prun-
ing watermelons, pumping water, digging sweet potatoes,
cutting firewood. They used whatever was around them for
their toys—steel barrel hoops to roll with a heavy wire
pusher, old disc blades on which to slide down straw hills,
slingshots to hunt with, homemade kites to fly or June bugs
leashed to a string—and there were corncob fights that took
place inside the barn with hay bales as fortification. They
raised welts on one another with the corncobs, and if they
were feeling especially aggressive, they dipped their ammunition in water, thereby increasing the stinging effect of a
direct hit.

The most prominent black citizen of Archery was William
Johnson, a bishop in the African Methodist Episcopal
Church, the pastor of the local congregation, the headmaster
of a small school and the executive director of an insurance
company that grew out of a black fraternal order. His church
was one of the centers of the community. Just across the
road was a tiny store built of wood but covered with flattened tobacco cans.

The other gathering place was the train stop. The tracks of
the Savannah, Americus & Columbus Railroad ran right
through the center of the community, a short stone's throw
from the Carter's front yard. The train, pulled by one of the
first diesel engines in the rural South, made one round trip
daily. If an Archery citizen wished to ride, he walked up the
tracks a short distance and placed a red leather flag in a
holder beside the rails. The engineer would note the flag

and stop in Archery to take on passengers. Because of the engine's peculiar shape, when compared with the traditional form of the steam locomotive, it was known as "The Butt Head." The fare from Archery to Americus, thirteen miles away, was fifteen cents. The single passenger car was segregated. Whites rode in the front.

Jimmy started to school in Plains in the fall of 1930. Because of the ordinarily lethargic tempo of the local economy, it was difficult to notice that the country was in a depression. Not much was different. Earl and his black tenants worked just as hard as they always had, Lillian ran the house and read her books and raised the three children— and life went on. Then the bottom fell out of the market for crops. Peanuts dropped to a penny per pound. Cash became scarce for most farmers. Credit was a necessity for almost everyone, but not for Earl. He had dollars—the dollars he'd earned over the years. He had held onto them and he owed no one. The Carters were in good shape. Earl built a tennis court between the store and the house and he bought Jimmy a pony for his eighth birthday in 1932. Lillian bought him books. The next month, Franklin Roosevelt was elected President. It had been twelve years since a Democrat had been in the White House. Earl and Lillian and Alton and Jimmy's grandmother, Nina, and his grandfather, Jim Jack Gordy, were pleased. Like the vast majority of Southerners, they were Democrats. "Yellow-dog Democrats," Alton recalled years later. "That means that we'd have voted for a yellow dog if it had been running as a Democrat."

They were doubly pleased by Roosevelt's links with Georgia. He had built a summer home at Warm Springs, about fifty miles from Plains, and had spent considerable time there bathing his polio-paralyzed legs in the tepid water of what had been a nondescript spa. He had taken the time to get acquainted with the local citizens and they had liked him, or so the reports from Warm Springs said. Earl was bothered a bit by the stories about Roosevelt's wife, Eleanor. Damned if she wasn't a lot like Lillian—always poking around in the black houses, seeing if everything was all right, checking on the babies, taking medicine and food. He called Lillian "Eleanor" once, as a joke. She did not think it was very funny. She thought he meant she resembled Mrs. Roosevelt physically.

By 1933, Jimmy's boiled-peanut business, and his systematic saving, had brought him enough cash to purchase five bales of cotton, but since cotton was selling so cheaply, his father advised him just to hang on to it. He stored the big bales in one of Earl's sheds and waited. The work continued. The Carters' farm was a veritable beehive of diversification. Not only was it producing watermelons, cotton, peanuts, sweet potatoes and corn, it was also producing honey and goose feathers and milk and eggs and wool and blackberries and other fruits and vegetables, and timber and meat from their hogs and their cattle and their goats and sheep. Earl not only sold his products through his own little store next door to the house but he began to sell to other stores as well. He exchanged the wool sheared from his sheep for finished blankets which he sold. He began to manufacture a sugarcane syrup bottled under the label "Plains Maid," and it soon became a favorite in many of the surrounding country stores. He separated sweet milk from his cows and sold cream and butter to the local groceries, along with chocolate milk in nickel bottles for other stores and service stations.

In the winter, the Carters slaughtered as many as forty hogs a day, and then, like a factory assembly line, would transform the bodies into merchandise—hams cured by the Carters, sausage ground by the Carters, souse meat spiced by the Carters, lard rendered by the Carters, pigs' feet pickled by the Carters. Peaches and wild cherries and blackberries and muscadines became jelly and jam and occasionally wine, and the tomatoes from the garden were used to make catsup. It was hard, hard work, but Earl Carter's family and tenants survived, month after month, with food on their tables and, for many of them, some undefined expectation that the new President—this Roosevelt who was a part-time Georgian—would change the country's luck. "Earl had high hopes for FDR," Alton remembered. "He was crazy about him in the beginning. Liked him a lot and liked what he was doing and Lillian was just as fond of him, too."

It was during this period that Earl became an informal banker for the area. Farmers would come to him for money, put up their land for collateral and walk away with the cash they needed. Later, when some of them could not pay him back, Earl's holdings expanded. The former owners became renters, joining the growing number of people around Plains who worked for Jimmy's father. The boy wasn't doing badly, either. In 1937, the year his brother Billy was born, Jimmy finally sold the cotton he had stored in Earl's shed. It brought him enough to purchase five houses in Plains. At thirteen, he was a landlord. The houses had belonged to the local mortician. Jimmy purchased them from his estate after his death. They provided $16.50 a month in rental income for him from then until the middle of World War Two, and he kept them until 1949, finally selling them to the tenants. Earl was proud of his son's interest in property. He had always been proud of his son, even though he had been a rather stern father to him. Lillian thought his sternness had prompted a great love for him from Jimmy, perhaps an even greater love for him than for her. She had been the gentle, indulging parent. She had read to the boy over the years and then taught him to read himself and bought the books he wanted—but at night when the children would come into the living room to say their prayers and their good nights, it was always at Earl's knee that they bowed.

The boy was obedient and hardworking, eager to please his father. As their lives unfolded, their relationship would deteriorate, especially when the boy left home and entered a world of technology and ideas that were alien to the father. But in those sunshine days of their lives together, they were as close as any father and son had ever been. Jimmy was so full of energy and ideas and laughter. He had his maternal grandfather's infectious grin and he seemed always to be on the move, finishing one project, planning another. Earl called him "Hot," a name he shortened from "Hot Shot," and Lillian remembered that her husband—a stolid man not easily given to tears—had once wept softly when Jimmy spent two weeks with the Gordys in Columbus where they had moved. "He said, 'I sure do miss ol' Hot,'" Lillian recalled. "Then he said it again. 'I sure do miss ol' Hot,' and I looked up from my book—we were eating supper, I believe—and I looked up from my book and I was never so surprised in my life. There were tears in his eyes. I just reached over and put my hand on his arm and told him Jimmy would be home before he knew it."

In the summer of 1938, Archery—like so many other communities around the country—was abuzz with speculation about the fight. It was called nothing else. "The fight" was sufficient. It would match a young black man named Joseph Louis Barrow against a young German named Max Schmeling. Barrow, of course, was Joe Louis. He had won the heavyweight title the year before by pummeling James J. Braddock for seven merciless rounds and then flattening him for good in the eighth. Braddock had won the championship from Max Baer in 1935. Baer had won it from Primo Carnera in 1934. Carnera had taken the crown from Jack Sharkey in 1933, and Sharkey had won it the year before that with a fifteen-round decision over Schmeling, after Schmeling had taken it in 1930 on a foul that may not have been a foul but which was declared to be so nevertheless by the officials. After Schmeling lost to Sharkey in 1932, he fought Louis in Berlin and beat him. It was the young black man's first loss, and he moved through a succession of opponents over the next few years before winning the heavyweight championship of the world. He was an instant hero among black people. A quiet, shy Alabamian, nearly illiterate, he exploded in the ring.

Louis had beaten everybody—everybody except Schmeling, who was a rather perplexing, bewildering symbol for much of white America. His country, or so a lot of journalists were suggesting, was governed by a megalomaniacal little man whose iron-fisted approach to government left little if any space for individuality of thought or civil liberties, including religious tolerance. There was even some talk that Chancellor Hitler and his National Socialist party members conceived of themselves and other Germans as members of a superior race, a notion that seemed rather farfetched to many white Americans, especially in light of the fact that it had been the Americans who had finally supplied the men and matériel for the defeat of the Kaiser in Earl Carter's war only a generation before. Besides, in the 1936 Olympics, staged grandly by the Third Reich in Berlin, an American sprinter named Jesse Owens had dealt rather handily with the best the world had to offer, including the Germans—and for many Americans, Hitler's talk of Teutonic superiority was just so much prattle. There was an initial inclination, when talk of "the fight" began, to oppose the German and fall in behind the native-born American from Mobile, Alabama. It just made good sense, even if Schmeling was not a Nazi.

Still, the presence of Louis on the national scene was discomfiting for many white people. He was the first black champion in his division since Jack Johnson nearly thirty years before, and since then, the heavyweight crown had been held by so many rather wonderful figures, all white, all American—Dempsey, Tunney, Baer, and the effervescent James J. Braddock—and it just seemed altogether appropriate that a white man should rule boxing in the same way white men ran the rest of the country. So, when Louis beat Braddock and the championship went to a black man, the word went out urgently for a new white hope. It was a fruitless search. Louis was so overwhelming, so strong, so absolutely the best in the world that his success was grievous to many whites.

America, after all, was a white country. America, after all, had already shown its mastery over the world. If times had gone a little bad for the country over the previous few years, well, hell, that was no reason everything had to go bad, and that included sports in general and boxing in particular. There were no black people in major-league baseball and none in the fledgling professional football leagues, and tennis and golf were exclusively white men's sports except for caddies and locker-room attendants. So why, why in the name of everything that was obviously American, was it necessary for black men to participate in pugilism?

Actually, it seemed unfair to many. Black men, as most everyone knew, were inherently stronger than most white men. Their anatomy was better suited to taking punishment. It was difficult to floor a black boxer by hitting him in the head. It was just—just an inequitable situation, and for many Americans it seemed a negative symbol of what was happening in the country. Times were bad for everybody, and they had apparently gone sour in boxing as well. This Joe Louis, this big black buck they called the Brown Bomber— this guy just wasn't as American as most Americans, and for many white Americans it was only a small warp of chauvinistic logic from there to turn their sympathies back to the German challenger.

After all, those stories of Hitler's persecution of Jews in his country seemed a bit overblown. No one would actually treat an entire segment of the populace badly simply because it happened to be a certain way or look a certain way. That sort of thing just wasn't done in a civilized world, and besides there was a growing suspicion that the international Jewish conspiracy was planting such rumors to stir up the rest of the world against the Germans. That was Colonel Lindbergh's theory, wasn't it, and who was to doubt the Lone Eagle's grasp of the international scene? If the Germans were good enough for Lucky Lindy, then Schmeling was a good enough champion for white America. Moreover, it was not insignificant for many Americans to remember that Schmeling had dealt Louis his only defeat. In white America, the German gradually became the favorite.

Still, in the black communities across the country—from his roots in south Alabama poverty to the teeming cities of the North—Joe Louis was a veritable god. Wherever he traveled, he was venerated as a symbol of achievement and accomplishment that was purely and simply racial—black. He was the great black hope fulfilled. He had done it. He had money, power, prominence, prestige. He stayed in the best hotels, and it didn't matter about his color. They never turned Joe Louis away, nosiree, and there was much gossip about how Joe could have just about any woman he wanted and had enjoyed himself that way with numbers of beautiful girls, including some who were white. Whatever was true or false about Louis did not matter. It was the appearance of things that was important—and black Americans worshiped him, adored him, could not hear enough about him, could not imagine a sufficient number of myths to satisfy their craving for vicarious achievement. If they did not quite understand why they felt such a deep loyalty to Louis—just as most white Americans did not grasp the reasons for their antagonism toward him—they did not concern themselves with the mystery. It was a joyous thing, rich in its psychological tapestries and rewarding for most black Americans.

There was, for instance, a young boy in Marshall, Texas—a child of poverty, himself, deep poverty—who hung on to every word of every account of every exploit of the fabled Brown Bomber. The boy was James Farmer, and although he would eventually become a notable spokesman and leader in the black struggles for equal rights in the 1960s, he would never forget how much Louis had meant to him when he was that little boy in east Texas. Years and years later, after Jimmy Carter had persuaded him and millions of other black Americans that he was a decent man who could be trusted with the power of the White House, Farmer would remember Louis as the first positive role-model of his life. "Lord God, there he was, a black man whipping white men all over the place," he would recall. "And every time he fought, it was the same thing all over again. When he won the title, I was so excited, I nearly wet my pants. He gave me a sense of dignity, I think, although I didn't know what to call it at the time. It was nothing more, nothing less, than black pride, I know now. There was old Joe Louis out there cracking all those white boys just like he didn't know—like nobody had ever told him that us black people were innately inferior to the rest of the world." For James Farmer and for thousands and thousands of other black Americans, young and old—but mostly young—Joe Louis was more than a boxer.

The same was true around Archery, on Earl Carter's land, in Earl Carter's shacks, where Earl Carter's black laborers lived their well-ordered lives. Their days were devoid of any symbols save those that represented the apartheid society around them: the bell that clanged in the early dawn, calling them from their straw-mattress beds; the rutted lanes, cut deep by wagon wheels and pocked by the hoof-prints of mules, that led only from their doors to the main road and Earl Carter's fields and back again; the big, white African Methodist Episcopal church that was the physical repository of a spiritual dream that envisioned some afterlife improvement in their lot in life (although in neither the white churches nor the black churches was there ever any talk of a social equality between blacks and whites in the heavenly hereafter; it was generally assumed, rather, that paradise, like everything else in the divine plan, was segregated); the little store, layered with a siding of flattened tobacco cans, where the black men found illegal whiskey for cash money and sweet surcease from the rote of their day's labors; the quiet nights on their front porches immersed in the liquid darkness, swimming with rural sounds—crickets, night birds, faraway hounds barking and baying, the moan of a train heading for Columbus or Savannah or Atlanta or God only knew where, and on most evenings, the music from the Carters' radio wafting across the fields, as though it were seeking the soft lights of the kerosene lamps in the windows of the little shacks and shanties. Then, the silence: the deep, ebony silence as the lamps were doused and sleep set in, the heavy-breathing sleep of the workingman, the working-woman, the working child, the ill-paid, ill-housed but oh-so-well-loved pawns in Earl Carter's day-to-day struggle for af-fluence.

He did not abuse them, of course—not in the sense of a Simon Legree—but he saw them as other Southern planters saw their own black farmhands: the God-given labor pool from which white landowners would forever profit by divine right. The era of legal slavery was long past, but the concept survived hale and hearty all across the American South, a region caught up in the mythology of its past, chained to it by its politicians, its preachers and its patrician planters. Even Bishop Johnson, for instance—the most successful black man around Archery and in the surrounding region—knew his place in the scheme of things. When he had mat-ters to discuss with Earl Carter, he sat in his car in front of the store while his driver walked to the rear of the Carters' house, knocked on the back door and asked if "Mistuh Uhl" was available to talk to the bishop. If he was, the two men would do their talking outside, never in the house as neigh-bors, standing beside the bishop's automobile, never seated together as friends or across a table as equals.

There was but one exception to the protocol. The bishop's oldest son, with the fruits of his father's relative success and influence, had left Archery as an adolescent to be educated in the North, a not uncommon hegira for the children of black status; and when he came home on vacations, he would come calling at the Carters', filled with tales of the outside world for Lillian and Jimmy—and the young man would brazenly walk across the sandy dirt-yard, up the steps to the porch and knock authoritatively on the front door. Lil-lian loved him a great deal and he was a wonder to Jimmy, with his stories of Boston and New York—and the three of them would sit in the Carters' living room and Lillian would serve tea and cookies and the questions and answers and stories would flow.

Earl, though, always left by the back door when the bishop's son came knocking at the front, driven from his own home by the mere presence of a black man in his parlor. For days afterward he would be dour and brittle. "But he never said a word to me," Lillian remembered. "He didn't like it—didn't like it at all—and he didn't understand it either. He didn't understand how I could do such a thing that was just against everything he'd ever felt or been taught or shown by example in his mother's house; but he wouldn't talk about it with me and he never once told me not to do it again. I guess he knew it wouldn't have made any difference. It wouldn't have done any good for him to have told me to stop seeing the colored boy in our parlor. I liked that colored boy and I respected him because he was smart and because he was out there trying to get an education and trying to make something out of himself. I wanted Jimmy to get to know him and hear him talk about his adventures and his schooling and all. I enjoyed it, too, of course, but really I wanted Jimmy to be exposed to something and somebody he was not normally going to be exposed to."

But if Earl kept silent about the bishop's son, he could not help talking that spring about "the fight." Schmeling looked like a winner to Earl, and if he could not bring himself to believe that wholeheartedly, at least he could hope for such a victory for the German. Wherever he went that week before the bout, he touted Schmeling's prospects. So enormously important was the fight to him that he went looking for someone to place a wager with—to no avail. "It was pretty near impossible to find a white man who'd put any money on Joe Louis," Earl's brother, Alton, recalled. "And no white man would ever bet money with a nigger. That just wasn't done."

On the long-awaited day, several of the younger black men who worked for Earl approached Lillian in the yard of the house and asked if she would seek the permission of "Mistuh Uhl" for some of the hands to come to the house that evening and listen to "the fight" on the Carters' radio. She agreed without consulting her husband, and that night the front yard of the house held dozens of young black people, eager to hear the next episode in their idol's systematic dominance of the white man. Earl and Jimmy—by then a thin teenager—sat on the porch steps next to the radio, its cables snaking across the wooden boards to the big battery, while the black visitors stood or squatted or sat in the sandy yard, waiting for the bell and their vicarious struggle with the boss.

It was a curious scene: the excited voice of the blow-by-blow announcer against the incessant roar of the crowd from faraway New York City—and the restrained, nearly silent little audience gathered around the radio in the lamplit darkness of Archery, Georgia. When Louis promptly dispatched Schmeling and the announcer's voice rose screamingly over the roar of the thousands at ringside, feverishly echoing the cadence of the referee's count of the fallen German, there was not a sound in the Carters' front yard. "The fight" was over. Jimmy smiled. His mother had expressed her sympathies for Louis. She had transferred them to her son. Earl sighed, reached over to the radio, clicked it off and bid a perfunctory good night to the crowd of young black people, still standing quietly in the yard. He turned away and began coiling the battery cable as Jimmy picked up the radio and took it inside the house.

The young black visitors left in a group, disappearing into the night, heading through the open fields together toward their shanties and their shacks. The evening silence settled in on the comfortable home of the Carter family. Earl went straight to his bedroom without bidding good night to anyone. Jimmy went into the parlor and kissed his mother before heading toward his little room at the right rear of the house. He undressed and crawled into the feather mattress.

Suddenly, in the distance, the quiet of the night was broken by an outrageous burst of cheers and shouting. The Brown Bomber had won and Mistuh Uhl's farmhands were celebrating that victory—not in his austere, pro-Schmeling presence, but in their own way, in their own company and in their own place. Years later, Jimmy would remember that evening and write: ". . . all the curious, accepted proprieties of a racially-segregated society had been carefully observed."

They always were, by almost everyone, almost all the time. There were laws on the books in the Southern states that dictated the extreme boundaries of racial relationships—laws against miscegenation, laws against integrated public facilities, laws against integrated classrooms, laws against equal opportunities—but there were also the proprieties, as Jimmy would later describe them. One limitation was *de jure*, the other was *de facto*. There was no difference, none at all, between the two forms of segregation, save the difference between typhus and smallpox, and although Jimmy Carter knew little of the rest of the country and therefore had no opinion at the time, his black neigbors—his father's laborers—were possessed by the notion that the rest of America was different from the South. They were wrong, of course. There was no distinction between the practical effects of *de jure* segregation and the practical effects of *de facto* segregation. Racially, America was generally as Southern as the South and the South was as American as America, give or take a little *de facto* here and a little *de jure* there. As Mrs. Lettie Leland, a native of the Mississippi delta who emigrated north in the late 1930s, remembered years later, "I been down in Natchez and I been down in Detroit, and the truth is, down is down, and it don't matter where you are or who it is that's putting you down."

Still, in those years, there was some effort to compensate. America liked very much to pretend that it heartily disapproved of the South for being the way it was, even though the way the South was was pretty much the way America was. So, the South tried very hard to pretend that it was not really the way it was, hoping that someday America would come to love it for appearing, at least, to be the way America liked to pretend that it was. It was all very confusing if you did not pay close attention—and over the years from the night of "the fight," with his mother's help, Jimmy Carter would pay very close attention. He would come to know how the South really was and he would learn to pretend, like his father, that it was not really what it was, and when in later years he would emigrate, like the bishop's son, to America, where he would live for several years, he would learn to pretend with the best of the rest of them that America was not really what America really was, and when Jimmy Carter came back home to the South years and years later, he would bring with him one of the most important lessons of his life. He would discover in the course of his years that, just like the South, America had an enormous tolerance for and perhaps even a grand appetite for hypocrisy. Jimmy Carter would never forget that. He would, in fact, come to understand its implications better than any politician of his day.

I have seen
A curious child, who dwelt upon
  a tract
Of inland ground, applying to
  his ear
The convolutions of a smooth-lipped
  shell,
To which, in silence hushed, his
  very soul
Listened intensely; and his
  countenance soon
Brightened with joy, for from
  within were heard
Murmurings whereby the monitor
  expressed
Mysterious union with its native
  sea.

    —William Wordsworth,
      "THE EXCURSION"

LATE ONE AFTERNOON in the first week of March 1976, a long procession of cars and buses streamed south from the airport at Jacksonville, Florida, headed down Highway 17 toward Green Cove Springs, a tiny rural community on the St. Johns River about thirty miles away. The people living in the houses along the road came to their front porches to watch the motorcade pass, drawn by the noise of the two motorcycles leading the way, the pulsating blue bubbles on the police cars next in line, the occasional wail of a siren and the long train of vehicles carrying the candidate and his aides and his operatives and his Secret Service protectors and his local allies and their wives and families and the reporters and photographers and television cameramen and technicians—the traditional inhabitants of an American presidential campaign. It was an impressive caravan, and as it rolled along toward Green Cove Springs, the people on the front porches waved happily and threw kisses toward the highway, more expressions of country cordiality than political affection.

The region through which Jimmy Carter's motorcade was

passing that day was tough territory for him. Some of the people he saw on the porches raised little homemade placards above their heads on which they had printed in crude block letters their instincts for the Florida Democratic presidential primary, only a few days away. "Wallace for Leadership," said one. "George Is Our Man," another proclaimed. "I'll Never Lie to You: I'm Voting for Wallace," read a third—and there were more as the trip continued. Wherever he went in Florida, Carter saw strong evidence of Wallace's strength and popularity. Some reporters were suggesting that the crippled Alabama governor, making his fourth presidential race, was merely a shadow of his former self, but Carter sensed that in Florida, at least, he was a formidable opponent. Despite its overwhelming ratio of transplanted residents to native-born, Florida was nevertheless a very, very Southern state. St. Augustine, just a few miles east of Green Cove Springs, was the scene in the 1960s of one of the meanest, bloodiest resistances to racial protest and demonstrations in the entire history of the civil rights movement, including Selma and Birmingham. Children and old women had been savagely beaten by roving gangs of enraged white marauders. The Ku Klux Klan and the White Citizens Council had invaded the community—the oldest in the country—and transformed it into a living hell for black people, those who lived there and those who had come there with Martin Luther King, Jr., to try to change its racist habits.

There were scores of big towns and little towns all up and down the Florida peninsula that prided themselves, even in the seventies, on their systematic, utterly effective subjugation of black people at every level and in every facet of their societies. At Starke, for instance, just a few miles west of Green Cove Springs, the entire state of Florida, through its governmental machinery, had conspired to keep two young black men locked up in the death row of a prison there for years after another man had confessed to the crime for which they had been convicted. They had been freed the

year before by a Federal court and over the outraged protest of the state authorities. It was sometimes difficult to tell,
in fact, where Alabama and Georgia ended and Florida began, so similar were their attitudes toward race—and Carter
knew all that that day as his campaign took him closer and
closer to Green Cove Springs, a little country town that
could have been anywhere in the American South, and
Carter knew that there, as in the rest of the state's rural and
small-town areas, George Corley Wallace was going to be a
hard man to beat.

The people were Wallace's people. They saw him as their
champion. They warmed to his words, even though they had
heard them before. They saw him as their representative,
the only politician who gave a damn about the lower-
middle-class white working people whose lives were being
constantly disrupted by an uncaring, unfeeling Federal bureaucracy. They believed it when he told them that they
were the backbone of the land. They loved it when he told
them that they were the ones who "paid their taxes, obeyed
the laws, loved their families, respected their religious traditions, served their land—and always wound up getting it in
the neck." They adored him when he said enough was
enough. "They cain't spit on us and call it dew," he would
say. "You open up one of them briefcases and all you'd find
is a peanut-butter sandwich," he would growl. "You take a
look at what's happenin' in our country, and you find out, if
you look real close, that the main problems we've got are
the problems that the liberal sob sisters have caused—the
same ones that like to come down here and ask us to give
them more power so they can go back to Washington and
continue to make a mess of things," he would mutter, and
they loved it, loved it because they knew that even though
Wallace couldn't talk about it anymore—he had evolved
from a snarling segregationist who pledged eternal fealty to
apartheid in his 1963 inaugural address in Montgomery to a
sturdy champion of "freedom of choice" in public education—what he was really all about was race.

Wallace had made his mark on the history of his times as a man who stood firmly and solidly for white supremacy, and it was sufficiently indelible that he no longer needed to proclaim it. It was just there, unspoken, but clearly a part of him. He had had no other credentials in 1964 when he had run with startling success in Democratic presidential primaries in Maryland, Wisconsin and Indiana, and he had offered nothing more of consequence in 1968 when he had been an independent candidate for President, and although the years had taught him to conceal cleverly what he was really selling with the accepted and familiar code words of the era, he was still the white man's candidate in 1976, and Carter knew that in Florida, as in Georgia and all across the country, there was still one hell of a market for just such a candidate. In 1972, for instance, before Wallace was shot, he swept the Florida primary over the best the Democratic party could offer at the time—Henry Jackson and John Lindsay, making his debut as a Democrat, and Hubert Humphrey, who moved so far to his right in response to Wallace that he spent a great deal of his time criticizing free lunch programs for minority children in public schools—and Carter knew that Wallace enjoyed a substantial residue of support and strength as the Florida voting approached, and he was worried.

Florida was the critical point in his blueprint for capturing the Democratic presidential nomination. If he could not beat Wallace in a Southern state as a native Southerner himself, he would probably cease to exist as a significant candidate, and although his polls were relatively favorable, the margin between him and Wallace as measured by Carter's own analysts was razor thin. But there was more to Carter's anxiety that day than Wallace's strength. Carter knew he had made a major mistake in seriously contending the Massachusetts primary. For the first time in more than a year, he had deviated from his carefully planned timetable and game plan for winning the nomination. He had intended all along simply to do as well as he could in Iowa and New Hampshire (he had not really expected to do as well in those two states as he had) and then move directly and quickly from New England down to Florida, the place he had to win if he was to remain a serious candidate. But he had done so smashingly in the Iowa caucuses and emerged from there as the tentative front-runner, and he had won a plurality in New Hampshire. Suddenly, he was the Democrat to beat in 1976.

Then he made his first mistake. He had allowed himself to be persuaded that the Massachusetts primary, held just a week after New Hampshire's and a week before Florida's, was his for the asking. He had been so buoyed by his quick, early successes that he was unable to resist the temptation, even though he had very little to gain in Massachusetts and a great deal to lose. He waded in, investing several days and several thousands of very, very important dollars, and he misread his potential—misread it badly. There was no carry-over effect from nearby New Hampshire, and Carter finished a poor fourth behind both Jackson and Wallace. It was a potentially devastating error. Not only had he lost time and money he could have spent in Florida—where it was really important—he also had lost much of the momentum gained from his victories in Iowa and New Hampshire. He was almost back where he had started again, and all because he liked the taste of success and wanted more and more.

Foolishly, after his defeat in Massachusetts, he had told reporters that he really hadn't made much of an effort there anyway—a claim they all knew to be false and a claim that showed them for the first time that Carter, like every other politician they had ever seen, could and would shade the truth when he thought it was helpful to his candidacy or his cause, and many of the journalists had written both perspectives: the impact of the Massachusetts loss on Carter's campaign and Carter's subsequent effort to minimize what had been a major effort there.

As the motorcade headed down Highway 17 that afternoon in March, he slouched in the back seat of his car, his face drawn, his chin resting in his hand, his elbow on the car door's armrest. He would not admit it to anyone then, but for the first time in his fourteen months of campaigning, he could see the whole thing slipping away from him, going right down the drain.

Greg Schneiders, his young personal assistant, sat in the back seat next to him, as silent as he. As the procession pulled into the outskirts of the little town where Carter was to speak to a crowd gathered for an annual fish fry, Schneiders leaned toward him and said two words: "Your uncle."

Carter stared at him blankly for a moment.

"Your uncle," Schneiders repeated. "You asked me to remind you about your uncle."

"Oh, yes," Carter said. "Uncle Tom. This is where they brought him, you know. Green Cove Springs, Florida."

"I didn't know that," Schneiders said.

"Yeah, this is where they brought Uncle Tom," said Carter. "It was truly a terrible thing to happen to a man. Mother said she'd heard him talk a lot about how he wished he'd been killed."

Thomas Watson Gordy was Lillian's younger brother, Jim Jack Gordy's pride and joy, named for old, weird Tom Watson, the fire-eating populist turned racist turned anti-Semite. Tom Gordy, like Lillian, grew up in Richland, not far from the Carters in Plains, and like many Southern boys, he saw the military as a chance to get away from the field and the farms and the clay and the dust and the stifling summers and the sunup to sundown rhythms that set the pace for everyone around him. But not Tom. When he was old enough, barely old enough, in fact, he enlisted in the United States Navy, and when he left Richland and southwest Georgia, he left all of that behind for good. He found a new home and he seldom came back. Still, the Gordys and Earl and Lillian followed his nomadic life at sea through his postcards, and no one was more fascinated by the record of Tom's travels than his skinny, scrawny little nephew, Jimmy. The stamps and the postmarks were objects of wonder and awe for the little boy in Archery—Marseilles, Gibraltar, Amsterdam, Athens, the Panama Canal, San Diego, San Francisco, Seattle, Pearl Harbor, Manila, Hong Kong, Pago Pago, Sydney—and Jimmy saved them all and read them and reread them until they were dog-eared and worn, and by the time he entered the first grade at the Plains Elementary School, something quite important had happened to him.

Jimmy had already formed the vague notion in his mind— wispy but definitely there—that someday, like his Uncle Tom Watson Gordy, he would see all those places himself. Someday, he told his mother, he would be a sailor, and she said, yes, of course, you will, Jimmy. Someday, he told his father, he would send them postcards from those faraway ports himself, and he said, yes, of course, you will, Jimmy. Years later, he would be unable to recall the precise point at which he specifically decided to make the Navy his career, but he would remember those postcards from his Uncle Tom Gordy as the genesis and germ of the idea, a concept that slowly took shape in his mind, layer on layer, until it became clear to everyone who knew him that, while he was still a little boy, his dream of going to sea was more than a childish whim. He was serious, deadly serious about it. He started checking books on the oceans from the library by the time he was in the fourth grade, and before he entered the high school at Plains in the autumn of 1938, he had already written to the United States Naval Academy at Annapolis, Maryland, for its entrance requirements. He had refined and enlarged the dream even further.

He told his father of his plans. Earl was pleased. After all, he had been an officer himself in the war to end wars, and it seemed appropriate to him that his son aspire to something more than a mere enlisted man's status. Moreover, Earl was happy—and relieved—that his son had decided on a college education that the Federal government and not he would

pay for. Jimmy would be the first of the Carters ever to graduate from college, and Earl was pleased and proud of him;
but the Depression, while less severe for him and his family
than for most of the people around Plains and Archery, had
not done much for Earl's bank balance. He had bought land
and extended credit at his store and lent money to hard-
pressed friends, and the prospect of shelling out several
thousand dollars for Jimmy's education was not exactly a
happy one for Earl. If his son could go to Annapolis, it
would give him more time to get back on his feet financially,
and for the first time since he and the daughter of Jim Jack
Gordy married, he began to take an active interest in
Congressional politics.

Earl decided in the mid-thirties, after Jimmy had told him
of his plans to attend the academy, to get behind the incumbent, Representative Stephen Pace. He contributed money
to his campaigns, got to know him as well as he could, discovered that he agreed with him on a great many issues,
dismissed as unimportant those on which they differed and
laid the foundations for the pursuit of Jimmy's dream. Earl
was a storekeeper, of course, but he was also a very successful farmer and he knew enough about politics—perhaps
from his father-in-law—to understand that if you want your
boy to get an appointment to the United States Naval Academy, you have to do your plowing and planting early. Without such preparation of the soil, there might not be any harvest at all.

Early one fine autumn morning in September 1938, the
boy got up early, dressed quickly, wetted his hair from the
basin on the back porch of the house in Archery, carefully
combed it and parted it on the left, rubbed an old rag over
his shoes and sat down at the kitchen table for his first
breakfast as a high-school student. He was thirteen years
old, and although he had begun to grow vertically, he was

still shorter than most of the girls in his class and still rather slightly built. "Skinny," Lillian remembered. "Just downright skinny, but not because we didn't feed him. He ate a lot, but it seemed like he'd burn it up before he got up from the table. He had so much energy and he was always into this or into that, planning some project or something or other. He was busy, busy, busy all the time—working for his daddy or working for me or playing or running—and he was healthy. There was no doubt about that. He was skinny, but he was healthy. Lord, he'd come to the table in the morning and his cheeks would be glowing like the coals from a fire."

By that morning in the fall of 1938, the Carter family was complete. Another son, Billy, had been born the year before and Lillian had decided there would be no more. With Jimmy getting into high school and Gloria and Ruth taking a great deal of her time, she thought it would have been foolish to have had more children. Besides, she was nearly forty years old by then, and her obstetric experience as a nurse was warning enough. She knew that even though Earl had often talked of having a larger family—perhaps six or seven or eight children—she was finished. It was too dangerous. She had never opposed Earl's plans, but the Depression had spoiled them, not she. Ruth had been born in 1929, the year the bottom began to fall out of the country's economy, and both she and Earl had agreed that with the pressures on both of them trying to keep things together, having another child would have been foolish. "But as soon as things began to look better, we began to talk about another baby," Lillian recalled, "and when I finally got pregnant with Billy, we joked about naming him for FDR, since we both thought he was the man who had helped us out of the Depression."

But there would be no more children, she resolved. She had spent the Depression years working ten- and twelve-hour days as a nurse, not only at the hospital in Plains but on free-lance, private assignments around the countryside—and she was tired. She wanted to spend some time with her own family, with her new baby and, of course, with her books. It seemed like years since she had actually spent the entire day reading as she once had—and she was right. It had been years: good years, not so good years, busy years— and for the country, and for the world, momentous years. Even Lillian, with her energetic efforts to escape isolation there in southwest Georgia—to know as much as possible about what was happening around her, no matter how large the circle—did not grasp the significance of those fourteen years since she had given birth to her first child in 1924.

Those were the years in which Lenin and Sun Yat-sen and Sacco and Vanzetti and Huey Long and John D. Rockefeller all died and in which Robert Kennedy and Malcolm Little (who became Malcolm X) and Fidel Castro and Ernesto Guevara and Nguyen Cao Ky were all born. Those were the years that brought power to Stalin in the Soviet Union, to Hitler in Germany and to J. Edgar Hoover at the Federal Bureau of Investigation. Those were the years of Lind- bergh's crossing of the Atlantic and the flights over the poles by Byrd and Bennett, of the first liquid-fuel rocket and the first computer and the first television picture tube and the first electric razor and the first iron lung and the first automatic pilot.

By that morning in September of 1938, as Jimmy gulped down his breakfast at the table in the kitchen in Archery, Hitler had annexed Austria, Chamberlain had negotiated an appeasement pact with him, John F. Kennedy was already 21 years old and nuclear fission had been achieved with uranium. Martin Luther King, Jr., was a nine-year-old preacher's boy going to a segregated school in Atlanta and George Corley Wallace, Jr., was enrolling at the University of Alabama in Tuscaloosa. Anne Frank was nearly ten years old and the pride of her parents' aspirations in Amsterdam, Leonid Brezhnev was a thirty-two-year-old Russian soldier, the same age as a young Nazi named Adolf Eichmann, Charles de Gaulle was the forty-eight-year-old commander of an armored outfit in the French Army, and Marguerite Oswald was pregnant again. She had decided to name her new baby, if it was a boy, Lee. Lee Harvey, she would call him.

The world seemed to be rushing madly through momentous changes it had no time to comprehend, but in Archery and in Plains, life was steady, predictable, still moving along to the cadence of the planting and harvesting seasons. The white children and the black children spent their days together, working and playing and scuffling and roughhousing, while the adults of both races labored hard to pull their livings from the flat, dusty fields. There had been births— Ruth and Gloria and Billy, for example—and there had been deaths. Bernece Watson, the oldest son of the only other white family in Archery, had died at the age of twenty in 1935 when a local doctor had diagnosed his ruptured appendix as constipation, and Bishop Johnson had died the next year, precipitating what Jimmy would recall many years later as "the most important event which ever occurred in Archery," his funeral.

So respected and revered was the old black clergyman that his last rites attracted scores of mourners, white and black, from miles around, including many who came from out of state to be present in the Archery church for the services. In the yard around the church and up and down the dirt road, they parked their cars—dozens of big cars: Cadillacs, Packards and Lincolns, Jimmy recalled—and went inside to listen to the several preachers and choirs eulogize the bishop. Earl did not attend. The next day he asked Lillian if she thought the bishop's son—the one who insisted on coming to the front door of the Carters' house—might come back to Archery to take his father's place. No, said Lillian. Good, said Earl. The congregation probably needed an older, more experienced man anyway, he added, and went back to his work.

All through the years of Jimmy's boyhood, the weeks of his life had been distinctly punctuated by the weekends— the lazy Saturday afternoons fishing on the creek banks, the ritualistic dressing-up for a visit to downtown Plains—a gathering of eight or nine business places, an occasional movie in nearby Americus, usually with his Cousin Hugh, Alton's son, and on Sundays, the interminable Sunday-school classes, the long-winded hellfire and damnation sermons and the traditional Sunday dinner at home with mounds of fried chicken and puddings and biscuits. After the meal, he would help his mother spread a large cheese-cloth and then a tablecloth over the food, guarding it from the flies and protecting it until the leftovers were eaten for supper that night. There were few breaks in the routine of work and worship and play. One came in the hard winter of 1936, the winter after the bishop died and the worst winter anybody could remember. It snowed in Archery, a rare occasion, and everybody—the youngsters and the adults, the blacks and the whites—instinctively called a holiday.

By then, Earl Carter had grown a bit chubby around the middle, despite the fact that he often played tennis on the court between the house and the little store, and still played baseball in the summertime with some of the younger men of Plains. Similarly, Lillian was noticing a few gray hairs and cursing the cumulative changes in her figure from child-birth. "Oh, I fretted about it," she remembered, "but I knew there was nothing I could do about it. Besides, I was still prettier than most women my age, and besides, having a family was something to be proud of, wasn't it? Well, any-way, I didn't take much notice. I always believed you ought to try like hell to take care of the things you can take care of and just let the rest of it go hang. That's the way the Carters have always been, and the Gordys too. We just always did the best we could with whatever we had to do it with."

She applied that principle to child raising as well. "The kids had everything they needed," she said. "We—Earl and I—always saw to that, but they were never spoiled. I guess if it had been left up to me, I would have spoiled them, but Earl took care of that. He insisted that they behave and he was pretty keen on them doing as they were told." Jimmy was occasionally mischievous, but seldom grievously bad.

Earl had spanked him only a few times—once that night he had fled his parents' party and refused to come down from his tree house and once the afternoon he had taken careful aim with his air gun and fired a BB into Gloria's bottom and once when he had come home from Sunday school with two pennies, having kept the one he was to donate and lifted another from the collection plate as well. But he was the sort of child parents enjoy. He did his chores, he kept up with his studies, he minded his mother and father, was courteous to and respectful of his elders and, Lillian remembers, he kept his little room at the back of the house in meticulous condition. "Everything had to be in just the right place," she recalled. "He couldn't stand for anybody to come in and pry around or change things. He kept it neat and he kept it just the way he wanted it. If anything was ever mislaid or missing, he knew it wasn't his fault."

Just before Jimmy started to high school in the fall of 1938, the Carters received a letter from his Uncle Tom. It was postmarked Pearl Harbor. Tom was assigned to the Pacific Fleet. He was married by then and he had learned to box in the Navy. A photograph was included in his letter. It showed Uncle Tom standing barechested in boxing gloves in front of a large group of other sailors. He had beaten them all in the process of becoming the fleet's lightweight champion.

It generally occurs in the South sometime around puberty.

The white boys abruptly move away from the black boys to take their positions in the semiadult world of apartheid. It is not a process that they notice when it begins. It is like seepage. Gradually, the lives of black and white children— children who, like Jimmy Carter and his black neighbors and friends, had spent countless hours and days together, spinning out their childhoods in innocent disregard of their society's strictures—are separated, and finally segregated. It just happens, slowly, as they grow, until finally there comes that day when the black children hang back a bit from the white at the door to the house, waiting respectfully for an invitation to share the water from the pail and the dipper, or deferentially allowing the white child to go through the barn-lot gate first or any one of a number of symbolic acts that seal their lives apart, forever and ever, with no questions asked and no answers given. It had always been that way and that was the way it was for Earl Carter's elder son. He had started to high school and he spent less and less time with the friends of his boyhood, most of whom were not even going on beyond the eighth grade. Those who did had to walk several miles to their own classroom while Jimmy rode a bus the two miles to his—to his new friends and new books and new challenges and, of course, new opportunities, leaving the children of Archery behind, irretrievably mired in the deep, sucking mud of a world they seemed unable to change.

Jimmy did not know what was happening to him or them, of course, because, like his parents, he harbored no ill will, no rancor at all, for the black people, adults and children, he had known and loved and liked in his young life; but, like his parents, he was nothing if he was not a genuine product of southwest Georgia. There was simply no point of reference for him against which he could measure the society around him against some other arrangement. For him and his white companions, and for the black children he left behind as well, what was there in Archery and Plains was all there was. He would be a grown man before he would ever again associate with black people in social or professional situations that even suggested equality, and another quarter of a century would pass in his life before it would occur to him that it was blatantly and brutally unfair for white children to ride to school on buses paid for with public funds while black children walked. "It is not easy to give up old habits," he would write many years later, looking back on those moments of separation from his first friends, "and it is

especially difficult when they are ingrained in almost unquestioned tradition."

It was unquestioned not only by the Carters and the other
white families of Archery and Plains but by the black families as well. Like most other Southern black people,
Jimmy's playmates and their parents had little if any idea of
the energy and the money and the sweat and the blood the
black movement was expending in those days. They seldom
saw a newspaper or heard a news broadcast, and when they
did they were given no information that suggested to them
that America was other than a racial utopia. The bishop's
son was dangerous because, like Jimmy in his later years, he
had emigrated beyond the Southern shores. The bishop's
son—this brazen young man who thought nothing of sipping
tea in a white man's parlor—had no doubt found a reference
point.

While the rest of America was not much more equitable
racially than the American South, it operated a racism that
could be dealt with, or so many like the bishop's son believed. There were no laws on the Northern books. There
was simply a separation that issued from natural selection or
preference. It was as brutal psychologically as *de jure*, and it
was as effective a means of segregation as the statutory
brand, but for the bishop's son and the thousands of other
young black people who began filtering northward, it was a
welcome difference. They saw it as such a striking contrast
to their origins that many never returned, believing that
Northern opportunities for blacks were based on personal
worthiness. It did not matter that that was not the case; what
mattered was the difference, the point of reference. There
were no laws on the books in the North and there were no
round-bellied sheriffs waiting around the next corner eager
to enforce them—and once that relative liberty was tasted
by a black Southerner, the comparisons would be dangerous. Earl Carter knew that, and so he was relieved that, as
far as Lillian knew, the bishop's son was seeking his fortune
somewhere else.

Earl Carter liked his Negroes just the way they were:

meek and pliable, obedient and respectful, poor but happy in the work he gave them, aware of only what they needed to know, blissfully unaware of Marcus Garvey and the Niagara Movement and the National Association for the Advancement of Colored People, their racial pride stirred by such remote and fleeting moments as a first-round knockout by Joe Louis over Max Schmeling. Earl Carter's life was well ordered, like the lives of planters and merchants all across the South, and its order was the product of a static social structure that was simultaneously strong and solid—sufficiently so to maintain a status quo amid churning change—and inherently weak—sufficiently so that one tiny alteration would produce its collapse. Its glue was tradition, as Jimmy later discovered, unquestioned tradition. Questions could be dangerous. Southern whites did not like questions. Southern blacks did not ask them.

Jimmy had spent much of the summer of 1938 wading through the thickest book he had ever seen, *War and Peace,* and when he walked out of the little house at Archery to wait for the bus that would take him to his first day in high school, he was proud of himself for having finished it. He knew Julia Coleman would be pleased, too. She was the superintendent of the Plains education system—a bright, gentle spinster who had become the personification of the local schools in the thirty years she had been a part of them—and the joy of her life was to discover some child in whom she saw potential and then to nurture the seed she recognized, watch it grow, tend it, fertilize it, pamper it and give it special attention. She was not an attractive woman physically, which may have accounted for her lifelong spinsterhood, and some long-forgotten childhood disease had left her with a pronounced limp; but despite that and the thick spectacles she wore to compensate for her weak eyesight, she was one of the most respected people in the community. She was, it seems, a natural teacher—that rare specimen of an educator whose single passion is the transfer of knowledge, the development of skills and, most importantly, the encouragement of curiosity. "She loved questions better than answers," Jimmy's Cousin Hugh recalled; and she also loved Jimmy, others remember. She recognized his quickness, his enormous reading skills, his discipline and his willingness to listen, and she focused her own gifts on him—challenging him, praising him, chastising him, prodding him. It was a positive chemistry.

Jimmy had never known a day in his life when the importance of education was not mentioned in his home. Both Lillian and Earl stressed its value for him and the other children constantly; his studies took precedence even over his chores, though he was intelligent enough to be able to dispense with his homework in short order, leaving sufficient time for the tasks his father assigned him on the farm and in the little store. And, in almost every case of a dispute, all of them minor, his parents reinforced his teachers, especially "Miz Julia." Her word was as much law as his father's. Whatever she suggested became a commandment, and as he responded obediently to Earl, he followed her instructions without question.

It was no wonder then that he had willingly tackled Tolstoy that summer, although he first thought the massive book she had assigned him for his vacation reading was a Western adventure tale, involving cowboys and Indians. When he saw he was mistaken, he was not the least bit disappointed. He read on and on, remembering that many of the books Miss Coleman had suggested to him before had been much more rewarding than their titles or covers might have promised. For several years, she had been providing Jimmy with long reading lists, and for every five books he read and reported on, she awarded him a silver star on a little chart she kept near her desk. For every ten books, Jimmy got a gold star.

"He was a gold-star boy," Lillian remembered. "He kept

count of how many he had, and whenever he got another one, he'd come home and tell us about it. Julia was a remarkable teacher, really remarkable. She knew exactly what she was doing with Jimmy and all the other children she took an interest in. She seemed to just know how far she could push them—I mean, challenge them—without breaking them down with a load they couldn't carry yet. Oh, she was wonderful."

Miss Coleman's bibliographies were spiced with a variety of books—histories, biographies, fiction light and heavy— and although Jimmy did not realize it at the time, she was building the eclectic reading habits that would follow him all through his life, even after there were no more gold stars for him. Years later, in the opening lines of his inaugural address, he would cite one of her favorite bits of wisdon: "As my high school teacher, Miss Julia Coleman, used to say," the new President would intone, " 'We must adjust to changing times and still hold to unchanging principles.' " She would retire from her post in 1958 after a tenure of half a century, and she would die before her star pupil became nationally and internationally prominent, but he would remember her as one of the people whose influence had shaped and changed his life. "She saw something in me, I think . . . a hunger to learn," he would say.

But the Plains High School, despite her presence, was not a complete academy. Miss Coleman's insistence that Jimmy and other students learn to handle themselves in debate (she would spring formal arguments on them without warning and grade their performance in discussing them) and in self-expression through writing (similarly, she would surprise them with instant essay assignments) and her efforts at least to introduce them and expose them to fine art and classical music and worthwhile books were simply not the sort of preparation a young man set on attending the U.S. Naval Academy required, and through the weeks and the months and years of high school, Jimmy never forgot his primary goal—to be a naval officer.

In a top drawer of his chest of drawers in the little bed-room at the back of the house in Archery, he kept the copy of the academy catalog he had sent for long before high school. He memorized the rules and the academic mini-mums he would need to get there, and he worried, worried a lot. There was, for instance, a mention of malocclusion, or overbite, in the section on physical condition. The Navy, it seemed, did not want officers with buckteeth, and Jimmy knew that while his were not malformed, they were large and prominent and he knew that he did have a slight over-bite. He knew that just from chomping into an apple—and it worried him. Moreover, the catalog mentioned something called "urine retention" as an important quality of those who would matriculate to Annapolis. Jimmy interpreted that as something much more complicated than a ban on bed wetters. "I was always ashamed to ask whether that last clinging drop would block my entire naval career," he wrote long afterward. The reference to flat feet in the catalog was enough to inspire him to herculean corrective measures, even though he did not know if such a condition was a prob-lem for him or not. He spent hours and hours as a high-school boy rolling his feet on soft-drink bottles, just to make sure.

What worried him most was lack of a full science curricu-lum at Plains High School, and the Annapolis catalog was very clear about that. The closest the little school came to a science course was agriculture—a course that bored Jimmy, his mother recalled—and with characteristic discipline the boy scoured the library and his teachers' shelves for any and all books he could find on chemistry and engineering and advanced mathematics. "I don't recall seeing Jimmy without a book or several books in his hands or somewhere close by all during his high-school days," his Cousin Hugh remem-bered.

Still, he was not regarded as bookish—not by anyone who knew him in those days. He seemed to find time for the other normal pursuits of adolescence, although he was not really a very passionate athlete. He was quick enough but not tall enough to stand out as a basketball player, and he spent his years on the school's team as a substitute. He played baseball as well, but again discovered that his size and lack of exceptional strength were handicaps. "I couldn't throw the ball hard enough," he would remember. "It just didn't hum." But his stamina and his speed were perfect assets for track, and both in high school and later, he made a respectable mark for himself as a runner.

Still, his recreation as a teenager was the recreation of a country boy—fishing and hunting and hiking and camping on the banks of the Choctawhatchee River and the Kinchafoonee Creek. Some of the most delicious fun was when the sucker fish were running. Sometimes called "redhorse fish," the "suckers were fearsome fighters," Jimmy would write. "The meat was delicious if slashed in thin strips so that the tiny bones could be throughly cooked." His father had also taught him how to shoot, and he enjoyed the early-morning hunts when he would go with Earl to join a band of grown-ups at some predawn gathering spot, drink a little coffee boiled over an open fire while the men fortified themselves with a few nips of whiskey, and then as the sun came up head out into the fields, the dewy grass soaking their trousers and boots, shotguns cradled across the front of their bodies, waiting for that whooshing flutter of the birds—and then the explosions of the weapons into the quiet, morning air. The men all had work to do and the hunts seldom lasted past midmorning, and Jimmy remembers that his father often drove him to school—no one cared if Jimmy Carter was tardy—covered with feathers from the kill.

"I never did quite understand that about Jimmy, why he loved to hunt so much," his mother puzzled years later. "It was just the expected thing, I suppose. His daddy loved to hunt and all the men loved it too and there was always some sort of hunting season on—legal, I mean—and there were always guns around in all the houses. I guess it was just the manly thing to do—but I didn't really like it, not all that much. I reckon it was sort of one of the rites of manhood Jimmy wanted to be a man, like every other boy, and out there hunting with his daddy—who most of the time was either his daddy or the church deacon or his boss on the farm or his boss at the store—sort of being equals out there with their guns and all, well, I guess that made him feel like a man, having his own gun and all, and getting up so early like that with Earl. I guess that's what it was."

Lillian also recalled that her elder son began to take an interest in his appearance at about that time, spending increasing amounts of time in front of the mirror, combing his hair and worrying about the absence of a beard on his still-freckled face. "He was so pleased when he finally found a little fuzz," Lillian remembered. "He shaved it off immediately."

The years skittered past for him, as they do for most high-school students, marked here by this flirtation and there by that athletic triumph, always underscored by the eternal, unceasing, relentless cycle of the agricultural rhythms—the plowing, the harrowing, the discing, the planting, the cultivation, the harvest, and then back to the plowing, with hog slaughtering and woodcutting and canning and preserving inserted for good measure. While his interests were rapidly expanding, what with all the prodding from Miss Coleman and the support, reinforcement and encouragement from his parents, Jimmy could still not escape his father's busy farm and his father's unyielding insistence that there was always work to be done and that Jimmy was one of the people who would have to help do it.

One of the most demeaning tasks for a boy who had begun to fret about his hair and his beard was the mopping of cotton, and years later, in his autobiography, Jimmy would remember it in precisely the fashion he came to dread it. "It was a job for boys and not men," he would write. Cotton mopping was necessitated by the advent in the South of the boll weevil, a creature that became one of the few villains in Jimmy's life, an enmity he must have shared with almost every other child of the rural South in those days. The boll weevil attacked the cotton buds, drilled his way inside and ruined them. It was one of the most devastating insects in the history of American agriculture and figured prominently in the substantial shift away from cotton as a major money crop in many parts of the South. To combat its boring, the cotton buds had to be poisoned. "The normal process used was to mix arsenic, molasses and water, to pour this conglomeration into a bucket, and to walk down each row of cotton with a rag mop on the end of a stick, dip the mop into the bucket and apply a small quantity of the mixture into the bud of each cotton plant," Jimmy would write years later. "After a few hours in the field, our trousers, legs and bare feet would become saturated with the syrupy mess. The flies would swarm around us and at night when we took off our trousers, we had to stand them in the corner because the legs would not bend." That was cotton mopping. "We despised it," Jimmy remembered. It was no wonder that he set his heart on a naval career. There are no boll weevils at sea.

As the years flew past for him, they also moved with great speed in the world around him, and he began to take an even greater interest in the newspapers that came to the house in Archery and the high-school library in Plains. Even at his age, he sensed that there was an inexorable movement in the headlines toward war. In 1939, Hitler first took Czechoslovakia and then, with Russia's assistance, stormed across Poland. There was some talk about President Roosevelt sending troops to Europe, a venture that Earl deemed foolish. Jimmy agreed, but Lillian recalled that her son began to read the international news avidly that spring. "He showed me a story about submarines, I recollect," she said. "It was all about how bad they were or something or other." It was, perhaps, a summary of a series of submarine accidents in the spring of 1939, just about the time Jimmy was ending the ninth grade and beginning his first summer vacation from high school. In late May, the *Squalus,* an American sub, sank and twenty-six men were lost. A week later, the British sub, *Thetis,* went down with ninety-nine men aboard, and two weeks after that, sixty-five French submariners drowned on the *Freund.* Lillian was more interested in—and shocked by—what she read that summer of a smallpox epidemic in India that killed nearly a half-million people, and an outbreak of the bubonic plague in Uganda that claimed more than two thousand victims—and more and more, she thought, the news from the world outside Archery and Plains was unpleasant.

The next few years would do nothing to change her perspective, and by the autumn of 1940, when Jimmy began his final year in the eleven-year elementary and high-school program at Plains, she was persuaded that even as her husband had marched off to war, so would her elder son. The League of Nations had collapsed. Its final effective act had been the expulsion of the Soviet Union for its invasion and capture of Finland. Germany was straddling Europe, Japan was moving south through China after having signed a non-aggression pact with Germany and Italy—and Roosevelt, running for an unprecedented third term, was simultaneously promising to do everything he could to keep the United States out of the conflicts in Europe and Asia while busily advocating its involvement.

Earl had broken with FDR by then. He had approved of almost everything his Administration had done, and he was particularly pleased with its involvement in the Tennessee Valley Authority and Rural Electrification Administration. The Carters now had electricity and running water in their house at Archery, and Earl was actively engaged in the management of the local electrical cooperatives. But he had turned sour on Roosevelt because of what he deemed to be unwarranted interference in his private life as a farmer through his agricultural production controls. Earl believed, as did many other Southern farmers, that FDR was meddling when the farmer was told by the government when to slaughter his hogs and how many to kill. Besides, Lillian remembered, Earl had never really liked Roosevelt from the beginning, especially after 1932 when he had built his little place up at Warm Springs and Eleanor had begun to make her presence known in Georgia. "I just really think that Earl's hatred for Roosevelt grew out of his dislike for his wife," she said. "He couldn't stand to see her picture in the magazines or the newspapers. It wasn't really very nice, but that's the way he felt."

If his father had some difficulty relating to Mrs. Roosevelt, Jimmy was having very little relating to the young women with whom he went to school. "He was never what you'd call a 'ladies' man,'" his Cousin Hugh recalled, "but he never had much trouble getting a date. Never had any trouble, to tell the truth. All the girls liked him, darned near all of them—but he didn't seem to ever latch on to any particular one, at least not for a long time. Must have been his last year before anybody ever thought he was seriously interested in a particular girl."

She was Eloise Ratliff, also the daughter of a farmer and the child of a much larger family than the Carters—a family that had not survived the Depression with quite as much financial health and vitality as Jimmy's. She was a strikingly pretty young woman, with dark, shiny hair, large eyes and a marvelous smile—and Jimmy was smitten with Eloise. "He was. He liked her a lot," Lillian remembered. "She was the only one I ever knew of that he seemed to care anything about at all, I mean, while he was still in high school. But I believe he did like her an awful lot. Of course, he didn't talk to me about her or anybody else for that matter. He'd just say, 'Mama, I've got a date with Eloise. Is that okay?' And I'd say it was all right with me and he'd be gone."

Eloise was a bit older than Jimmy, and not only were they good friends but they became academic competitors as well. She was one of Miss Julia's favorites: bright, quick, disciplined—and she received as much attention from the superintendent as Jimmy. All through their years together, they had been narrowly separated academically. One year, Jimmy's grades would be slightly better and the next year she would manage a slim superiority—and when the grades were posted for the last time in the spring of 1941, Jimmy once again had edged her out. By the narrowest of margins, he would be the valedictorian of the Class of 1941. Eloise would be the salutatorian.

It never seemed to bother either of them, Jimmy's sister, Gloria, remembered. "It was just a friendly sort of competition. Nobody ever got mad or got hurt, not that I know of anyway," Gloria recalled. She knew something about competing with Jimmy, since both of them had given up trying to compete with Ruth for their father's attention. Ruth—blond and big-eyed and giggly and little-girlish—completely captivated Earl. She could do no wrong. Gloria and Jimmy went at it with each other. "We didn't fight, but we did compete," she said. "We couldn't stand for the other to get ahead. It must have helped both of us, though there were times when I wondered whether brothers and sisters were supposed to love each other or constantly try to beat each other."

One day, during the final week of school for the tiny class of 1941, Jimmy and several other boys decided it was much too nice an afternoon to spend in a classroom, and off they went to the Americus highway and hitchhiked their way the eleven miles over to the county seat for a movie. They were caught red-handed and hauled back to Plains, where they received an ultimatum. "We either had to take a licking or not graduate," Jimmy recalled. "The fellow who was going to give the punishment was very handy with the paddle and some of us gave serious consideration to becoming dropouts the week before graduation. But, in the end, we decided to take the punishment—and that's exactly where we took it: in the end."

That minor difficulty resolved, the Class of 1941 graduated intact. Jimmy was sixteen years old and, because he had finished at the top of the class, he was awarded a scholarship to Georgia Southwestern College in Americus. Eloise, who desperately wanted to go to college, won nothing. Jimmy gave her his scholarship. After all, he was going to the United States Naval Academy. Earl had been talking to Congressman Pace, and the Congressman had been saying he was doing all he could but that appointments to Annapolis were hard to come by what with the world going to hell and all and everybody trying to get their sons into the military academies. Besides, it wouldn't hurt the boy to wait a year, the Congressman suggested. He could grow a little bit, put another few months of maturity on him, get better grounded in the science and math he missed at Plains High School, and then hit Annapolis at full speed. Earl didn't like the idea at all, but there was nothing he could do. Jimmy did not seem to mind. It would come. He would go to Annapolis sooner or later, one way or another. In the meantime, Georgia Southwestern didn't look all that bad to him. After all, with the scholarship he had given her, Eloise was headed there too.

Sometime that summer there was a card from Uncle Tom. He had been reassigned from Pearl Harbor to Guam. It was certainly "a really pretty island," he wrote. "You all will have to come and see me some time." Uncle Tom was still boxing and still seemed to be enjoying himself in the Navy. Lillian told Earl it might have been nice to have spent so much of one's life traveling like Tom—to have seen so much and to have been so many different places, to have heard so many languages and dealt with them all and to have seen so many sunsets and sunrises over so many varied horizons. "And Earl just stared at me and grunted like an old boar hog," she recalled. "Just snorted, that's what he did—and then—you know, he was like this: he would react to me immediately and then change all of a sudden, like he remembered something he'd forgotten—and then, after he'd acted like I hadn't made any sense at all about my brother, Tom, he broke into a big old smile—Lord, if you'd have seen him smile, you'd know why I loved him so much—and then he said, 'It's kind of hard to make a crop if you're always running off to here and yonder, isn't it?' and we both looked at each other for a long, long time and then we both just died laughing."

That summer there were several more postcards from Uncle Tom, who seemed quite happy in his new assignment on Guam, and all of them ended up in Jimmy's top drawer in the back bedroom. There was another letter from Congressman Pace who said it looked doubtful that he would be able to arrange an appointment for the next academic year, but he had every reason to be optimistic about the following one. Earl was dubious. He wrote out a tuition check to Georgia Southwestern and Jimmy's transcript was forwarded by Miss Coleman to the little state school in nearby Americus. "He is an exceptional student," she wrote in an accompanying note. "I am truly sorry to have him leave my classrooms, but I am genuinely happy that he is moving on to a higher challenge."

It was not a propitious time to be passing what was taken then to be the final step into American manhood. Jimmy's high-school years coincided with what seemed to be an inexorable movement toward world war, and by the time he graduated that spring of 1941, much of Europe was being threatened by the Third Reich's rather insatiable hunger for more and more territory. Poland had fallen, the Battle of Britain had begun, Germany and the Soviet Union had signed a nonaggression pact which Hitler had promptly violated by invading from the west, Dunkirk had been the point of departure for thousands of Allied fighting men abandoning the continent, and President Roosevelt, in the midst of his successful campaign against Wendell Willkie, had made a deal with England, trading American warships for naval bases in the Atlantic from Newfoundland all the way down to Trinidad and British Guiana. That summer, Roosevelt and Churchill met at sea and mutually agreed to put an end to the German aggression, while the United Auto Workers banned all "Communists, Fascists and Nazis" from holding posts in the union.

Lillian and Jimmy kept up with the details. Earl knew only the broader brushstrokes. He was worried, though. He wrote the Congressman again. The answer was the same. Mr. Pace was working on the appointment. It was not an easy task, he said, but it would come, eventually. As a matter of fact, the Congressman noted, with the way things were going in the world, the appointment would probably be easier to get as the weeks went along. It looked as though there was no way the United States was going to be able to keep out of Europe's problems, he said, especially with Roosevelt and Churchill getting together and making all sorts of secret deals nobody in the Congress knew anything about; but Japan, wrote the Congressman, seemed to be taking a much more accommodating position. It didn't look as if the country were going to be drawn into anything serious in the Pacific.

That pleased Lillian, of course, for she thought often of her younger brother somewhere out there in the ocean's wilderness—she could not always remember the name of the island—and she wrote him and told him of the Congressman's optimism. "But it was just being Pollyanna," she remembered so many years later. "I knew full well there was going to be a war, and I knew Tom Gordy was going to get into it, and there was Jimmy, too, just the right age to have to go. I worried a whole lot about it all the time, but I didn't talk much about it to Earl. I knew he was already worried enough."

The concern of Jimmy's parents was a common burden for mothers and fathers all over the country, including a small, prim woman who lived not more than an hour's drive from Plains, across the state line, in Barbour County, Alabama. Her name was Mozelle Wallace and in that autumn of 1941 she had been a widow for nearly four years. Her three sons were all away at college. The middle one, George—named for her late, ne'er-do-well husband—was beginning his final year in law school at the University of Alabama in Tuscaloosa. He was twenty-two years old. She knew he would have to go if there was a war, and although she was not a student of current events, the talk around Clio—the little village where she had raised her sons—was that it sure looked as though there was no way to avoid it. She ran a sewing room in one of Roosevelt's New Deal social centers, a far cry from her talents as a pianist and a music teacher, but a symbol of the independence she had sought since her husband had died in 1937 and left her with a heavily mortgaged farm and a desk drawer full of bills. George had volunteered to drop out of his first year in college when his father died, but Mozelle would not hear of it. She was determined to be self-sufficient. She had lived so long, tied to the fortunes of her erratic husband, and she was not about to turn her back on her first opportunity to live without that burden.

So George went back to Tuscaloosa to college, to a campus that regarded him as something of an oddity. He was a pugnacious, determined young man with no money, a collection of odd jobs that provided but a mere survival, no particular place of residence—sleeping here for a few weeks and there for a few weeks, always moving on to the next place that would have him—and an aggressive aversion to the symbols of campus acceptance: the fraternities, the formal parties and dances, the clubs and the capers. He was dark, almost swarthy, and he carried himself with such a ferocity that he had few friends. He was a boy accustomed to violence, unaccustomed to direction, a stranger to discipline, an enemy of friendly counsel. He would go his own way, his acquaintances on the campus realized quickly, and he would fight anybody who interfered with his course. Still, there did not seem to be a course for him. He did not struggle academically, but he did not excel either. He made neither dean's list nor honor roll and cared nothing for either achievement. He was simply there, eking his way along, driving a taxi, driving a laundry truck, running—badly—a boardinghouse, and during the summers heading up to Kentucky and Tennessee and West Virginia to sell magazine subscriptions. He seldom spoke of home—of Clio or Barbour County or his late father or his solemn-faced mother, Mozelle. It was as though there were no yesterdays for him at all.

There were, of course, and like Jimmy's boyhood days, they were a collection of Huck Finn pastimes and pursuits in an integrated, rural setting. George and his brothers, Jack and Gerald, swam and fished and fought with black children and thought nothing of it until that adolescent point of departure when their playmates' color separated them and segregated them. But unlike Jimmy Carter, George Wallace grew up lacking the stability of a home in which there was encouragement, friendship, support, flattery, warmth and direction. George's father dreamed of being a man of power and position but seldom pursued either with much passion. Jimmy's father had no such grandiloquent dreams, but pursued similar goals nevertheless with the plodding persistence that made their attainment possible. Jimmy's father was the disciplinarian. George's father played no such role in his life. Mozelle and Earl administered the punishment in their respective families, and both preferred the branches of peach trees. Unlike those in the Carter orchard, the peach trees in the Wallace's backyard produced no fruit.

George's father was at rather constant odds with George's mother—over money, over alcohol, over how best to deal with their sons, over the boxing gloves he bought George one day when he went to Columbus, just across the river in Georgia. That was important to George's father—the ability to inflict physical punishment. He was a small man, racked by illnesses and stooped by defeat. Most people called him "Sag," but most people knew that George's father would fight over most anything. He would argue awhile, and then he would lash out, flailing and whirling and seldom doing much damage to anyone, usually losing, always building another hostile cubicle in a corner of his mind, gathering enemies like some farmers gather their crops.

But George's father had little time for work that provided an income for his family. He was always chasing the profitless rainbow, while Mozelle taught music in the public school and paid the bills and bought the food and watched her husband borrow and borrow and borrow and mortgage and mortgage and mortgage until there was no hope—none at all—that they would ever see the light again financially. George's father held a few minor, appointive political jobs in Barbour County, but he achieved neither wealth nor position through them. He remained until his death simply a man people called "Sag" Wallace. He had taught George little. The boy had not worked regularly during his boyhood. The farm provided little opportunity or even need for that. It had been scratched over for so many generations that there was little left in the soil. George's father left him but one legacy. He taught him to box—and, occasionally, during his summer trips to Appalachia, he would go at it in some murky pool hall or basement with a local champion, dispatch him in no time at all and disappear with his money.

But all of that was behind George Corley Wallace, Jr., in the autumn of 1941. As Jimmy entered his first year of college at Georgia Southwestern, George began his final year of law school at the University of Alabama. Shortly before either of them completed the final examinations for the first semester, the anxiety shared by Lillian Carter and Mozelle Wallace and hundreds of thousands of other mothers in the country was realized. The Japanese attacked Pearl Harbor, and on the same December afternoon they bombed Guam, where Tom Watson Gordy was stationed. At first, there was no word from the little island in the Marianas. Then, Tom's wife, Dorothy, who lived in San Francisco with their three children, was told officially that her husband was missing in action and presumed dead. The news reached Lillian sometime in January. Her grief was equaled by Jimmy's. The idea that Tom Watson Gordy, his idol since he could walk around the living room—the strapping young man grinning out at him from the treasured photograph, standing there in the picture in front of all those fellows he'd so heroically thrashed during his wonderful ascent to the fleet boxing championship—was no longer a part of his universe was almost beyond the young man in Archery.

That summer—1942—the letter finally arrived. The Congressman said that while Jimmy had prepared himself at Georgia Southwestern, he had been working diligently himself. His efforts in Jimmy's behalf had paid off, he was happy to announce. Jimmy had received an official appointment to the United States Naval Academy, not for the coming year but for the following summer, the summer of 1943. Jimmy was greatly disappointed. He had felt certain that he would be off to Annapolis in 1942, but he was cheered by the fact that it had finally happened. He was going. Gradually, his gloom about the delay was replaced by his anticipation. On the advice of a teacher at Georgia Southwestern, and with the consent of his parents, he enrolled in the Georgia Institute of Technology that summer—Georgia Tech— and was accepted in the Navy's ROTC program at the Atlanta school. When he finally arrived at the academy, he wanted to make sure he would be ready. He told Eloise Ratliff the good news, and she was pleased by it, although, as Lillian recalled years later, the young woman seemed to sense that Jimmy would not only be leaving Archery when he went away to Georgia Tech, he would also be leaving much more behind in the wake of his first eighteen years.

And in Tuscaloosa, a friend—one of the few he had made there in five years—asked George Corley Wallace, Jr., what plans he had made, now that he had graduated and earned his law degree.

"Well," he said, "Ah was thinkin' about runnin' for guv'nuh."

That was taken for granted, the friend said, realizing that

almost everything that George had done during his tenure there had somehow—and sometimes almost manically—related to his often expressed ambition of becoming the governor of Alabama, thereby following in the footsteps of his political idol, Bibb Graves, a former governor whose success as a statewide candidate was attributed almost solely to his ability to make race the motivating factor in all his electoral contests.

"You mean right now?" the friend exclaimed. "You're fixin' to run for governor right now?"

Wallace grinned. "Naw," he said, "after the woah."

What then, the friend asked, was he planning to do with himself in the summer of 1942?

"Well," said Wallace, "Ah'm fixin' to join up."

"The Army?"

"Nope, Ah think the Ayuhcoah," said Wallace. "I b'lieve Ah'll be an Ayuhcoah sergeant."

The dark, stumpy young man from Alabama had never seen an airplane close up in his life. The fair-skinned boy from Georgia had never seen the sea.

Three summers later, a nervous Air Force sergeant dropped from the belly of a B-29 at a sparse military air base on Guam, his hands shaking from one more bombing mission over Japanese-held islands in the Pacific. He had been flying such missions for nearly eighteen months and the toll was beginning to show on him. He was a flight engineer, responsible for the various systems in what was then a prime showpiece of America's aeronautical ingenuity—the long-distance, heavy bomber—and, day after day, week after week, he had climbed the three-step ladder into the womb of the plane, listened through the muffled earflaps of his soft helmet to the deafening roar of the engines cycling for take-off, and then, eyes closed, trembled with the craft as it hurtled down the runway carved between the rows of palm

trees and lifted finally, clumsily—laden with its burden of
bombs—into the air, headed invariably into deadly nests of
Japanese pursuit planes and Japanese antiaircraft fire that
spawned bursts of flak around his young life.

He occupied himself in the long, but not long enough,
interludes between missions with his memories and his
dreams—his remembrances of his brothers and his mother
and his dead father who had deposited him as a bashful sixteen-year-old on the steps of the state capitol in Montgomery, Alabama, with the express instructions to "go to it,
kid." His objective had been a job as a page in the state
legislature and he had set himself to the task and won the
post and sealed his own fate forever. He would, by God, be
the governor of Alabama, he swore there on the island
where the Navy said Jimmy Carter's uncle had died—but
the visions were not enough to thwart the pressure of flying
frequently into the jaws of death. The very sound of an airplane engine sent shudders through his body, but he flew,
nevertheless, every time, and every time he shoveled himself through the little trapdoor in the belly of the plane at
the end of a mission, he prayed in an abstract way that it
would be the last.

On the morning of August 7, 1945—three summers after
he had joined the Air Corps—it seemed very likely that his
prayer had been answered. He glanced around him and noticed little clutches of men talking and shouting and laughing. Some were drinking, a rare public sight on an Air Corps
base. George Corley Wallace, Jr., had become an astute observer of human behavior. Something was up, he knew.

On that same day, on the other side of the world, on another ocean, Jimmy Carter, by then in his second summer as
a midshipman, was serving his U.S. Navy apprenticeship
aboard a decrepit destroyer in the North Atlantic. It was his
second summer at sea, and although he was not yet twenty-
one years old, he saw himself as something of an old salt.
The ship's public address trumpeted a screeching notice to
the regular and the supplement of would-be officers and

gentlemen from Annapolis, and Jimmy, like the scores of other sailors aboard, prepared himself for another routine announcement from the executive officer. But like his shipmates, Jimmy Carter's attention increased when after the hortatory prefix—"Now hear this! Now hear this!"—the voice on the loudspeaker announced a message from the President of the United States. Jimmy and the others seated themselves on the deck to listen, and Harry Truman's Midwestern twang chirped nasally through the audio system and into history.

With utter solemnity, the new President, in office less than a hundred days, made it clear that a scientific landmark had been passed and that, as he put it, "the age of atomic energy" had been introduced the day before by America's deposit on the Japanese city of Hiroshima of an atomic bomb more powerful than twenty thousand tons of TNT, a destructive force equal to the capacity of more than two thousand of the B-29s George Wallace was reluctantly flying out of the Marianas. Truman rationalized the moment. "It was to spare the Japanese people from utter destruction that the ultimatum of July 28 was issued at Potsdam," he said, referring to a joint statement issued by him, Chiang Kai-shek and Prime Minister Clement Attlee the week before in which the terms for the Japanese surrender had been outlined and a warning of worse things to come submitted. "Their leaders promptly rejected that ultimatum," Carter heard Truman say over the destroyer's loudspeakers. "If they do not now accept terms, they may expect a rain of ruin from the air the likes of which have never been seen on the earth." There were looks of disbelief and wonderment around Jimmy as Truman's words sank in. "The force from which the sun draws its power has been loosed against those who brought war to the Far East," the twang continued—and the puzzled men aboard the destroyer began to murmur and mutter as the President spoke. What the hell was it? they asked each other and no answers were available.

They had argued among themselves that summer about
the end of the war and how it would come. The prevailing
view—and, of course, about the only view available to those
who were not privy to the capacity the United States had
harvested from the deeply secret Manhattan Project—was
that after continued saturation bombing by B-29s, including
the one that George Wallace had come to hate by that time,
Japan would finally surrender or be crushed beneath an invasion. Their studies of Shintoism at the academy had persuaded most of Jimmy's shipmates that surrender was the
least likely possibility and that, in the end, the only way to
win World War Two was to send American troops ashore, a
prospect that raised another lively argument whenever they
discussed it that summer. How many casualties would there
be? They had already read of Iwo Jima and Okinawa and of
how the Japanese had fought almost to the last man and, like
sophomores at Princeton discussing the dimensions of infin-
ity, they talked and talked and talked about the number of
deaths required to bring Japan finally to its knees. Most of
them, including Jimmy, felt sure the war was far from over.
Many of them hoped it would last long enough, if that was
the way it had to be, for them to get a taste of it. Now, President Truman was telling them about something they knew
absolutely nothing about. "There was no way to
understand," Jimmy wrote years later. "We had never heard
even a rumor of this quantum leap in destructive power."

Neither had George Wallace. The first he knew of it was
that morning when he sauntered around to several of the
tiny gatherings of Air Corps personnel on the fringes of the
strip where his pockmarked, flak-scarred B-29 had just
landed. He was not all that interested in what it was that
was so captivating to everyone else. He had just flown his
last mission—at least for a while, he was sure. He was going
home, at least for a while, he knew. The news that "a big
bomb" had been dropped on Hiroshima cheered him, and
the speculation that it would probably end the war brought
him great comfort, but the principal thrust of his mind that

day was the fact, the blessed fact, that he had survived and he was going home, home to Alabama. He left that afternoon for Hawaii and California, and by the time he arrived in San Francisco, a second atomic bomb had been dropped on Nagasaki, a city Wallace knew quite well from ten thousand feet.

"The news of Japan's surrender came while we were still at sea," Carter wrote in his autobiography in 1975, remembering his days as a midshipman three decades before. "We were especially envious of those who were celebrating the victory in Times Square." The magic words had moved electronically around the curving facade of the Times Building on that evening of August 14, just a few minutes past seven o'clock. "Official: Truman Announces Japanese Surrender," they flashed, and after five days of rumors and distortions—five agonizing days since the second bomb had prompted suggestions that Tokyo was about to lay down its arms—it was over. The ritual euphoria Jimmy Carter and his shipmates regretted missing jammed midtown Manhattan with a throng estimated by police to be in excess of two million happy people, and all across the country, in cities and hamlets, millions more were celebrating with similar abandon.

In Mobile, Alabama, George Wallace, who had arrived there the day before after a week of travel and a 10 percent mental disability discharge—the toll of all those missions— spent the triumphant evening serenely ensconced with his new wife and baby in the home of his in-laws, the Burnses. The next day, he hitchhiked to Montgomery, got a job as an assistant attorney general and began laying his plans to run for the Alabama legislature the next spring. He would win, easily—the first of many victories in a career that would eventually make him one of the most adored and abhored men in American politics. Years and years later, his disability discharge would be raised as evidence of the insanity of the racial doctrines he would preach.

Late in the winter of 1977, after he had been President for

several weeks, Jimmy Carter—the candidate who had promised the nation that he would never make a misleading
statement—paid a benevolent call, as commander in chief of
the armed forces, to the Pentagon, where he told an enthusiastic audience of Defense Department employees that he
had voluntarily "served in two wars." It was unarguable, of
course, technically undeniable. During the waning days of
World War Two, his enrollment at the academy in Annapolis
made him a bona fide member of the country's military; and
during the Korean conflict a few years later, he was a lieutenant stationed on the eastern shore of the United States,
halfway around the world from the war.

The young man standing on the deck listening intently to
President Truman's announcement that afternoon in the Atlantic Ocean had traveled quite a distance in the three years
since he had packed his bags and headed up to Atlanta and
Georgia Tech, leaving Archery and Plains behind for a long,
long time. To the ROTC student and future midshipman, the
Navy became his unofficial curriculum adviser in that first
year away from home, and he worked hard, very hard, getting his feet wet in a number of engineering and mathemati-
cal disciplines that had been unavailable to him in Miss
Coleman's classrooms or on the tiny, ill-funded campus in
Americus where he had spent his first year as a collegian.
Years later he would judge his studies in Atlanta to be much
more difficult than the challenges posed for him by his instructors at Annapolis; and, in the process of his studies at
Georgia Tech, he seemed to be laying the basis for the single-minded focus that would characterize most of the rest of
his career, both public and private. His steadiness and relentless determination to achieve and succeed impressed
classmates and teachers in Atlanta; yet it was not such a
rigid passion for perfection that a healthy, busy social life
was disallowed. He came into contact with a sizable circle

of friends and acquaintances, on and off the campus; he wrote Eloise, who was still back in Sumter County, with some regularity and dated her when he returned to Archery on weekends; still, as Lillian had anticipated, their relationship became less and less important to both of them. "You could see it coming," Jimmy's mother recalled.

The year passed quickly for everyone. Georgia Tech, as usual, had one of the better football teams in the country, and Jimmy frequently passed up a trip home for a Saturday afternoon in the stands, watching the Yellowjackets demolish another hapless opponent. His grades were high, his work consistently excellent and his ambition to carve out a place for himself as a gentleman and officer in the United States Navy grew with each day's war news. The American forces under Lieutenant General Dwight Eisenhower landed in North Africa in early November, while British bombers struck heavily at Italian targets and the U.S. Air Corps concentrated on German installations in occupied France.

The Germans, in turn, were bombing London and the surrounding countryside almost every day, with Churchill, as the prime minister, lumbering about urging the citizenry to hold fast. Japanese-Americans had been rounded up by then and imprisoned in camps in California and New York—with the tacit approval of the American Civil Liberties Union—and in the Pacific, the Americans at Bataan and Corregidor had been overrun, while the Marines had captured the tiny island of Guadalcanal in some of the bloodiest fighting the war would produce. There was still no official word on Uncle Tom Watson Gordy. He was still listed as missing in action. The Japanese still held Guam. There was no way of telling.

Many of Jimmy's classmates at Georgia Tech left school that year to enlist in the armed forces, and on more than one occasion, he considered following their lead. The initial confidence that the United States would deal quickly with Japan and Germany had faded by then, but there was considerable dread among many of the young men his age that the war would be over before they got their chance to get into it. Despite the temptation, however, he reinforced his decision to go to the academy with even harder preparatory work. The ROTC instructors in Atlanta had already given him a vague idea of the rigorous sort of schedule that would face him at Annapolis, and Jimmy was determined that he would be as ready for it as humanly possible. His academic pursuit was accompanied by a regimen of physical training—daily calisthenics and intramural sports and a training-table diet—and as his year at Georgia Tech drew to a close, he believed he was as ready as he would ever be. He was eighteen years old. He stood five feet six inches and weighed less than 130 pounds. He was instructed to report to Annapolis in mid-June. "It was," he would say years later, "a dream come true."

Still, even at that age, Jimmy Carter was not a great romantic who believed that his dreams would be fulfilled because of some inexorable destiny. What dreams he had, he pursued with the calculated passion and patience of a hungry panther on the stalk, and he seemed always capable of involving others in his pursuits. His father's courtship of Congressman Pace was but one example. Without that assistance, which eventually produced the opportunity to fulfill his dream of becoming a naval officer, not much of the rest of his efforts would have had much value—but given that leg up, he was single-mindedly committed to the objective he had established so many years before. Whatever needed to be done, he did—and if that meant rolling his feet over soft-drink bottles or doing a hundred sit-ups every morning, then so be it. If it meant he had to become proficient in plane and solid and analytical geometry, not to mention advanced calculus and algebra—then so be it. As far as he knew at that point in his life, there were few things he would not do, no sacrifices he would not make, to get where he wanted to go. His uncle Alton noticed that about him, even as a younger boy.

"The thing about Jimmy was that he just wouldn't quit," the old man said in the summer of his nephew's presidential race. "I mean, now, that boy just wouldn't give up on anything. Didn't make no difference what it was, he'd hang right in there and stick to his guns—and there was another thing about him, too: you couldn't argue him out of anything. I recollect one time that Jimmy and my boy—that's Hugh, Hugh, Senior—I recollect that one time they was both set on going over to Americus one Saturday afternoon to see some movie. I don't remember what it was but they were both hot to see it. But the problem was that Hugh had spent the money he needed to get in and so I just suggested—I wasn't really serious about it, you know—but I said to Hugh, 'Hugh, why don't you ask Jimmy to loan you the money?' Now, old Jimmy, he always had money—always did. He worked hard and he didn't spend very much. Course, wasn't much to spend it on. At any rate, I says to my boy, Hugh, 'Why don't you just ask old Jimmy to lend you the money for the movie,' and so he did, and Jimmy just got this hard-down stubborn look on his face and said, nope, he didn't aim to do it. Well, they argued back and forth for a while, but old Jimmy, he wasn't about to part with a small loan. You couldn't a pried that money out of him with a crowbar. I believe he'd a soon died as to part with it; and finally, Jimmy says to Hugh, 'Why don't you go borrow it from your daddy?' And so, that's what happened. You know, I do believe old Jimmy would have just as soon been strung up by his heels as give my boy that money."

Lillian does not demur at her brother-in-law's appraisal. "He was tight with his money, all right," she recalled, "but I think it had something to do with the way he looked at everything. You know, he wouldn't take money for nothing. I mean, he didn't like for his aunts or his uncles or Earl's mother to give him a penny or something just to be giving it to him. He saw money as what he got for work. A sort of fair exchange, I think is the way he saw it—and that's about the way he looked at everything else. He thought if you really worked hard enough at something, you would be rewarded for your work, maybe with money you earned or with something else. I think I've always believed that, more or less, and his daddy and I tried to teach all our children that too, so it was just natural that he'd think that way, I suppose. I'll say this about Jimmy, though: I don't ever remember hearing him say he couldn't do something. He might not just come right out and say he could do it, but he'd never say he couldn't. He'd just wade right in and start trying to do it. Come to think of it, I don't ever recall that he wound up not doing whatever it was he set his mind on doing. He was always that way. He was that way with his peanuts. He was that way with his wanting to get into the Naval Academy. Lord, I don't remember when he wasn't that way. I sure don't."

More than three decades after Jimmy finished his first two years in college—one at Georgia Southwestern and another at Georgia Tech—and got ready to leave Archery for Annapolis, none of the stubborn determination was missing from the man the tightfisted boy became, and by the time the long motorcade roared into Green Cove Springs, Florida, that afternoon, some of the grim, sour depression that had settled on him during the long ride had been replaced by a calm steeliness that had become a familiar demeanor to those who had followed his campaign. He left the car as soon as it stopped moving and waded with a grin into a huge crowd of people, attracted not only by a presidential candidate but by mounds and mounds of fried fish and hush puppies and coolers crammed with soft drinks. They weren't accustomed to being courted for their votes in a primary election. Even Wallace—who, despite his confinement to a wheelchair, seemed to be everywhere in Florida that March of 1976—had not been to Green Cove Springs. If this Carter fellow had something to say and had come all the way from

Jacksonville to say it, well, the crowd reasoned that the least they could do was listen. After all, he was a Southerner, too, wasn't he? and after all, he was a rural type himself, a farmer and all.

"I'm very glad to be here," the candidate drawled. "I feel like I have a very special relationship with Green Cove Springs. It's a town that played a special part in our family." The audience stared blankly at him. As far as they knew, the few Carters who lived in the area had nothing to do with the Georgia Carters from whence had sprung this fellow on the stage in front of them. He continued his story:

"You know, my Uncle Tom—my mother's younger brother—how many of you have heard about my mother, Lillian?—well, her younger brother, Tom, was in the Navy, you know. As a matter of fact, I believe that he was the inspiration for my own career in the Navy. He was stationed on Guam when the war—that's World War Two, for some of you younger folks—when the war started and, as you know, the Japanese attacked Guam the same day they did Pearl Harbor, or the next day, I believe."

The people in the audience were still bewildered. What was this fellow up to? Who was this Uncle Tom he was going on about and what in the world did he have to do with their little town in central Florida? Carter continued:

"Well, first they told Uncle Tom's wife that he was missing in action, you know, because the Japanese had captured the island of Guam and there was no way to tell what had happened to him. Then, about two years later, I believe, after we had retaken Guam, they told Uncle Tom's wife that he had been killed. My aunt was living in Plains with my family and her children by then, and of course we were all grieved to hear the news, but in a way, I think, my Uncle Tom's wife was relieved that at last she knew he was dead. As many of the relatives of the Vietnam missing in action and the prisoners of war know, it is sometimes better to know one way or the other than to be kept hanging in suspense like that. My aunt remarried along toward the end of the war, but when it was over, they found my Uncle Tom working for the Japanese on a railroad somewhere in Japan. He had been a prisoner of war ever since the day the war had begun. He was in very, very poor physical condition and, as many of you may remember, there was a veterans' hospital right here in Green Cove Springs and they brought him back to the States and sent him here to recuperate."

Uncle Tom had survived, but he had paid a terrible price. He weighed less than a hundred pounds when he arrived at the hospital in Florida. His mind was almost shattered. He had lost his wife and his children. He often told his sister, Lillian, that he sometimes wished he had been killed that very first day when the fighters had come in low over Guam, strafing, and the bombers had sown such devastation all around his radio shack and the Japanese troops had come ashore. "I'd be a whole lot better off if I was dead," Lillian remembered him sobbing. The Gordys and the Carters never quite forgave his wife for acting as though he were.

Consider them both, the sea and the land; and do you not find a strange analogy to something in yourself? For as this appalling ocean surrounds the verdant land, so in the soul of man there lies one insular Tahiti, full of peace and joy, but encompassed by all the horrors of the half-known life. God keep thee! Push not off from that isle; thou canst never return!

—Herman Melville,
MOBY DICK

ON AN OUTRAGEOUSLY beautiful morning in the late spring of 1977, the nuclear submarine U.S.S. *Los Angeles*, trailing a long, aquamarine wake off the Florida coast, gradually began to disappear beneath the surface of the Atlantic Ocean, its twenty-foot conning tower and bridge cutting darkly through the sea like a shark's dorsal fin. Abruptly, they too were gone, the wake had vanished and there was no evidence at all of the vessel's previous presence. Inside the sleek, black craft, now coasting gently on a sloping course deeper and deeper into the murky quiet, the *Los Angeles*'s crew busied itself with the intricacies of the dive, eyeing the gauges, reading the meters, adjusting a valve here and a pump there—all under the watchful gaze of a wizened little man in a baggy, civilian suit and a younger, better dressed man who had been President of the United States for little more than four months. The *Los Angeles* was the showpiece of the nation's nuclear navy, the prototype of a new class of attack submarines designed to augment a system of national defense that relied heavily on the potential use—and therefore, the potential threat—of missiles fired from beneath the sea to targets on a faraway shore.

The *Los Angeles* was the little man's pride and joy, and he knew the ship like the back of his hand from its rounded bow all along its tubular, 110-yard, airplane-like fuselage to its finned stern. He knew it intimately, like a man knows every curve and indentation in the body of a woman he cherishes—and on that good morning in May of 1977, as it slid silently downward in the Atlantic, he was showing off the love of his life to the President of the United States, a man who had once been his own subordinate but who was by then the commander in chief of the country's enormous armada. The *Los Angeles* was the President's ship to command, but as it leveled at the bottom of its dive, the man in charge of it was clearly neither its captain nor the President but the little fellow in the baggy, civilian suit, Admiral Hyman G. Rickover—one of the Navy's largest figures, a sour-faced, brittle iconoclast, loved and hated wherever sailors gathered. Among other names, he was called "the father of the nuclear navy," a designation he neither denied nor discouraged. He thought it was utterly, uncontestably true. By the sheer dint of his acerbic personality, he had forced his beliefs in nuclear sea power on those whose support was required. He had begged and borrowed and bullied and berated, all in the name of the importance of that force unleashed in the awful explosion the President of the United States had heard about on another naval vessel more than thirty years before—and the admiral had succeeded. He had had his way.

Still, like Billy Mitchell's battles with the Army Air Corps in the 1920s, Rickover had had to fight every inch of the way to enforce the wisdom of his vision on the men who held the purse strings for the nation's defense investments. It had not been easy nor had it always been pleasant. No one had seemed to understand what he was talking about in the late 1940s and early 1950s. He found it difficult to believe that they were that ignorant, that naive, about the necessity for

constant progress in the development of the instruments of
war. They seemed intent on fighting the next one with the
weapons of the last one, ignoring what Rickover knew to be
the simple truth of human conflict—that the next one is always different from the last one, and probably worse. If the
Navy was to move ahead as a fighting power in the world
community, the ignorant civilians would have to be educated and sensitized, Rickover decided and, for years and
years, he had spent a great portion of his time and energy
doing just that. He was a lobbyist for his dream, and there
was probably no one in Washington more effective as a special-interest spokesman than he.

The *Los Angeles* and the rest of the nuclear navy were
proof of his stubborn persistence and persuasive dogged-
ness. Loaded to the gills with the most sophisticated gear
the nation's technological catacombs could produce and deliver, the *Los Angeles* was the crowning achievement of the
admiral's years of diligence, and although he seldom smiled,
he was actually observed by several aboard the vessel that
day to be grinning, if ever so slightly, as he took the President on a tour, continuing his lobbyist chores.

The President—a man who in stark contrast with the admiral seemed to smile much more often than necessary—
was also genuinely elated to be on the *Los Angeles,* far beneath the choppy surface, gliding smoothly, noiselessly
along on the silent power of the nuclear generator, taking
him back in his mind over the long years since he himself
had served aboard a submarine—the long, long years since
he had last heard the hatch on the conning tower clang shut
above his head and the banshee Klaxon screech out its
warning of an imminent dive. It was not the first time he
had been aboard a submarine, but the *Los Angeles* was a
distinctively different machine from the one on which he
had spent so much of his time as a younger man.

"You know," the President told Rickover as they shuffled
down a narrow passageway deep in the bowels of the boat,
"the thing that I really like about these nuclear subs is that

there's no diesel smell." The admiral nodded. He also remembered the old subs. "If there was one thing I hated
back then about the submarine service," the President continued, "it was the odor. You couldn't escape it. You just
couldn't get away from it at all, no matter what you did or
where you went. It just stayed right there with you all the
time, even when you went ashore." The admiral nodded
again. "I can still smell it sometimes, even now," the President said, making a face, and Rickover nodded again, this
time with a hint of impatience. He was a man religiously
devoted to schedules, and the President's olfactory reminis-
cences had delayed them long enough. There were many
new techniques of operation and pieces of equipment and
gear to be shown to the President that day—and they didn't
have all day. The submarine service had changed drastically
over the years and there had been many more important improvements than those the President could appreciate with
his nose.

"Do you smell something?"
"Yes, I must say I do. Most unpleasant."
"Utterly nauseating, isn't it? What could it be?"
"Well, if I'm not mistaken, I believe it is the odor of a
plebe."
"I believe you're absolutely correct. It is a plebe. You can
smell them a mile away, and it is without a doubt the foul-
est, most sickening smell in the world."
"I don't believe anyone would ever argue with you on
that point. It is indeed the worst odor God has ever allowed
on the earth. Do you suppose that God actually created
plebes?"

He was one of nearly a thousand men-children deposited
onto the sprawling bosom of the United States Naval Acad-

emy in the early summer of 1943, and although he had been Miss Julia Coleman's favorite student and Eloise Ratliff's knight in shining armor and Lillian's pride and joy and Earl's hope for the future of the Carters, on that June day and on many more to come, Jimmy Carter was nothing more than a plebe, the academy's designation for a first-year student. It was derived from a class distinction in ancient Roman society, but it is doubtful that its definitions were ever more starkly and strenuously applied at any point or place in history than at Annapolis. The plebe was the lowest form of human life, if indeed that much was granted. He was to be treated accordingly, which meant that he was to be subjected to constant humiliation and hazing. The upperclassmen were skillful practitioners, having endured the same miseries, the same ridicule and scorn, themselves.

For a plebe, there was never a moment's peace. In tandem with the heavy academic schedule and the strict military discipline imposed on all students, the academy's unceasing, ruthless pressure on its plebes produced numerous dropouts in the first few months of any term. As was the case at the United States Military Academy at West Point, New York, the Army's officer-womb, the strain at Annapolis was often evidenced in emotional breakdowns, fits of depression and occasionally by bloody brawls. Some of the plebes simply disappeared overnight, leaving behind a bed unslept in, a career uncarved. All were quickly forgotten. None was mourned. They could not take it, ergo, it was best that they left. There were no reprieves and there was little, if any, counseling. Once a midshipman expressed some disaffection for the treatment he was receiving, the die was cast. The punishments and harassments were accelerated and exaggerated, even beyond their originally absurd proportions. Annapolis was an adult world. There was no room at all for boys, even if they were still boys.

His hair clipped, his arms and buttocks sore from inoculations, his back as ramrod stiff and straight as he could possibly make it, Jimmy Carter began his naval career—a slight, nearly frail, freckle-faced Southern boy, nine hundred miles from the comfortable little house in Archery, the fields of his father's farm, the wonderful aromas drifting out from his mother's kitchen, the friends of his childhood. The year he had spent at Georgia Tech had helped, of course, as had the first year of college at Georgia Southwestern; but nothing could completely prepare anyone for the storm of abuse and the sadistic Prussian disciplines that were in the very air a plebe breathed at Annapolis. The sense of adventure that had motivated him for months and months quickly evaporated as the days of terror marched past. The hazing blurred in his mind. Again and again, his hands would instinctively clench into fists and then quickly relax. The homesickness welled in him, but he kept it there, inside. His letters home to Lillian and Earl were crisp and occasionally officious. He did not suggest to either of his parents that it was an arduous, nearly maddening life that had befallen him.

What he would later call his "lifetime commitment" was sustaining him. He had conceived and maintained a psychological stance that served as a deterrent to most of the plebe's traditional ailments. The hazing he treated as a joke, he would recall. He merely refused to take it seriously. Over and over, he told himself that it would not last forever, that the only strength he required was the strength needed for the moment, not for the long haul. He dealt with each incident, each moment of abuse and punishment, individually, he remembered, and somehow it proved an effective approach. The stubbornness and the determination he had learned from his days as a pint-sized peanut salesman in Plains became his chief assets in his day-to-day battle with an environment that proved too hostile for many of those who entered Annapolis with him.

Jimmy would not quit. "It never entered my mind," he would say many years later. "I mean, not once. I just didn't consider quitting to be one of my options." He would not give his tormentors the satisfaction of driving him out. Those postcards from his Uncle Tom lay somewhere on a shelf in his mind, next to his image of Earl's proud smile when Congressman Pace finally announced his appointment to the academy. The classwork, he decided, was not all that difficult, particularly for someone who had devoted himself so diligently to the demands of his instructors at Georgia Tech; and his military orientation in the ROTC gave him an edge over many of his classmates as well.

Still, with or without such advantages, they all lived in Bancroft Hall, the world's largest dormitory and the center of life at the academy. There were nearly two thousand rooms in its eight separate wings and a mess hall that seated almost four thousand people simultaneously. It was a community complete unto itself, with a cobbler's shop, a library, bowling alley, barbershops and a radio station. The vast grounds, with the statue of Tecumseh as a centerpiece, stretched across nearly three hundred acres of good, flat, Maryland land beside the Severn River, not far from the state's historic capitol. The domed chapel, where Jimmy and every other cadet worshiped regularly (godliness being as harshly mandatory as cleanliness), rose majestically over a crypt in which rested the mortal remains of Captain John Paul Jones. That particularly impressed the young plebe from Georgia. Having begun his naval reading as a small boy, he had come to know a great deal about the sea and its heroes, including Mr. Jones, and he wrote to his parents about the crypt and its contents with more enthusiasm than in most of his letters. He also suggested to Earl and Lillian, though with little detail, the pace and place of his new life: his small room and the fierce necessity to maintain it in precise conformity to academy rules and traditions, his schedule (as a farm boy, he had another advantage in that he was accustomed to an early rising), the food and the mealtime formations that brought the nearly four thousand midshipmen together on the quadrangle in front of Bancroft Hall prior to their breakfasts, lunches and suppers.

But he did not tell his parents much about the fate of a plebe at the tables in the enormous mess hall. It was, perhaps, the most vexatious part of the first-year student's life. "We never ate a peaceful meal," he remembered and wrote years later. "There were constant questions, research, songs, poems, reports on obscure athletic events, and recitations required of us. Poor table manners, any interesting facial expression, mistaken answers, or off-tune notes were reasons for instant punishment." Sometimes, their food was withheld from them. Occasionally, they were forced to eat their meals while sitting beneath the tables. At times, they were marched from their bunks in the early-morning darkness—before reveille—and chased at breakneck speed through a nearby obstacle course.

Some of the more sadistic upperclassmen indulged in purer forms of corporal punishment. Their victims were required to grab their ankles while their inquisitors pummeled their backsides with heavy aluminum bread pans or brooms or long-handled serving spoons. The plebes endured extra drill duties, were assigned to row large, heavy boats in the Severn—against the current—and given lengthy sessions of salute practice, an opportunity to spend several hours doing nothing but raising their hands sharply to their foreheads, over and over, again and again. A common mealtime punishment for a real or imagined infraction of the rules, or a violation of the academy's traditions, was the demand that the guilty plebe assume a normal sitting position at the table without any part of his body touching his chair. "There was no way to escape," Jimmy wrote in his autobiography, "not even for the best behaved of midshipmen. It was sometimes a brutal form of training and testing. If one ever showed any weakness, he was assaulted from all sides with punishment and harassment, and forced out of the academy."

But not Jimmy Carter, of course. He was determined that whatever he was asked to do, he would do, and he would do it with no whimpering, no complaining, no carping and no rebellion. If possible, he would do it with a smile, no matter how painful. He would get through it somehow, he vowed, an oath he reaffirmed a thousand times during that first year.

He maintained the posture without exception until the evening some upperclassmen called him from his tiny room into the corridor of Bancroft Hall and demanded that he sing. It was not the singing he minded—he had sung for them before—it was the song. From the very first day he had arrived at Annapolis, from the moment he opened his mouth, his roots and origins were clear. He was a Southern boy. He spoke differently from most of his colleagues. He drawled. His voice was soft, his vowels rounded, his enunciation pure southwest Georgian and his diction twanged and was tinted with the accents of his heritage. He became the farm boy, the hick kid from the sticks, the hillbilly, the hayseed. "Johnny Reb," some of his colleagues there called him—and the upperclassmen who hailed him from his room that evening demanded that he entertain them with what they considered an appropriately rural song of Jimmy's homeland. "Sing 'Marching Through Georgia,' " they ordered.

Now, there are still places in the American South, particularly in Georgia, where the very mention of William Tecumseh Sherman's name—unless preceded by a deprecatory oath—can prompt immediate combat or the threat of it. Of all the Union generals who invaded the Confederacy, none was more hated than he, and it was an antagonism that had survived for more than a century, principally because of his "march to the sea" after he had burned Atlanta. Mile after mile, tramping roughshod over farm after farm, the Federal troops under Sherman's command moved eastward toward Savannah, leaving behind a trail of arson and utter destruction, so complete that it became a legend—and as a legend, it inspired a song, "Marching Through Georgia." Sing it, the midshipmen demanded of Jimmy that night in Bancroft Hall. He shook his head from side to side.

He was not an avid student of the Civil War (or as some genteel ladies in Savannah and Augusta still call it, "the late unpleasantness"), but his Grandfather Gordy had spoken to him enough times about it, and the Carter-family stories about the participation of his forebears had given him an appreciation for the less subtle forms of natural, regional loyalty. He was not about to sing a song about the Yankees ravaging their way from Atlanta to the ocean. Nosiree, he decided, then and there. He would draw the line. He would take whatever punishment ensued, but he would damn well rather defame his family's good name than hum even a single bar of that dirty little ditty. "No, sir, I won't sing that one," he replied, and he did not. His Yankee tormentors insisted, but he would not retreat an inch.

For the rest of his days as a plebe, his punishments became increasingly severe. He paid dearly for his Confederate sensibilities, but he did not sing the song. Years and years later, during his campaign for the Presidency, a high-school band in Phoenix, Arizona, welcomed his arrival one afternoon by striking up "Marching Through Georgia." He interrupted his loping gait toward the platform, cocked his ear and listened for a moment. His grin disappeared and he shook his head grimly. "Doesn't anybody realize that's not a Southern song?" he hissed.

A few days before the end of his first full year at Annapolis, Jimmy and a small group of plebes gathered around a radio in Bancroft Hall to hear the voice that had been such an enduring symbol of authority for him, the same voice he had first heard slicing resonantly through his parents' battery-operated radio in the little farmhouse in Archery. The midshipmen had learned earlier in the day that Roosevelt was scheduled to speak that night and that he would make an important announcement about the war, and like the group around Jimmy, most of the other students at the academy were eagerly awaiting the President's words, wondering what he had on his mind. Abruptly, the answer came.

Roosevelt informed the country that the Allies—by that time, they were being called "the United Nations" by the President and other American officials—had not only captured and liberated Rome but had literally swept through the city, across the Tiber and northward up the peninsula, driving the Germans before them. "One up and two to go," said Roosevelt, reminding his audience that the fall of one Axis capital did not mean that the war effort could be relaxed at home. His fifteen-minute address was notable for its lack of heroics. "The victory," he concluded, "still lies some distance ahead. That distance will be covered in due time. Have no fear of that. But it will be tough and it will be costly."

Only a few who heard him speak that night knew, as he did, that a substantial portion of the cost he mentioned was about to be paid that very night on the beaches of France. It was June 5, 1944, and as Jimmy finished his studies late that evening, it was already the next day in Europe, and the Allied invasion was under way. The next morning, when the news reached Annapolis, there were mixed emotions on the sparkling, sprawling campus. The midshipmen were jubilant, of course, for D day marked a turning point in the war—the beginning of the end of Germany's domination on the continent; but many of the young men at the academy were also depressed by the news, for it meant that the primary fear in their minds for many months was one step closer to reality. The war could very well be over before they had their chance to fight in it. Jimmy shared that dichotomy. Even under an accelerated, three-year curriculum, he was still two years away from graduation—two more years of hard work in the classroom, two more years of disciplined practical experience in gunnery, navigation, astronomy, engineering, seamanship and naval tactics. He felt sure that in two more years the war would be history.

If Congressman Pace hadn't been so slow, he would already be finishing his second year and heading into the final one and there just might be some war left for him. But, of course, what was done was done. There was no remaking of the course and sequence of events that had placed him belatedly in the academy's Class of '46. He would do the best he could with what he had been handed. That's what his father always advised; besides, there seemed no alternative other than leaving Annapolis and volunteering for active duty. Jimmy quickly dismissed that option. He had invested too much of himself in that first year, that unbelievably harrowing plebe year, and he had no intention of letting it all go for nothing.

That summer of 1944, while the Allies pushed deeper into France, heading toward Paris, Jimmy got his first assignment at sea. Along with scores of other green midshipmen, he sailed out into the Atlantic aboard a creaking old battleship, the U.S.S. *New York*, bound for patrol duty up and down the East Coast of the country and down into the Caribbean, with such ports of call as Jamaica, Puerto Rico, the Virgin Islands and Trinidad. "We worked at learning everything from naval strategy to 'holystoning' the wooden decks (rubbing a white brick back and forth on the deck to polish the wood)," he wrote years later. "For cleaning and maintenance chores, the regular ship's crewmen gave the orders, and we carried them out. At times, we were rationed as little as one gallon of fresh water a day, and we used salt water for bathing and washing clothes.

"Sleep was scarce, and we constantly yearned for it. We slept topside on the decks, and an instant after reveille sounded, the salt water hosers would begin to wash down the deck. We had to scramble wildly to keep ourselves and our blankets dry."

The U.S.S. *New York* was assigned to a routine combat status all during the cruise, despite the fact that she was carrying a large complement of the young midshipmen, many of whom had never before seen the outside, much less the inside, of a battleship. The students were given rotating duties every so often so that in the course of their maiden voyage they would learn as much as possible about the ship. Nevertheless, battle stations and cleaning stations were permanent. For Jimmy, it was an arrangement that once again provoked mixed emotions. His battle station was at a forty-millimeter antiaircraft battery, and he was pleased to be there. His cleaning station was the "after head," the toilet in the rear of the ship. He was not pleased to be there. Two

troughs were attached to the walls in a wedge-shaped compartment, and a constant stream of salt water flowed into
them, washing the human wastes into the sea. During rough
weather, however, the motion of the ship sloshed everything onto the floor of the compartment. Jimmy's job was to
keep it sanitary. "This was not a favorite cleaning station,"
he recalled.

In fact, his first tour of sea duty was a rather rude intro-
duction to that life he had lived vicariously for years,
through his uncle's postcards, letters and stories. Everything
aboard ship was a problem: it was a problem to wash one's
body, a problem to wash one's clothes, a problem to eat
one's meals, a problem to urinate, to defecate, to walk, to
sleep. Especially sleep. Since they were required to wear
their life jackets at all times, most of the midshipmen slept
on them at night, cozying in as best they could near their
battle stations on the deck. One afternoon, Jimmy saw one
of his classmates accidentally lose his life jacket over the
side of the ship. He stepped to the rail, looked down into
the churning sea and watched the filthy jacket sink beneath
the waves. It was "disconcerting," he remembered.

A few days later, the ship detected what was thought to be
a German submarine and immediately began a series of violent maneuvers, zigzagging at top speed, attempting to escape the unseen enemy vessel. Suddenly, the ship was
jolted and shuddered from bow to stern. No one was certain
then—or now—what had happened, but one of the blades
on one of the ship's four enormous screws was broken off,
either by a torpedo from the German submarine or by a col-
lision with a hidden reef during the evasion tactics. It was
the closest Jimmy Carter would ever come to hostile action.
The Navy awarded a combat ribbon to everyone aboard, including all the midshipmen from Annapolis.

Not long afterward, the *New York* was ordered back to
port for repairs to its damaged propeller. As she headed for
home, every revolution of its broken screw caused the ship
to lurch. Down in the after head, the boy from Georgia, who

had just finished a miserable year as a plebe, spent the entire return voyage trying unsuccessfully to maintain a sanitary toilet. "Every time the broken propeller would turn over, the rear end of the ship would jump just high enough to slosh the salt water onto the floor," he wrote. "In spite of heroic efforts, the cleaning situation deteriorated drastically."

At the end of the summer, Jimmy returned to Archery and Plains for a brief vacation from his new career as a student-sailor. "He hadn't changed much that I could tell," his mother recalled. "He still seemed just a bit too young to be doing what he was doing and, of course, I still thought of him as my little boy. Earl, well Earl treated him like a man, I suppose, but I treated him just like I always did, like my little boy. I think he liked that. I know he sure liked eating some home cooking again. He said he had just about given up on food altogether up at school. He wasn't home all that long. I tried to fatten him up, you know, but it wasn't much of a project. He was still sort of thin. He seemed like he was enjoying being home. He ran around a bit with some of the boys he knew who were still around and him and his daddy went fishing or hunting, I think, and then it was time for him to go back. He seemed like he was ready to leave again."

By the middle of his second year, it was fairly clear to Jimmy that he was going to miss the war. Roosevelt was already talking about establishing an international monetary fund and a world bank that would become the pillars of postwar reconstruction, and by February 1945, after the Yalta Conference—where much of shattered Europe was divided up by Roosevelt, Churchill and Stalin—the date for the organizational convention of the United Nations had already been set. In that same month, General George Patton's Third Army crunched into Germany and headed toward Berlin, a city whose postwar occupation had already been charted by the Yalta participants. Russia was considering the prospect of getting into the war against Japan (later, Stalin would claim that it was this threat of Soviet intervention, not the atomic bomb, that persuaded the Japanese to surrender), and Field Marshal Sir Bernard Montgomery was telling his troops in the European campaign that they had come "to the last and final round." "We want and will go for the knockout blow," he said. Americans had seized a greater part of Manila by St. Valentine's Day of 1945 and over the next weekend, the Fifth Fleet, under the command of Admiral R. A. Spruance, launched more than fifteen hundred planes against the Tokyo and Yokohama areas in a surprise attack that destroyed more than five hundred planes and three dozen ships. On the next Sunday, the Marines invaded Iwo Jima, a tiny volcanic island less than 750 miles from Tokyo.

In the meantime, Jimmy's studies at the academy were progressing at the steady pace of a midshipman's march. Relieved of the pressures of hazing and harassment, he found the academic demands to be far less than he had anticipated. He had little difficulty with any subject and, in fact, discovered during his second year that he did not have to spend as much time studying as most of the rest of his classmates. He was quick and inventive, although he was far less industrious than many of his colleagues. He did not have to be, he found, and although he was never slothful, he allowed himself plenty of hours for pursuits that pleased him and whetted his personal interest.

For instance, he became one of the academy's experts in the identification of ships and aircraft. Using spare time earned by serving occasional guard duty, he would show up at a naval base across the Severn River and spend entire days doing nothing but studying the silhouettes of Allied and enemy planes and vessels flashed on a screen for a split second. There were hundreds of different profiles to memorize and recognize. "I worked hard at it until I had mastered them all," he recalled.

At the same base, adjacent to the academy, Jimmy also

received flight instruction. Under the supervision of active-duty pilots who used the teaching time to fulfill their flight-pay requirements, Jimmy learned to handle several different types of naval aircraft, including a two-seater scout plane and the big and reliable but old and slow PBY, a long-range plane used for ocean patrols and sea-rescue missions. His flight lessons were by far the most exciting part of his life at Annapolis to that point and his letters to Earl and Lillian reflected his enthusiasm for the new adventure. "But you know me," Lillian recalled, "I just couldn't stand the idea of my little boy flying an airplane out over the ocean. I could still remember how worried I got when he just drove our old pickup truck into Plains." Occasionally, Jimmy wrote a note to Miss Coleman about his studies and his self-improvement program of using the money paid him as a midshipman ($4 monthly the first year, $7 monthly the second) to purchase classical phonograph records. He told his former teacher too that he had chosen Spanish as his foreign language requirement and was thoroughly enjoying his first exposure to a different tongue.

His native tongue was a different matter, though. A year and a half in Maryland had not softened his Southern diction, and he still retained enough of his backwoodsy shyness that the necessity to speak before a group frightened him. As a result, he thoroughly dreaded one of the oldest academy traditions, the demand for midshipmen to practice after-dinner speaking. It was "most fearsome" to him, he wrote. A large group of midshipmen would get together for a formal meal—presided over by a senior officer—after which a few of them would be called on at random to deliver a speech, ostensibly entertaining. "Cold sweat was everywhere," he remembered. The dance lessons were more to his liking. Like his father, he enjoyed the chance to fox-trot, waltz, samba and rumba, and if there were no women to dance with during the academy lessons, he did not seem to mind. It was the dancing that he enjoyed at that point, he recalled.

While his size prevented him from participating in most of

the intercollegiate sports played at the academy, his speed and the stamina he had nurtured in his rural boyhood were welcome on the cross-country squad, a pursuit he enjoyed but at which he did not excel. He was gradually gaining the reputation around Annapolis of a young man who always got the job done. If he happened to like the job, he did it extremely well. If it was of less than passing interest to him, he performed accordingly—but he always did the job. He studied as much as was necessary on the courses and subjects whose merits he doubted, bore down on those that attracted him and willingly helped those classmates who asked him for assistance. He was liked, though not well liked, and he was not remembered on the campus as a man of distinctive traits, tics or triumphs. He had few enemies and few friends. Some who disliked him perceived him as a snob who thought of himself more highly than he ought. Both allies and adversaries considered him a tightwad.

The news came after dinner one evening in mid-April, in the spring of 1945, at the end of his second year at the academy. About an hour's drive from Archery and Plains, in a little white house in Warm Springs, Georgia, Franklin Roosevelt had died. About an hour's drive from Annapolis, in the Cabinet Room of the White House, Harry Truman had become the thirty-third President of the United States. Nearly half a million American troops were moving rapidly toward Berlin and Leipzig. The Russians were already near enough to begin focusing artillery on the German capital. In the Pacific, the Japanese suicide flights had begun and American gunners were having field days. The organizational meeting of the United Nations was less than two weeks away in San Francisco. On the day it convened, the Russians surrounded Berlin and the British dropped six-ton bombs on Hitler's mountain retreat at Berchtesgaden. The end was in sight, and only three weeks after Roose-

velt's burial in Hyde Park, Germany surrendered uncondi-
tionally in Eisenhower's schoolhouse headquarters at
Reims. The war in Europe was over, but the talk in Bancroft
Hall the night of the surrender was all about the continued
fighting in the Pacific. How long could Japan hold out? the
midshipmen asked each other. Long enough perhaps for
some of those who were about to graduate to get a taste of
the war? Probably, Jimmy concluded, but not long enough
for members of the Class of '46, he knew. He had settled all
that in his mind before he boarded another battleship that
June for his second summer cruise. Before he stepped
ashore again in late August, World War Two was over.

Plains and Archery seemed never to change. He had not
been home since Christmas of 1944 and he had spent a cumulative total of less than two months there in the previous
two years—but somehow it seemed precisely the same as on
that day he had left. Uncle Alton's store was still one of the
busiest places in town. The men still idled their hours away
at the service station just across the tracks. There were still
baseball games on Sunday afternoons at the high-school
field and Miss Julia was ready to begin another year guiding
the academic interests of the community's young.

It was autumn 1945. The war was just over, the world had
turned upside down—but it could well have been the end of
any previous summer. Jimmy felt comfortable there again
and Earl and Lillian, of course, were pleased to have him
home and doubly pleased that the two years he had spent at
Georgia Southwestern and Georgia Tech before going to the
academy had kept him out of harm's way. Not everything
remained completely constant, though. Eloise had not
waited for him as she had once promised. Late in 1944, she
had married Lonnie Taylor, a local boy who was two years
older than Jimmy. He had been drafted early in the war and
had risen to sergeant by the end of it. Eloise was pregnant,

Lillian told Jimmy, having heard the news from the wonderfully efficient communications network indigenous to any small town. Jimmy was not disturbed. He had written to Eloise, of course, but they had moved steadily away from each other in their separate passages toward maturity.

She was a Sumter County girl who dropped out of college to get married and have babies. He was a midshipman with a combat badge. He had stepped ashore at exotic Caribbean ports. He had fired deadly weapons and flown large airplanes and was on his way to becoming an officer and a gentleman. "Is that right?" he said nonchalantly when Lillian told him about Eloise, and years later he would minimize his feelings toward the young woman. Lillian, though, insisted she knew better. "I could be wrong, but I think it sort of bothered him a little bit," she said. "At least, I think it did for a little while." She was learning that she could not always be certain of her son's feelings. He was not only a quiet boy. He had, she thought, become a very private person. That was the primary impact of Annapolis on her son. He had never gushed out his innermost feelings, but he had never been guarded either. The hazing, with its insistence on a silent acceptance of its miseries, seemed to have transformed him. It was difficult for Lillian to know what he was thinking when he came home. It was even harder for Earl.

On the day before he was to end his vacation and return to Annapolis for his third and final year at the academy, Jimmy and a friend spent the afternoon cruising around the community in an old, rumble-seated Ford. They chanced to drive past the Plains Methodist Church—just across the street from the little house Earl and Lillian had rented in the first years of their marriage—and spied Jimmy's sister, Ruth, and another young woman in the churchyard. "The other girl was Rosalynn Smith," he wrote years later. She was younger than Jimmy by three years, and although he had seen her around his house with Ruth several times, he had paid scant attention to her. "She was an insignificant little girl," he recalled. At loose ends, though, that afternoon, and looking for a diversion that evening, the two young men-about-town asked the girls to go to a movie in Americus that night. They accepted.

Rosalynn Eleanor Smith was a pretty, dark-haired, eighteen-year-old sophomore at Georgia Southwestern College, where Jimmy had spent his first year after high school. Like Jimmy, she was the oldest of four children, but unlike Jimmy, she had grown up in hardworking if genteel poverty. Her father, Edgar Smith, a mechanic, had died of leukemia in 1940, leaving her and her quiet, bright mother with the responsibility of caring not only for the immediate family but grandparents as well. Allie Smith, Rosalynn's mother, had cut short her own college studies to marry Edgar and had, over the years of their marriage, become a seamstress of some reputation in the community. Her wages, earned with pricked and swollen fingers, supplemented her husband's only to the degree that the family survived the Depression with food on the table and not much more.

The Smiths were known around Plains as hardworking, honest folk—dependable, reliable, steady, churchgoing people, a part of that larger bloc of the local citizens who lived from week to week on the work of their hands and the strain of their backs. Edgar detested the grit and grime and grease that covered him in his day's labor—etched and burrowed deeply into his body and soul—but he seldom complained and never spoke at all of his distaste for the dirt of his job. He did speak frequently of the virtues of work. It was his only source of self-esteem, it seemed, and when he discovered he was ill in the spring of 1940—sufficiently sick that he could work no more—the fierce force that had kept him trudging through the Depression waned and disappeared.

Early one Sunday morning that year, he summoned Allie and his four young children into his bedroom and told them he was dying. They never forgot his words to them. "My working days are over," he told them. It seemed a death sentence to a diligent Scotch-Irish descendant. "I want all of you to go to college," he said. "I want you to do better in life than I have." It was the dream of every parent, of course, not unlike Earl's own aspirations for Jimmy, but it was spoken with the finality of a man who knew that whatever his dreams had been for himself, they no longer had validity and could only be salvaged by transfer to his children. Earl was hard at work that spring of 1940, working to build his growing business as a grocer and land speculator and warehouser, and his dreams were still real and reachable. Edgar knew his were quickly vanishing, like a man's breath on a cold day. He could justify them only by stretching them at least one more generation. College was the magic solution, he thought. If his children would only get themselves educated, they would never, ever suffer the indignity of coming home every night to their own children covered in grease and oil, smelling like the shop where they worked.

He died in the fall. To everyone's surprise, he left a little money. It was enough to get his children started at least in college and it was earmarked for that purpose. His wife went to work at a grocery store in Plains, leaving the children in the care of her ailing, aged mother. Within a year, her mother died. Rosalynn was fourteen years old when she became her mother's surrogate at home. She was called "Sister" by the other children.

Her younger brother, Murray, remembers the years just after their father died. "You know, it was the afternoons when we were alone there at the house when she was really the mother. Mama was working, you know, and we'd come home from school and Sister would just take over. She was old enough then to keep us all in the straight and narrow so to speak, and that's what she tried to do. I guess the thing about her that sticks in my mind now is how she loved to dance. I can see her now. I can see her dancing in the house to records or to the radio. Sister loved to dance."

She also liked to study. Like Jimmy, her mind was quick. Plains High School was fairly simple for her, and when she graduated in the spring of 1944, she was eager to obey her father's wishes that she extend her education beyond Miss Coleman's classrooms. She enrolled in a secretarial course at Georgia Southwestern, the only one in her high-school graduating class to go to college. She lived at home and commuted daily to the junior college in Americus. "I didn't know what I really wanted to do," she remembered. "I had thought about being a teacher and I had given some thought to being a nurse like Miss Lillian and I had also considered the idea of becoming an interior decorator. But really, I didn't know what I wanted to do."

She did know, however, that she wanted very much to get out of Plains. She did not know quite how she would manage it, but she knew it was important for her to leave. Whether she saw Ruth's older brother, the young midshipman home from the Naval Academy, as her passport, she did manage, as she put it, to "hang around, trying to get him to notice" her. She saw in him something quite different from the standard Sumter County product. Most did not finish high school, and if they did they went off to the Army, like Eloise Ratliff's new husband, and came back to work the family farm or get a job at one of the new factories the war had brought to Americus. But Jimmy Carter wasn't going to follow that course, she knew. Why, Ruth had told Rosalynn that Jimmy had started writing letters when he was twelve years old to people he hoped would be of some assistance to him in securing his appointment to Annapolis. He was a young man who had left little to chance, and more importantly, he had managed to get out of Plains himself. Rosalynn knew there was more to the world than the block-long row of stores and Earl Carter's peanut warehouse and Alton Carter's general store and the service station across the tracks where the idlers whittled and chewed tobacco and spat on the ground, leaving rich brown quagmires as evidence of their indolence, and drank soft drinks spiked with whiskey. She had not seen any of that other world, but she knew it was out there and she wanted desperately to get a look at it.

Still, even though she had had her eye on Jimmy, she was a bit taken aback when he and his friend asked her and Ruth to the movies that afternoon. Her mother easily remembered the young midshipman who came calling. "He was really a good-looking fellow in that white uniform," she said years later. "And he had all those amazing teeth, so white, so white." Jimmy did not try to kiss Rosalynn good night on their first date that night. Instead, he took her home to the modest little house where her father had died five years before and asked her for a late date the next night. She was uncertain. Hadn't he told her he was going back to Annapolis the next day? Sure, he said, but he didn't plan to leave until late in the evening. But he already had a date with someone else for the next night, she pointed out. Sure, he said, but he was asking her out afterward. She was still unsure that that was the proper way to behave, but she liked him a great deal and finally she accepted. After his first date the next night, he picked her up and they simply drove around—and around and around and around—and he finally left Plains for his last year at the academy in the wee hours of the next morning. Rosalynn went back to her secretarial course at Georgia Southwestern, but her heart was not in it. The letters flew between them, and when he came home at Christmas, they saw each other every night—and no one else. They seemed utterly smitten with each other, although they were almost strangers.

Jimmy told Lillian about his new sweetheart. His mother mildly protested, pointing out that Rosalynn was "just a little girl," one of Ruth's many young friends. "But what I was really trying to tell him was that I thought he was probably too—too, too sophisticated for her," she said. "You know, he'd been off up there in school for quite some time before he met her and he'd been going out with Northern girls, you know, and well, with older girls, I knew, and well, you know, I knew they were different from Rosalynn. I just thought maybe he needed a little talking-to, just to keep him straight. But he wouldn't hear any of it. He said he was fixing to marry Rosalynn. I just shook my head. I asked Ruth what it was all about and she said it looked to her like it was something really serious."

One night, just before Christmas, Jimmy sat with Rosalynn in his car in front of her house. He looked over at her and told her she was beautiful and told her he loved her and told her he wanted to marry her and asked if that seemed to be a good idea to her. She said no. Jimmy was chagrined and a bit puzzled. There he was, the most eligible young bachelor in town, about to become an officer and gentleman in the United States Navy, offering this daughter of a mechanic a chance to see the world with him—and she had turned him down.

"I was so young," she remembered. "I hadn't made up my mind about much of anything yet—a career or anything, you know—and this was something that I hadn't even thought about at all: getting married—and at my age. I wasn't about to make up my mind on something like that on the spur of the moment."

He learned something about her from her refusal. She was clearly not as sophisticated as some of the young women he had dated during his four years away from Plains. Her experience and her education were limited, but Rosalynn Eleanor Smith was not a girl to be rushed into anything. She was not impulsive. She had never been and she never would be. She had goals and purposes, even if they were vague, and she was as committed to reaching them as he was to achieving his. He liked that about her. It was a strikingly attractive quality in a woman, he thought. He went back to the academy after Christmas, still smitten, still determined that he would marry her, and when she came to the academy over the Washington Birthday holidays—always a festive occasion at Annapolis—he asked her again. His letters had been carefully calculated and crafted to prepare her for the second proposal. Appreciative of her yearning to leave Georgia, he had written to her of the vast possibilities of life with a naval officer, of the ports and places they could share, and apparently it was an effective approach. She accepted, there on the banks of the Severn River, nine hundred miles from home. Her mother was pleased. His mother was dubious.

His last three months at the academy flew by for him, and as June 1946 approached, the country was settling fretfully into peacetime. There were strikes and threats of strikes in the news almost every week. There had been lusty demonstrations among American soldiers still in the Pacific and in Europe who wanted to come home. The United Nations had officially opened its first round of deliberations in London and had chosen Paul-Henri Spaak, a Belgian diplomat, as the first president of its General Assembly over the Norwegian, Trygve Lie. There was street fighting in Teheran and few days passed without the explosive sounds of terror in Jerusalem and Tel Aviv. Little of the world's events held much interest to Jimmy, though, that spring. He had focused narrowly on two targets: his graduation and his marriage to Rosalynn. Now, as both approached, he found himself facing as well a career assignment he did not greatly relish.

He had finished fifty-ninth in a class of more than eight hundred midshipmen (at the top of the academic list that year was Stansfield Turner, who first became an admiral, as everyone more or less expected, and then was appointed to be the head of the Central Intelligence Agency by the classmate who became President, which no one had expected), and although he considered his ranking quite respectable, he found it did him absolutely no good in the matter of getting his first assignment. The billets were based on random drawings of midshipmen's names, and Jimmy's was drawn far down the list. There were few interesting assignments left. He got a place on an experimental radar and gunnery vessel operating out of the huge naval facilities at Norfolk, Virginia.

His parents and Rosalynn came to Maryland for his graduation, and after he and his classmates had walked across the stage to receive their bachelor's degrees and their commissions as ensigns in the U.S. Navy—there was no official certification of their standing as gentlemen—and after they had all hurled their white hats into the humid air, Lillian and Rosalynn had snapped the ensign's bars on his shoulders and they had all gone home to Plains and Archery to get ready for the wedding. They were married on July 7, 1946, in the Plains Methodist Church—Rosalynn's church—and although Jimmy had always been a devoted disciple of punctuality, the woman at the piano had to play the wedding march twice while the guests fidgeted and waited for the groom. Jimmy blamed the piano player. "Her watch was fast," he said.

He was twenty-one years old and Rosalynn was not quite nineteen. They left their childhood home on a hot, heavy afternoon and drove north together after the ceremonies, north toward Norfolk and a new life. Rosalynn couldn't have been more excited. She was finally leaving Plains for good, or so she thought. Her new husband was similarly elated. His Uncle Tom would have been proud of him, he knew. Jimmy was a Navy man. From that day on, he would be the one sending postcards back to southwest Georgia, and someday, he knew—he believed it firmly, just as he'd always believed he would go to the Naval Academy—he would be Chief of Naval Operations.

Seven years later, they drove back into Plains in a little Studebaker loaded with their earthly possessions and three young sons. They had come back to stay. Jimmy had changed dreams in midcourse. Rosalynn was bitter. Their life as a Navy couple had been neither simple nor easy, particularly for her—but she had taken all the bad along with all the good, and she had survived the separations, the loneliness, the meager salary and the frequent moving—and she felt cheated by his decision to quit and go home to Plains, back to that hot and dusty little griddle of a town with the one row of stores and the railroad tracks down the middle and the gossips and the town drunks and the Carters and the Smiths, just waiting to interfere in what had been a well-ordered and deliciously pleasant life. She did not understand how Jimmy could give up what both of them had worked so hard for—the independence, the adventure, the promise of better things to come for both of them—just when his career was beginning to blossom.

It had begun that July day in 1946 when they arrived in Norfolk to take up residence in their tiny apartment. Jimmy reported for duty almost immediately, practically living aboard the U.S.S. *Wyoming,* a decrepit battleship that had been converted into a floating laboratory for the testing of new electronics and gunnery equipment. It bristled with experimental prototypes of recent improvements in navigation, radar, communications and fire control. Ensign Carter was not only the ship's electronics and photography officer, a job in which he learned to use a thirty-five-millimeter motion-picture camera to record on film the accuracy of the new weapons tested aboard the *Wyoming,* he was also the officer in charge of the education of the ship's enlisted men at the high-school and college levels. He liked his work and went about it with characteristic thoroughness, learning to repair the complicated electronic equipment and to prepare statistical performance analyses of the experimental gear they were testing.

"The work was interesting, but the duty was terrible," he recalled, remembering that in those first two years of his career, while he was fulfilling his mandatory surface-ship duty, he spent almost all his time at sea on the old ship. It was in such bad shape that when it sailed into port at Norfolk, it was banned from the regular piers in the navy yard and had to anchor for safety reasons on the opposite side of the harbor. While it was in port, the crew was kept busy moving and installing and modifying the gear to be tested during the next week's cruise. "I seldom saw my new bride," Jimmy remembered.

He saw her often enough that she became pregnant within three months of their marriage. They were both elated by the prospect of becoming parents, although Rosa-lynn knew she was not going to spend her first pregnancy ensconced in the lap of luxury. Their little place in Norfolk cost $100 a month, one-third of Ensign Carter's salary. The Navy charged him $54 each month for his food aboard the *Wyoming*, and he and Rosalynn religiously purchased a $75 savings bond every month, leaving Rosalynn, who by de-fault had become the family accountant and treasurer, with about $70 for the rest of the monthly expenses. Still, she managed and managed well, they both agreed, and as her stomach swelled gradually over the months of their first winter together, their excitement grew in proportion.

Their first child was born in the nearby Portsmouth Naval Hospital. They named him John William Carter, after Rosa-lynn's grandfather, but began almost immediately to call him Jack. Jimmy was delighted with the pace of his life and what had happened to him in little more than a year: he had graduated from the Naval Academy, acquired a smart and pretty woman for his wife, assumed line-officer responsibili-ties on a seagoing vessel of the U.S. Navy and become a father.

If all that pleased him, the state of the postwar Navy did not. It was in "bad shape," he said. At the end of the war, there had been three million men in the Navy, but by the time Ensign Carter's first son was born in 1947, the number had dwindled to less than a million. More than two thou-sand ships had been deactivated and assigned to reserve fleets during the same period and at least seven thousand ships had been declared surplus. Most of the active vessels, like the *Wyoming*, were miserably undermanned, operating with crews two-thirds and occasionally one-half the normal size. "It was a time of great discouragement," Jimmy remembered, "because . . . the nation was relaxing after a long and difficult war, and funds allocated for naval operations were meager." Despite the fascination of his assignment, he became "disillusioned" with the military in general and the Navy in particular. He gave serious consideration simply to resigning his commission, an indication of the extent to which he was disappointed. Since Annapolis graduates were serving "at the pleasure of the President," however, that option was not available to him. He suffered in silence, though, and seldom mentioned his dissatisfaction to Rosalynn on their brief weekends together. "Ecstatic reunions," Ensign Carter called them.

"If Jimmy was unhappy back then, I certainly never knew it," Rosalynn recalled one day during her husband's presidential campaign. "He didn't like that old ship but he seemed completely immersed in the work he was doing, and we were making new friends all the time and really enjoying ourselves, I thought—and when the baby came, it just added another dimension to our enjoyment, you know. And I think we were as happy, individually and as a couple, as we could possibly have been. I know I was. It was hard, but I was happy; and another thing, too, was that I was growing and I knew it, and that really made me happy. I was finding out that I could do just about whatever I set out to do, which is a wonderful thing to know about yourself, especially at such an early age. I wasn't even twenty, you know, when Jack was born, and there I was alone up there in a strange city and pregnant almost from the time we got there, and I was handling our money and paying our bills and saving and scrimping and making do with what we had—and I know it was one of the most important periods in my life. I feel like I probably grew up in Norfolk, or close to it anyway."

As Ensign Carter's two years of required surface-ship duty began to dwindle to a few months in the spring of 1948, he was faced with the necessity of choosing once again the direction of his naval career. He chose the submarine service, that branch of the Navy considered most elite and most dangerous. It was also judged by most of Jimmy's contemporaries to be the quickest route for promotion. He was still unhappy with the state of the postwar Navy, but he had resigned himself to do the best he could with what he had—to invest as much of himself as possible, hoping that conditions would eventually improve and that ultimately he could pursue his dream of becoming the Navy's chief of operations in a better environment. If the submarine service offered better odds on personal achievement for its young officers, then that was where he ought to be, he decided. He applied, was accepted and in July of 1948—while Harry S Truman and Governor Thomas E. Dewey were being nominated as the principal presidential candidates for that year's election—the three Carters packed up and moved farther north to the Navy's submarine school at New London, Connecticut.

Jimmy and Rosalynn were as excited as they had been when they had moved to Norfolk two years before. After all, this was what they had envisioned for their lives together: new places, new people, new challenges, new opportunities. Ensign Carter was by then Lieutenant Carter (junior grade) and he was feeling better about the Navy with every passing day at submarine school. "There was an elite group" of sixty-one men in his class, he said, "and the competition was intense." His teachers were World War Two submarine veterans, a proud complement of officers and enlisted men who regarded submarines as the only decent, honorable place to serve in the Navy. Their students, none of whom had even been inside a submarine before, were inundated with the disciplines and the details of this strange life beneath the sea. Each one had to learn thoroughly the various systems aboard—fuel, hydraulics, air pressure, fresh water, electricity, diesel engines, radar, fire control, torpedoes, gunnery, sonar, communications, and there were long sessions on underwater strategy with mock battles fashioned after real submarine actions in the war just behind them.

Jimmy and his classmates were taught how to escape from a submarine in trouble, entering the bottom of a huge water tank through an air lock and then rising individually through a hundred feet of water to the surface. At first they were provided with artificial breathing apparatus; later they made the ascent without such assistance. Every day's work brought new ideas and new questions, and Jimmy was enjoying himself more than he ever had at the Academy. He was learning everything there was to learn about his new environment. He was in the process of becoming again, a condition that seemed to suit him perfectly. All through his life he would discover that he derived the most satisfaction from situations in which he was becoming something else. He was gradually getting to know himself as a chronic overachiever, a man ever reaching, straining, grasping, groping for some new level. It was an urge that would intensify rather than wane as he grew older. There would be few moments in his life in which he would be pleased or satisfied with his life the way it happened to be at the moment he stopped to look at it.

A month before his graduation, as an absentee registrant in Plains, he cast his first presidential vote for President Truman. "Dewey went around acting as though he was already the President and I think that was the reason he lost," he said. "Truman won because people were already tired of Dewey as President." Of the sixty-one officers in his class at New London, he was, he said, the only one who openly supported Truman. He finished submarine school just before Christmas of 1948, loaded up the Studebaker again with his wife and son and their gifts for their families and drove south to Georgia to spend the holidays.

He heard about it when they arrived. Lonnie Taylor, stationed at Fort McPherson near Atlanta, had been flying his young family back to southwest Georgia around Thanksgiv-

ing just about a month before. Their plane crashed near But-
ler, Georgia and all four died. Eloise Ratliff Taylor, her husband and her two children were buried together in the little
cemetery just down the road from the Carter house in Archery. She was twenty-four years old, Jimmy's age. Her son,
Tommy, was two. Her daughter, Patricia, was not quite a
year old when the four of them died together.

Jimmy had been out in the world on his own for nearly six
years, first as a student and then as Ensign Carter of the
U.S.S. *Wyoming* and finally as Lieutenant Carter of the submarine service, and during that period he had spent very
little time back in Plains and Archery. It was as though he
had abruptly severed the cord to his boyhood and his beginnings, and in so doing, he had moved a considerable distance from his father. For nearly six years, their individual
experiences had been so strikingly different that each of
them had found it difficult to talk about them with the other.
Earl's role had been traditional: authority figure, disciplinarian, supervisor, superior. Jimmy's part in the relationship
had been predictable as well. When his father called, Jimmy
usually answered. He had always been an obedient boy and
he had tried hard to please his father. He respected him and
loved him, but he discovered that for nearly six years they
had been moving in different directions. Earl's place in his
life had been supplanted by the Navy. They found it most
difficult to communicate. Earl would chat about the peanut
business, something Jimmy knew little about, and Jimmy
would recount the intricacies of the newest Navy gadget he
had discovered or the principles of ballast in a submarine—
and Earl would nod silently, unable to relate it to his life
there on the farm. It was an awkward situation for both of
them and they tried eventually to resolve it by sticking
mainly to small talk or allowing Lillian to carry the conversation.

At Christmas of 1948, most of Lillian's talk was about her idea to buy a house in Plains. She had her eye on one just down from the Methodist church and just across the street from the house where they had begun their married life. Earl generally just grunted when she mentioned the new house, but he did not seem to oppose the idea of moving. After all, it did make a certain amount of sense. A large portion of his business had gradually shifted away from the farm and into Plains. It was probably the smartest thing to do, he finally told Lillian. They bought it and moved in that spring.

Soon after Christmas 1948, early one morning, Jimmy piled his personal gear into the Studebaker, parked in the dirt yard where the young black tenants had crouched and squatted that night to hear Joe Louis flatten Schmeling, kissed Rosalynn, Lillian and Jack, shook hands with Earl and drove away in the predawn darkness, headed toward California and his maiden assignment aboard a submarine. His wife and baby would follow in a few months, after he had settled in their new quarters in Hawaii. Rosalynn was excited again. California! Hawaii! It was precisely what she had dreamed their life would be. Jimmy drove carefully and leisurely into Alabama toward Montgomery, where George Wallace was about to begin his first term as a state legislator. He picked up Highway 80 on the outskirts of the Alabama capital and headed west, eventually passing around a slight curve that bounded a wide right-of-way where, nearly seventeen years later, a housewife from Detroit would be shot and killed because she happened to be riding in a car with a black man.

He arrived in Los Angeles just after New Year's Day 1949, arranged to have the car shipped to Honolulu, then boarded a plane and flew to Hawaii where, at Pearl Harbor, he reported for duty on the U.S.S. *Pomfret*, his first submarine. A couple of days later, the sleek black boat throbbed out through the narrows, turned south around Oahu and headed west, bound for the China coast. It was to be an exciting voyage for the young lieutenant from Georgia, and almost fatal.

A day out of Hawaii, the barometer began to drop, the winds shifted to the northwest and a malevolent storm began churning the ocean. It raged around and over the *Pomfret* for five days. Lieutenant Carter was racked with seasickness. The insane movements of the submarine combined with the foul odor of diesel fuel and human beings locked together in cramped quarters were too much for his stomach. He was not precisely an ideal role-model for the younger, enlisted men, but he did not care. He thought he would probably have to feel better in order to die and he thought perhaps he might become the first naval officer to succumb to mal de mer.

It was during his spell of sickness that he climbed one night through the hatch and onto the conning tower. The *Pomfret* had surfaced to charge its batteries for underwater operations. "I was on the submarine bridge about fifteen feet above the level of the ocean itself, holding on as tightly as I could to an iron pipe handrail inside the bridge shield," he wrote in his autobiography. "An enormous wave rose around us to a level of about six feet or so above my head. I lost my grip as the force of the wave tore my hand from the handrail, and I found myself swimming literally within the huge wave, completely separated from the submarine." He swam, he said, for what seemed an eternity before the wave receded and deposited him on the barrel of the five-inch gun located about thirty feet behind the conning tower. He hung on desperately until he was able to lower himself carefully to the deck and return to the bridge from which the huge wave had plucked him. "Had the currents been even slightly broadside instead of from forward to aft, I never would have landed on the ship . . . and would undoubtedly have been lost at sea in the dark storm," he wrote.

Years later, he was asked if that incident had frightened him. Incredibly, he said it had not. "I know enough about myself that I wasn't afraid," he said. "I could have disap-

peared in the ocean and no one would have noticed, but I
didn't. I survived. I'm a fatalist, I guess."

Whether Lieutenant Carter was vulnerable to fear or not,
others aboard the *Pomfret* were. It was such a monumental
siege of weather in the Pacific that several ships of various
nationalities were lost, and the pounding sea ruined the
submarine's radio equipment. It was unable to transmit its
daily position report back to the fleet headquarters in Pearl
Harbor. The communications specialists in the radio room
could hear incoming calls but could not respond. One message they received was an alert to other ships in the area to
keep an eye out for debris from the *Pomfret* "believed to
have been sunk approximately 700 miles south of Midway."
The skipper turned the submarine toward Midway to report
its existence. It was not lost at all, of course; it was simply
mute. During the three or four days it took to reach the island, many of the crew members' wives, waiting in Honolulu, were informed that the *Pomfret* had probably gone
down. Rosalynn, still back in Georgia with Jack, was spared
their temporary grief.

From Midway, the *Pomfret* resumed its course toward the
China coast. The government of Chiang Kai-shek was totter-
ing and Communist troops under Mao Tse-tung had effectively isolated Nationalist soldiers in the coastal cities. The
Pomfret moved up and down the coast between Tsingtao
and Hong Kong. When it docked at a mainland port, it
pointed its bow toward the exit from the harbor to the sea.
The Communists' campfires could be seen in the hills
around the cities, many of which had become ghost towns as
a result of the fierce fighting. Nationalist troops were draft-
ing "volunteers" at gunpoint and there were frequent moments of random violence. The skipper of the *Pomfret* was
riding in a jeep one afternoon in Tsingtao when, for no apparent reason, Nationalist soldiers opened fire on the vehicle. One bullet tore through the jeep's canvas roof. For most
of its three-month tour in the Asian waters, the *Pomfret*
served as an underwater practice target for American and

British surface vessels polishing their antisubmarine skills. Lieutenant Carter was, as usual, learning everything he could about his new environment, and in a few weeks he had become "intimately familiar," as he put it, with every facet of the vessel. Moreover, he had quickly come to grips with the essential premise of life aboard a submarine. It was interdependence. Every man aboard was critically dependent upon every other man aboard. Life among the enlisted men was sharply compartmentalized. Each was a specialist, an expert in his particular area of responsibility, but the officers' duties were much broader. They had to know every aspect of the ship and every crew member's individual job.

Lieutenant Carter enjoyed that weighty commission and took it in stride. He was at his best as a generalist and he took great pride in mastering every specialized post on the *Pomfret* by the time it slid back into Pearl Harbor in April. His ship, he had persuaded himself, was the best in the Navy—and if that was not totally and completely true, it was nevertheless the most practical perspective available. Pride was a submariner's most valuable possession—pride in himself as an elite specialist, and pride in his vessel as the finest in the fleet. Without the pride, the days and weeks of close quarters (they slept in tiered racks that made turning over a difficult task for most men and impossible for those of a large stature) would have been maddening. It was a lesson Lieutenant Carter would not forget: any enterprise is best shaped and charged in an atmosphere of pride, even if the pride is exaggerated.

Rosalynn and Jack arrived in Hawaii a week after the *Pomfret* docked in that April of 1949, and the three Carters set up housekeeping again in Oahu. Things were looking up for them. He had received a small raise with his promotion from ensign and the cost of living in Hawaii was relatively inexpensive in those days, compared to the prices in Norfolk and New London. Moreover, the young couple found their new assignment "an ocean paradise." Rosalynn became pregnant again that August and found, to her delight, that the second nine months were easier than the first. Jimmy spent a great deal of time at sea, as he always did, but managed to be ashore in April of 1950 when his second son was born in Tripler Army Hospital in Honolulu. He was named James Earl Carter 3d, but the nurses thought he so resembled his father that they called him a "chip off the old block." The baby was known from that day forward as "Chip."

Less than two months after Chip was born, North Korean troops invaded South Korea and President Truman ordered units of the U.S. Navy and Air Force into action in support of the Seoul government and in coordination with troops from member countries of the United Nations. It was to be a "police action," Mr. Truman said, and his decision to inject American forces into the Korean fighting was merely an effort to enforce a UN resolution for a cease-fire. The President ordered a Navy cordon around Formosa, the island retreat where the defeated Nationalist Chinese had taken refuge from Mao's armies, and increased American military presence in the Philippines. Moreover, Mr. Truman ordered an acceleration of U.S. military assistance to French troops engaged in a long war against Communist insurgents in a little country called Vietnam.

All of the President's actions were carefully calculated under an umbrella of United Nations approval or, in the case of his unilateral moves, to avoid any direct confrontation with the Soviet Union. Still, it was obviously a showdown in the Cold War which, said Truman, had passed from a tense but passive state to "armed invasion and war" for which "communism" was to be blamed. "The attack upon Korea makes it plain beyond all doubt that communism has passed beyond the use of subversion to conquer independent nations," he warned. General Douglas MacArthur announced soon afterward that U.S. planes had begun bombing and strafing missions below the thirty-eighth parallel against Russian-sponsored North Korean troops.

It may have been called a "police action" by the President, but at Pearl Harbor it was called war. Lieutenant Carter was apprehensive but anxious to sail east again on the *Pomfret,* but in late July, the submarine was transferred to San Diego, the wrong direction for combat. "Jimmy was disappointed, I think, that he didn't see any action during Korea," Lillian remembered. "We went out to San Diego to see them that fall—that was 1950, wasn't it?—and he talked a lot about the Korean War and about how useless submarines seemed to be in it. I remember he said once that North Korea didn't even have a navy." Still, however disappointed Lieutenant Carter was, he and Rosalynn and their two young sons tried hard to enjoy themselves in Southern California. The area was crowded because of the large military presence there and housing was hard to find. They finally settled in a small apartment in a civilian neighborhood popular among Mexican immigrants. Characteristically, Jimmy remembers that residency as a time for learning. "I got to practice my Spanish a lot," he said. While his parents were visiting that autumn of 1950, he got new orders. He was to leave the *Pomfret* and report back to New London to become the senior officer for the precommissioning detail on the construction of the Navy's first postwar submarine, the U.S.S. *K-1,* an experimental vessel designed to function as an antisubmarine submarine—a sub killer, it was said. The Carters packed up again and drove across the country. The lieutenant was really quite proud. It was an important assignment, he thought, and he had earned it. There were few young men in the Navy who knew more about a submarine than he did—about its engineering weaknesses and strengths, about its mechanical failures and potential—and it was exhilarating to know that the Navy had recognized his expertise. His personnel file was unblemished. It suggested that he was the sort of officer who always did the job to which he was assigned.

Rosalynn was happy about the move, too. She had not wanted to leave Hawaii, but she was never quite comfortable in San Diego and she knew that Jimmy's transfer to the

East Coast would put her back in a military community. New London would be better, she hoped, and it was. When people asked her what her husband did, she said, "Jimmy's building a submarine." She was right, in a way.

Actually, the *K-1*, Jimmy's new billet, was being built by the Electric Boat Company of New London, and his specific responsibility was to act as the Navy's agent during the final installation of its new equipment. For several months, he was the sole military representative assigned to the project, and he spent his long days checking and rechecking the long-range listening sonar and the other sophisticated gear going aboard the vessel. Moreover, he was the planning officer for the testing procedures to be applied when the submarine finally went to sea for the first time, that critical maiden cruise when every system would be evaluated.

"I was intrigued with the innovative and experimental nature of this work," he said, and although other officers much more senior than he were eventually assigned to the *K-1*, he often thought of it as exclusively his boat. He, after all, knew more about it than anyone who came aboard for its shakedown cruise off Cape Cod in the early winter of 1950. All went well during the first tests, including the first dive and the first surfacing. But when a practice torpedo was fired near the end of the cruise, Lieutenant Carter's carefully calculated testing plans were slightly upset. A small boat was attempting to recover the dummy torpedo as it bobbed up and down in the waves when suddenly the heavy metal tubing punctured the side of the wooden boat. It promptly began to sink and had to be run aground near Provincetown, Massachusetts, to prevent its total loss. It was the first and only kill for the *K-1*, Jimmy recalled. No combat ribbons were awarded.

He spent long weeks at sea aboard the new boat as it perfected its techniques for locating and disposing of other submarines. "We would stay submerged for long periods of time," he remembered, "working in stockinged feet with no machinery in operation, controlling our depth simply by raising or lowering the periscope a few inches at a time. With a constant ship weight and a slightly varying amount of water displaced, the submarine would rise or sink very slowly as the periscope was moved. This fine balance took a lot of skill, experience, and luck, but gave us a platform of almost complete silence from which to listen to our prospective targets. We could hear all kinds of strange sea creature sounds and could detect other ships at extraordinary distances." With the addition of a snorkel, the *K-1* did not have to resurface to charge its batteries and so was able to remain underwater for extended periods.

On one occasion, after having been submerged for nearly three weeks, a member of the crew—an electrician's mate— had an emotional breakdown. He "went mad with claustrophobia," Jimmy recalled, and was tied to one of the bunks to prevent him from hurting himself or anyone else, and fed intravenously until he was transferred to a helicopter somewhere south of Bermuda. It was the first time Lieutenant Carter had seen a submarine defeat a man. He had heard tales about such things, but they had not rung true to him. After all, it had never really bothered him, and it had not seemed to have much of an effect on any of the people with whom he had previously served, either on the *Pomfret* or the *K-1*. It was, perhaps, an imagined weakness, he thought—but the young man's insane behavior before the helicopter arrived to rescue him persuaded him finally that it could happen. One could never tell the sort of colleague in which an inherent weakness might suddenly make itself known.

He took his family back home to Georgia for Christmas 1950, the first he had spent in his parents' new house in Plains, and discovered that the distance between him and his father had grown considerably in the two years since he had last visited. It was increased even further when Earl seemed bewildered by Jimmy's story of a recent visit of the *K-1* to Nassau. The British officials had invited the entire crew ashore for a party but, shortly before the event was to begin, had sent a message to the submarine explaining that, in accordance with Bahamian customs, only white crew members were welcome. Jimmy and the entire crew boycotted the party. As he told the story, he sensed that Earl did not understand. They never spoke of racial matters again.

He left New London early one morning in January 1951 for a quick flight down to Washington and an appointment with a man named Hyman G. Rickover—Captain Hyman G. Rickover, who was in charge of the country's infant atomic submarine program. There were, in fact, no atomic submarines at that point, but under Rickover's prodding, Congress had authorized the construction of two prototypes the year before, and the power plants for the *Nautilus* and the *Seawolf* were already being assembled. Jimmy had read of the new program in 1950 and had recognized its potential for a young officer already on his way up in submarine engineering. He applied for a transfer and, as was the case for all potential recruits to the atomic submarine program, he was ordered to Washington for a personal screening by Rickover himself. It was the first time the two men had met. The lieutenant was twenty-six years old. The captain was fifty-one. The job applicant remembered the interview in detail more than a quarter of a century later:

". . . we sat in a large room by ourselves for more than two hours, and he let me choose any subjects I wished to discuss. Very carefully, I chose those about which I knew most at the time—current events, seamanship, music, literature, naval tactics, electronics, gunnery—and he began to ask me a series of questions of increasing difficulty. In each instance, he soon proved that I knew relatively little about the subject I had chosen.

"He always looked right into my eyes, and he never smiled. I was saturated with cold sweat.

"Finally, he asked me a question and I thought I could

redeem myself. He said, 'How did you stand in your class at the Naval Academy?' Since I had completed my sophomore year at Georgia Tech before entering Annapolis as a plebe, I had done very well, and I swelled my chest with pride and answered, 'Sir, I stood fifty-ninth in a class of 820!' I sat back to wait for the congratulations—which never came. Instead, the question: 'Did you do your best?' I started to say, 'Yes, sir,' but I remembered who this was, and recalled several of the many times at the Academy when I could have learned more about our allies, our enemies, weapons, strategy, and so forth. I was just human. I finally gulped and said, 'No, sir, I didn't *always* do my best.'

"He looked at me for a long time, and then turned his chair around to end the interview. He asked one final question, which I have never been able to forget—or to answer. He said, 'Why not?' I sat there for a while, shaken, and then slowly left the room."

Rickover, Lieutenant Carter learned, had graduated at the top of his Annapolis class in 1922. He had served aboard submarines, although he had never commanded one of his own, and had made his reputation in the Navy as a brilliant, demanding officer whose electrical engineering expertise was probably without equal in the entire Navy. After the war, during which he had served in the Pentagon as chief of the Navy Department's Bureau of Ships, he was assigned to Oak Ridge, Tennessee, as the assistant director of the Manhattan Engineering District, a post to which he came blissfully ignorant of even the most rudimentary knowledge of nuclear fission and from which he left six months later as a disciple of atomic power as a means of bringing the U.S. Navy into the new age. He had also become in that short span of time a budding nuclear physicist, he said, and often in later years, though his degrees were in electrical engineering, he would call himself that in public. "I'm a sailor, a submariner, an engineer and a nuclear physicist," he would sometimes tell his audiences, and they were, as he knew they would be, suitably impressed.

From his days at Oak Ridge, immersed in the possibility of nuclear power as the source of naval propulsion, Rickover gave himself completely to the concept of atomic submarines, probably at the expense of his smooth transition to admiral. By 1950, with his nuclear submarine dream almost in his grasp, he had been passed over twice for promotion, a signal that mandatory retirement was in the cards. Still, he declined to lie still for those he had offended with his often obstreperous insistence that he was right about atomic submarines. He made friends—important and powerful friends—with his arguments in Congress, and they took his case to the White House where President Truman, as the ultimate arbiter of naval promotions, decided that Rickover had been a captain long enough.

Truman had been the first American President to deal firsthand with the awful truth of atomic power, and in the painful process of his nuclear education, he had become an ardent devotee of the nuclear sub, and this thin, sour-faced little man was probably just the fellow who would make sure the country had them. Truman was damned if he would allow the Navy brass to force Rickover out, just because he showed so little respect for their authority and their rules. He would make him an admiral. There would be no retirement for Rickover then and not even twenty-five years later when he was seventy-six years old and the young lieutenant who had come to his office for an interview that day had become the President of the United States.

In 1977, Rickover would still be on the job, selling nuclear submarines to presidents, taking the commander in chief on a personal tour of his pride and joy beneath the choppy waters of the Atlantic, just off the Florida coast, hearing Jimmy Carter's gratitude for the lack of a diesel odor and remembering how far both of them had come in the previous quarter century.

Lieutenant Carter got the job with Rickover, despite his misgivings about the interview, and a promotion to lieutenant (senior grade), the Navy's approximate equivalent of an

Army captain. He was euphoric, having already decided that it was probably the finest billet then available to any officer of his rank. He once again found himself on the ground floor of an engineering project in which he would be not only a naval officer with considerable responsibilities, but a student as well. Again, he found himself in the process of becoming something other than what he had been, and if in later years, before, during and after his campaign for the Presidency, he habitually exaggerated what it was he became ("I'm a nuclear physicist," he would say, although he was nowhere near any such scientific status), he comfortably mastered the stiff new challenges hurled at him by his new discipline and his new commanding officer.

Lieutenant Carter became the senior officer for the crew being assembled for the *Seawolf* and was assigned to Schenectady, New York, the site of one of Rickover's four operations offices and of the Knolls Atomic Power Laboratory where General Electric engineers and technicians were building the *Seawolf*'s nuclear power plant. He began teaching a variety of subjects to the enlisted men in the crew, all of whom—like him—had been handpicked and personally interviewed by Rickover. Their curriculum included reactor technology and physics—and all the while, their teacher, the young lieutenant with the Georgia drawl, was taking special graduate courses in reactor technology and physics himself at nearby Union College. It was a tough, demanding assignment. He hardly had time to learn any group of concepts himself before he had to teach them to his men.

The admiral, ostensibly headquartered at the Atomic Energy Commission in Washington, seemed never to be there at all. Invariably, he was popping up one day at the operations office in Chicago and the next day at the offices in Pittsburgh and the next day at the Idaho offices where the *Nautilus* reactor was being built (and where, twenty years later, Lieutenant Carter's eldest son, Jack, would be dismissed from the Navy after being caught smoking marijuana at the same Idaho post), and the next day, perhaps, at the plant near Seattle where plutonium was being manufactured.

Rickover was a stern taskmaster, and at times an unmitigated martinet. Few of his men liked him. In fact, he had only a tiny circle of friends in the Navy at all, even after so many years. Still, he was both respected and feared, and that, it seemed, was precisely what he was seeking. It was his thesis that leadership required some of both, sometimes more of the latter than the former. It was an effective chemistry for Lieutenant Carter who saw Rickover as "unbelievably hardworking and competent, by any measure a remarkable man, probably the greatest naval engineer this nation ever produced."

When the admiral showed up in Schenectady to inspect his work, he never praised Jimmy for his excellence but simply looked at what he was doing and walked away. "However, if I made the slightest mistake, in one of the loudest and most obnoxious voices I ever heard, he would turn around and tell the other people in the area what a horrible disgrace I was to the Navy and that I ought to be back in the oldest and slowest submarine from which I had come," Jimmy remembered. "We feared and respected him and strove to please him. I do not in that period remember his ever saying a complimentary word to me. The absence of a comment was his compliment; he never hesitated to criticize severely if a job were not done as well as he believed it could be done. He expected the maximum from us, but he always contributed more."

There was one occasion that stuck in the young lieutenant's mind. He and the admiral and several other officers had worked all day in Washington and then, late in the afternoon, boarded a Navy plane for a cross-country flight to Seattle for more work there the next day. Rickover immediately opened his briefcase and began reading and making notes as soon as they were airborne. The others did the same. As the night closed in around them, they glanced furtively at the admiral to see if he was still working. He was. They continued their work as well, but as the Mississippi passed beneath them and the evening turned past midnight, Rickover's young charges grew tired. One by one, they went to sleep. When the plane landed in Seattle the next morning, the first thing they noticed on their awakening was their boss, still hunched over his briefcase, still scribbling away on a mounting pile of notes.

Since July of 1949, Rickover had been getting the "pinks" from every typewriter in every office in his command—the tissue-thin carbon copies of every memo, every message, every letter, every document produced by every single person in the project—and he read them all. Whether it was true or not, the legends that grew about him insisted that he knew where every nut and bolt was at any given point in the process of construction, whether they were actually in place on the power plants or in transit to the construction sites. "He always insisted that we know our jobs in the most minute detail," Jimmy remembered, "which is really a necessary, basic characteristic of a good submariner."

Another basic characteristic the young lieutenant learned from the acerbic admiral was functional isolation. In the spring of 1951, the President had dismissed General Douglas MacArthur as his Far East commander and installed General Matthew Ridgway as his successor. Rickover was appalled and shocked at Truman's move, for although he did not know MacArthur personally, he respected his grit and determination. He felt some kinship with the general and no little antagonism for Truman. But the admiral said nothing, and he instructed his charges to keep silence as well. After all, he reasoned, it was neither his fight nor theirs. The fish they were frying were their only concern. To take a stand on another issue as volatile as MacArthur's dismissal could jeopardize their relationships with Congress and with the President himself. Rickover maintained his silence. He was as mute on the subject as the *Pomfret* had been during its voyage to Midway after the storm. That was functional isolation. Lieutenant Carter remembered that stratagem, and it would serve him well in his later career. It was not always necessary, he learned, to speak one's mind on every contemporary topic and issue. Discretion, he learned, was a primary ingredient of single-mindedness. Worthwhile pursuits required some sense of concentrated proportion, and almost any enterprise was vulnerable enough without taking added risks.

Always rather instinctively methodical, Lieutenant Carter came to appreciate systematic planning even more under Rickover. Once, he and several other young officers in the program were assigned to repair a ruptured nuclear reactor near Chalk River, Canada. The reactor had gone out of control, producing more heat than its insulation could withstand, and had melted, allowing the escape of radioactive material into the atmosphere. No one had been injured in the initial accident, but the reactor core had to be disassembled to prevent further leakage.

Rickover was asked to provide a team for the job and Lieutenant Carter was among those chosen. It was not a simple task. No one could spend more than about a minute and a half near the core at any given session of repair. There was no time for mistakes, for fumbling with a bolt or a valve connection. Each step had to be taken with precision and dispatch. The admiral's young men assembled an exact duplicate of the crippled reactor on a nearby tennis court. While television cameras monitored the real reactor, buried far beneath the earth, Jimmy and the rest of the team rehearsed each individual step aboveground before going down for the real thing—and each time a fitting or a nut was removed from the real core, the corresponding piece was removed from the mock-up on the surface. It was tedious and scary, but it worked. The reactor was safely disassembled and the danger of substantial leakage averted. Rickover's men saved their urine and feces for several months after they had finished the job so that they could be examined and analyzed for traces of radioactivity. There were none of any consequence. More than ever, Jimmy had seen the efficacy of meticulous planning, of leaving absolutely as little as possible to chance. It was Rickover's way. It became Lieutenant Carter's as well.

In November 1951, while she and Jimmy were living in Schenectady, Rosalynn became pregnant for the third time. Jack was four years old by then and Chip was barely past a year. She was busy enough with the two of them and preparing for the new baby so that Jimmy's long absences from home did not seem to bother her. Hers was an active life with a broad circle of friends, both military and civilian. She was talking in those days of going back to school after the new baby was born. Jimmy said he thought it was a fine idea. That winter—the coldest either of them had ever endured—George VI, the king of England, died, his daughter, Elizabeth, took the throne, and leading figures in both the Democratic and Republican parties were talking about persuading Dwight Eisenhower, the president of Columbia University, to run for President.

But Lieutenant Carter was fairly oblivious to politics and world events and to almost everything except the U.S.S. *Seawolf.* It consumed most of his waking hours, and he was crushed when he learned that the *Nautilus* would probably be finished first. He and Rosalynn drove from Schenectady over to New London for the keel-laying of the *Nautilus* in mid-June of 1952. President Truman was there along with Admiral Rickover. The President chalked his initials on a bright yellow keel plate, a Navy welder burned them permanently into the metal, and the country's first nuclear submarine was officially under construction. Truman was the first President Jimmy had ever seen and the only Democratic President he would ever personally see before he became one himself.

On the drive back to Schenectady from New London that day, Jimmy and Rosalynn had a long talk about his career. Gone were the days of deep depression and disillusionment that he had endured during his days on the *Wyoming* just

after the academy. Everything was going swimmingly, much
better than they had ever expected. Jimmy was not yet
twenty-eight years old and already he was up to his hips in
significant responsibilities in the most exciting and most
promising part of the U.S. Navy. He would, no doubt, have a
berth on the *Seawolf* when it was finished and eventually
command of a submarine himself. The importance of the nuclear navy was such that it was not unrealistic to expect that
a future Chief of Naval Operations would come from the
ranks of those familiar with nuclear power as a naval asset.
Rosalynn was not quite twenty-five years old and already
had two strapping sons and another child on the way. Both
her boys were healthy, her husband's salary had become adequate if not enormous, they were still buying savings
bonds every month and had a comfortable little nest egg
stored away. In six years of marital partnership, they had
done fairly well, they agreed. "And Jimmy talked a lot about
the admiral that day," she said later. "He told me how lucky
he was to be working for him and how he was such a wonderful officer and manager and planner and all. Jimmy respected the admiral so much. He just was so pleased to be
part of his project, I could tell."

Rickover, in turn, was satisfied with young Carter. Although he was but one of dozens of officers working under
his command, the admiral was aware of Jimmy—not to any
special extent, not beyond his appreciation for the others,
but to the degree that he allowed him to remain on the job.
That was the admiral's way. If he was happy with a subordinate's performance, he allowed him to stay. If he was displeased, he arranged a transfer, quickly and without any fan-
fare or ado. There were no recriminations and no second
chances. It was as though Rickover thought of his disciplines as so rigorously special that it was no real shortcom-
ing to have failed them. It was no great shame to be a common man. Lieutenant Carter agreed. "I knew we were doing
what others either could not or would not do," he remembered. "I was proud—not in a vain way, I don't think—but I

was proud to be doing something that so few others could or would. I suppose we all need to believe we are involved in a special enterprise and that need was rather thoroughly filled by the admiral's project. It was just where I wanted to be."

That summer, Jimmy took a keen interest in a piece of political news. It came neither from the Democratic national convention that nominated Governor Adlai E. Stevenson of Illinois and Senator John Sparkman of Alabama as its champions, nor from the Republican convention that named Eisenhower and Senator Richard M. Nixon of California as theirs. It came from southwest Georgia where James Earl Carter, Sr., had been elected as the Democratic nominee for the state legislature. Jimmy was proud but surprised and amazed. His father had never talked about getting into politics as a candidate. He had made sure that Jimmy was exposed to the political atmosphere of the region, of course, and had carefully nursed his friendship with Congressman Pace to ensure Jimmy's appointment to the Naval Academy, but he had never indicated the slightest interest in actually presenting himself for public office. Nevertheless, he had done just that in that summer of 1952, and he had won the Democratic primary with hardly a vote cast against him. Since there were fewer Republicans in his district than blacks who voted, his primary victory meant that the office was automatically his, and he was elated by the prospects of going up to Atlanta to serve—almost as elated as he was when Jimmy called to announce the birth of another grandson, Donnel Jeffrey Carter, born in mid-August 1952.

Lillian was blissful, too. Her Gordy instincts had played a substantial role in persuading her husband to agree to become a candidate. She knew, even better than he, the extent of his popularity and influence in the local community. Without intentionally doing so, Earl had accumulated the ideal assets for a local politician. He was well known as a member of various boards and committees—rural electrification, library, public education—and he was highly visible as a businessman and as a pillar of the Plains Baptist Church where he was both a deacon and a Sunday-school teacher. He was regarded as honest, generous, hardworking, smart and pious. He was, Lillian believed, a shoo-in. "And I was so surprised at how naturally he seemed to take to politics," she remembered. "Oh, I don't mean he got out and shook every hand and patted everybody on the back everywhere he went, but he did take a great interest in talking to people about the job and what he might be able to do in it. He didn't have to work very hard at being elected. Most everybody already knew who he was and knew what sort of a man he was. But he worked harder than he had to, I think, because he found out it could be fun."

Late that year, after winning the Democratic primary and the general election, the fun went out of Earl Carter's life. He had cancer. He was dying—slowly, but inexorably.

"He accepted it," Lillian said. "It liked to have killed me, but Earl, he just acted like he'd just got the market report or something. He said if it was God's will then he could accept it without questioning. I've never been that kind of person myself, but he was and it was a good thing too because it like to have killed me and I turned out to be the weak one. He supplied a lot of the strength for me."

Jimmy came home on emergency leaves several times that winter and the two of them—father and son—talked about their lives in the decade they had been so far apart. They talked about the boys—Jack and Chip and Jeff—and they talked about Jimmy's sisters—Ruth, by then twenty-three years old, and Gloria, twenty-six, were both married—and about Billy, Jimmy's fifteen-year-old brother, a bright, mischievous but slightly untamed boy who talked about nothing but the U.S. Marine Corps. They discussed church matters and politics and Admiral Rickover and nuclear submarines and this awful new weapon they called the hydrogen bomb and they talked about how well Rosalynn was doing and how quickly Jimmy's career had blossomed in a peacetime Navy and they talked about some of Earl's adventures as a World War One officer and about how the New York Yankees, winners of the last four World Series, would probably go on winning forever and they talked about how Eisenhower was doing as President and how difficult it had been for Earl to vote for Stevenson—he had voted for him, he said, but Lord it had been a difficult ballot—and they talked about how Lillian had loved Stevenson and had been delighted to put a mark by his name, especially with Sparkman, the Southerner, being on the ticket with him.

All through the weeks, as the word of Earl's illness spread through Plains and Archery, a steady stream of visitors came to the Carter house, bringing cakes and pies and casseroles and dishes of fried chicken and words of encouragement for Lillian. The long talks partially assuaged Jimmy's feelings of guilt about the long vacuum between him and his father. It had not really been possible for him to spend much time at home in the years since Lillian and Rosalynn had pinned his ensign's bars on his shoulders at Annapolis; still, he wondered if he might not have offered more of himself to Earl during that period. Rickover's generosity to Lieutenant Carter during the long weeks and months of Earl's illness was striking. He spent extended leaves in Plains while his father grew progressively weaker. Stalin died, Dag Hammarskjöld became the United Nations secretary general, Edmund Hillary climbed Mount Everest, East Berliners revolting against the Communist regime there were put down by Russian tanks, the Rosenbergs were executed—and finally, in mid-July 1953, James Earl Carter, Sr., died. The tenants on the farm at Archery wept and wailed when Jimmy made the rounds of the little shacks, telling them Mistuh Uhl was gone.

The Plains Baptist Church was crowded the afternoon of his funeral, and so was Jimmy's mind. It was crammed with new information about his father. He had seemed such a phlegmatic man, almost without passion at all except perhaps for dancing and bridge. Yet in the two days since he had died, stories about his zealous interest in the welfare of his neighbors began surfacing in the community. Earl was a closet philanthropist, it seemed. Every year, when the high-school commencement called for the young women graduates to wear white dresses, Earl privately purchased the appropriate frocks for those whose families could ill afford them. Every year, he invested money secretly in the further education of young high-school graduates who might not have started to college without such assistance. He still had accounts receivable on his books from before the Second World War—Depression credit—and in the long months of his dying, he had canceled several large notes, including some he held on money owed to him by his black tenants. Jimmy was impressed but bewildered. His father had never seemed to be that sort of man, and even Lillian was a bit surprised by her late husband's generosity. "I knew about the dresses," she said, "but most of the rest of it he just kept to himself."

Jimmy stayed in Plains for a few days after the funeral, helping his mother settle herself as a widow. While he was still there, several local political leaders dropped by and suggested that Lillian ought to assume the seat in the state legislature her husband had held. She declined. She would be much too busy with her teenage son, she said—but she and Jimmy knew that other matters would also be competing for her time. Earl's business acumen was not what it had seemed to Uncle Alton and most of the rest of the family and the community. His philanthropy had endangered everything he had worked for over all those long years since he had returned to Plains from World War One. Not only were there sizable debts to pay from the estate he left, but Jimmy was shocked to learn from his mother that Earl had allowed his accounts receivable to climb to nearly $100,000 over the years.

What Lillian and Jimmy knew that they did not tell the

political leaders who dropped by that day was that unless something was done and done quickly about the family's business, it could be lost. They had plenty of land—more than a thousand acres, in fact—but little cash. Lillian could not take over ("My husband owned the business and I was just his wife," she said), Ruth and Gloria were married and gone, and Billy was a hell-raising adolescent. That left twenty-nine-year-old James Earl Carter, Jr., Lieutenant (senior grade), United States Navy, senior officer of the U.S.S. *Seawolf,* and perhaps, he thought, future Chief of Naval Operations. "I asked him if he wanted to come home and take over," Lillian recalled. "He said he didn't know, and I know it was a hard decision for him. He wanted to, you know, but he didn't want to. He said he'd let me know as soon as he decided."

Nearly twenty years later, when he was governor of Georgia, Jimmy reached back into his boyhood for a rhetorical anecdote he thought addressed itself to the subject of difficult decisions. "I remember when I was a child," he said, "I lived on a farm about three miles from Plains, and we didn't have electricity or running water. We lived on the railroad— Seaboard Coast Line Railroad. Like all farm boys, I had a flip, a slingshot. They had stabilized the railroad bed with little white round rocks which I used for ammunition. I would go out frequently to the railroad and gather the most perfectly shaped rocks of proper size. I always had a few in my pockets and I had others cached away around the farm, so that they would be convenient if I ran out of my pocket supply. One day I was leaving the railroad track with my hands full of rocks and my mother came out on the front porch—this is not a very interesting story, but it illustrates a point—and she had in her hands a plate full of cookies that she had just baked for me. She called me, I am sure with love in her heart, and said, 'Jimmy, I've baked some cookies for you.' I remember very distinctly walking up to her and standing there for fifteen or twenty seconds, in honest doubt about whether I should drop those rocks—which were worthless—and take the cookies that my mother had prepared for me, which between her and me were very valuable."

As he drove back to Schenectady that July following his father's death and funeral, he was caught again in a moment of decision. "I began to think about the relative significance" of his father's life and his own, he wrote. "He was an integral part of the community and had a wide range of varied but interrelated interests and responsibilities. He was his own boss, and his life was stabilized by the slow and evolutionary changes in the local societal structure. My job was the best and most promising in the Navy, and the work was challenging and worthwhile. The salary was good, and the retirement benefits were liberal and assured. The contact with Admiral Rickover alone made it worthwhile."

But there was more involved than the simple merits of his father's uncomplicated life as a small-town agribusinessman and community leader as against the simple merits of a promising military career. There was also the worried look in his mother's eyes when she told him after the funeral that, financially, things were not as they appeared. Jimmy had never experienced that sort of anxiety. There had always been sufficient money or assets for the Carters to live the way they wanted to live. When electricity had become available, they had been among the first to install the lines to their house. When plumbing was feasible, they had built a bathroom and a kitchen sink. They had the first radio in the community, and when television became popular a few years before Earl's death, they had the first set in Plains. They had cars and trucks (Jimmy's first date was in a pickup truck with his grandmother's neighbor's daughter when they were both thirteen) and clothes and books and records and a man-made pond for swimming and fishing and a house by the pond with a jukebox and a kitchen—and through all the years of his father's working life, the Carters had become leading lights, a family of substance in Plains.

Now, as Jimmy drove north toward Schenectady, he considered the possibility that all of that could disappear because of his father's surprisingly inept business practices. By the time he arrived home, he had all but made up his mind. He would take Rosalynn and the three boys and go home—home to Plains and Archery and the peanut fields and the Plains Baptist Church and Main Street and Uncle Alton and Cousin Hugh and Lillian and Billy and a failing family business that he knew almost nothing about.

Years later, in the fashion of most human beings, he remembered the decision differently. "You only have one life and I began to wonder if I should spend mine engaged in war, even if I could rationalize it as the prevention of war," he said. On another occasion, he thought of his decision from another perspective. "When I went back home to where I had lived and saw what my father's life meant—in the view of those who knew him best—his service on the school board, his working on a new hospital, his dealing with the education of farmers who bought seed and so forth from him, his life in the church and his life in politics . . . well, I could see then a pull on me that was almost irresistible to go back and re-cement my ties to my birthplace." The choice, he said, was between two questions. "Did I want to be the Chief of Naval Operations and devote my whole life to that one narrowly defined career, which was a good one, or did I want to go back and build a more diverse life with a lot of friends, permanence, stability, in a community, in a relationship, in the life of a whole group of people? I chose the latter."

Nevertheless, when James Earl Carter, Jr., late of the United States Navy, his wife and three sons drove into Plains on a cold, drizzly afternoon in November 1953, it was for reasons other than roots. He had come home to salvage the family solvency.

I came into this world, not chiefly to make this a good place to live in, but to live in it, be it good or bad. A man has not everything to do, but something; and because he cannot do everything, it is not necessary that he should do something wrong.

—Henry David Thoreau
CIVIL DISOBEDIENCE

THE CAMPUS of Oklahoma University was buzzing that September afternoon in 1976 when the Democratic presidential candidate's motorcade rolled into the little town of Norman, and headed for the school's cavernous field house where several thousand students were gathered to hear him speak. He had become in the short span of less than six months a very important national figure, a man who had come from nowhere to somewhere in American politics, and wherever he traveled, the crowds were getting bigger and bigger. He was enjoying it all immensely: the applause, the adulation, the outstretched hands, the screams of the women and the children, the uproar he caused when he made his appearance—and he was proud. He had often said that if he had lost the nomination to some other Democrat, he would simply have gone back home to Plains again and taken up his life again where he had left it, but that was an unlikely plan for such an uncommon man, a man of such pride. Those who knew him well flinched at the indignities heaped on him by an American presidential campaign: the absurdities, the clowning, the mandatory shoulder-rubbing with local politicians he knew to be either corrupt or incompetent or both, the hyperbolic introductions, the ridiculous gifts (they were arriving every day back home in Plains, everything from a giant plastic peanut, standing over eight feet high, to the world's largest postcard, a slab of plywood the size of a Ping-Pong table, covered with signatures, postage paid from somewhere in Wisconsin), and that strange but rather inescapable penchant of local leaders for forcing the candidate to wear a hat of some indigenous significance.

Jimmy Carter hated most of that part of a campaign, but he tolerated it with hardly a grimace—except for that afternoon in Norman, Oklahoma, when he was greeted at the university field house with an enormous roar and a red baseball cap emblazoned with white initials, O.U. He flashed his by-then famous grin and waved and took the cap reluctantly and then put it on with a flourish, still smiling, still waving, still pointing, still shaking hands with dignitaries on the stage until he suddenly realized that many of the cheers had gradually turned to tittering giggles. They spread from the top of the large arena to the floor where the stage had been built, a wave of good-humored snickering and outright laughter accompanied by a few fingers pointing toward the Democratic presidential nominee wearing a red baseball cap much too large for his head and drooping comically down around his ears. Abruptly, as he fathomed the meaning of the laughter, the smile vanished from Carter's face. He jerked the cap from his head and stood there for what seemed an eternity, grim-faced, red-faced, seething and steaming inside, struggling to regain his composure. He was angry. He could tolerate almost everything, but he could not accept ridicule, and he was easily embarrassed.

He had been but a small boy when, on the eve of a visit to his maternal grandparents in Columbus, Georgia, his father had decided to cut his hair with the large trimmers he also used on his mules. They were bulky, clumsy, awkward shears, and his father's hand slipped and removed a large chunk of the little boy's hair. To compensate, Earl simply cut off most of the rest of it. Jimmy was nearly bald and utterly mortified. He found an old cap, put it on before he boarded the train for Columbus and kept his head covered during the entire visit. Pride was a precious commodity—to a little boy visiting his grandparents, to a presidential candidate caught up in a difficult campaign and to a young man, fresh from the Navy, back home again to save his father's business and his family's reputation.

The Carters would not be embarrassed, he vowed, no matter how much work it required or how long it took to restore some fiscal substance to his father's estate. They would not lose their honor, their land or their standing in the community, not if Jimmy Carter could help it—not if he had to work all day and all night every day of every week of every month in that long and steady southwest Georgia cycle. "He never let on once to me if he was disappointed or not about leaving the Navy and coming home," Lillian recalled. "I think he was, but he never said a word about it to me or anybody else that I know of. He just drove in one day with Rosalynn and the kids and went to work."

He and Rosalynn and the boys lived with Lillian for a few days in November of 1953 and then moved into a recently built public-housing project nearby. His mother remembers that it was she who suggested they find another place to live "because no house is big enough for two women." Rosalynn remembers the move as her idea, but for the same reason, and Jimmy recalls that it was something he insisted that they do because he disliked living under a roof for which he was not paying.

The savings bonds they had so carefully accumulated during their Navy years became their only source of income as they settled into the tiny quarters and started to pick up the pieces of Earl's shaky legacy. Jimmy knew hardly enough about the business to know where to begin, but he began, nevertheless, and whatever his regrets about the career he had left behind with the admiral and the nuclear submarines, he soon found himself immersed once again in the process of becoming something he was not. Nearly a dozen years before, he had left Plains as a farm boy intent on becoming a naval officer. Now, he was a naval officer determined to become a farmer. The pursuits may have appeared contradistinctive, but he ignored such impediments. The stubbornness and steady patience he had learned from his chores as a boy had sustained him during his aborted naval career. He knew that and appreciated it, just as he knew that the single-minded disciplines he had absorbed at the academy, aboard the *Wyoming* and the *Pomfret* and the *K-1* and under the admiral were valuable to him as he tried to turn his life around again.

He may have regretted leaving the Navy but he did not regret having served. "That was an opportunity for me that paid off," he said. "I had a chance to travel extensively. I read and studied everything from, you know, music, drama, art, classical music and so forth. I stretched my mind and had a great challenge." He knew the habits he had learned were productive ones. "The academy is heavily disciplined, and life on a ship—particularly as a junior officer—is a heavy discipline, and to move into the submarines is an even heavier discipline—and then I met Rickover," he remembered, "and he demanded from me a standard of performance and a depth of commitment that I had never realized before that I could achieve. I think, second to my own father, Admiral Rickover had more effect on my life than any other man."

There had never been any passionate, intimate link between the young lieutenant and the admiral, but it had been a productive relationship based solely on Rickover's cold, impersonal demands for perfection from his officers. It was the fledgling farmer's greatest asset. He had absorbed Rickover's faith in the possibility of difficult projects. Like the admiral, Jimmy had reached the conclusion that almost anything was possible, given realistic commitment and work. Like Rickover, Jimmy had found in himself the ability to remain chronically dissatisfied with himself. He had discovered within himself a capacity for great joy only when faced with a difficult problem that required large portions of his energy and intellect—and the new life he had chosen required sizable portions of both. He grilled everyone he could corner for more than a few moments on the intricacies of farming. His Uncle Alton had some answers and the tenants on his father's land had others. The Sumter County agricultural agents were of great assistance and the books they gave him were a fertile resource.

As it had almost always been for him, while he was learning, he was simultaneously applying his lessons. The business was dual. There was the pure farming side—the eternal process of planting and cultivating and harvesting and selling the peanuts and the other crops—and there was the merchandising side, with the warehouse for storing other farmers' crops and the supply of feed and seed and fertilizer that was so important to his customers. It was an exhausting grind. His days often spanned sixteen and eighteen hours, and he would come home to the little housing-project apartment and collapse in a chair for a few moments, gobble down almost without noticing Rosalynn's offering for supper and then read himself to sleep on the latest farming techniques and innovations. "It was hard on him and on everybody," Rosalynn remembered, "but it wasn't too long before he seemed almost as happy as he'd been in the Navy with the same kind of awful schedule."

Rosalynn was coping, too. She had been stunned when her husband had come back to Schenectady from Earl's funeral and suggested that it was necessary for him to resign his commission and return to Plains. They had gone through the usual tensions in the first seven years of their marriage, but they had never had a disagreement like the one sparked by his decision to leave the Navy. How could he? she bristled. How could he give it all up? she yelled. Because I have to, he answered, bristling himself. Why do you have to? she countered. Because I have to, he explained. Well, I won't go back, she pouted. He heard all of her arguments but refused to compromise. He had seen his mother's face.

The dispute was not settled quickly. It festered between them for some time until Rosalynn eventually and begrudgingly gave her assent to the return to Georgia.

Understandably, she had feared the loss of the autonomy she had found and nurtured in her life as an officer's wife. She may have been Lieutenant Carter's spouse, but she was in many ways—a sufficient number to satisfy her—her own person. Jimmy was gone so much, she was forced into the role of decision-maker for the family. She paid the bills, she managed all the finances, she took care of the car, she handled the children's medical appointments and arrangements for kindergarten—and she made the major choices for the use of her time. She answered only to Jimmy and the needs and demands of the children.

In Plains, she knew it could be different. There, she would be subject to the restraints and interferences she thought she had escaped once and for all: her own mother and Lillian and the Plains Baptist Church and the First Methodist Church and Miss Julia Coleman and Uncle Alton. She had not known what she had been reaching for when she had ached so hard seven years before to shake the dust of Sumter County from her heels, but by the summer of 1953, she knew quite well what it was. She had been seeking her independence, and she had found what she believed to be a reasonably acceptable facsimile of it as Lieutenant Carter's wife. Now it was in jeopardy and although she finally agreed to go back with Jimmy, she was determined not to let the change in her environment reduce the individuality she had already achieved and the additional independence she was still seeking. She would be Rosalynn Carter of Plains, Georgia, if that was what Jimmy thought was absolutely necessary—but she would not be the average Plains, Georgia, housewife. She did not quite know how she would manage to preserve the blossoming values she so treasured, for the homecoming would be as significant a transition for her as for her husband—but she damn well meant to do it, somehow.

Many years later, when she was her husband's surrogate during his presidential campaign, she was often characterized as a mere mimic of his carefully stated views and positions. It was an accurate image, but it overlooked the rather basic essence of Rosalynn Eleanor Smith Carter. She was, in her own view, a woman of great independence. She was tough, sturdy, reliable and operated on an underlying basis of firm, unshakable resolve to remain precisely what she was, and it had begun years before when Jimmy had plucked her from the Navy life-style she cherished and in which she was growing, and rather unceremoniously dumped her back into a milieu she feared. He wanted to take over his father's business, to follow in his father's footsteps. Fine, she said, at last, but neither his father's business nor his father's ghost—nothing, in fact, she resolved—would keep her from continuing the process she had begun with their marriage.

Fortunately, Jimmy made it easier for her when they returned—perhaps unconsciously but nevertheless with a substantial effect. He suggested that she help him with the business, and asked if she would mind taking over the bookkeeping. She agreed. From then on, she was as important to the Carters' financial fortunes as Jimmy or anyone else. She was surprised at the ease and quickness with which she adjusted to and met the intricate demands the world of agribusiness made on her accounting abilities, and it did not take Jimmy long to recognize that their enterprise would be substantially less promising without her counsel and her competence. It was a new bond between them and added a new dimension to their marriage. He was pleasantly surprised at how much more he enjoyed her company as a semiequal. He had only minimally appreciated her role as a partner during his Navy years, mainly because of his absences. He simply did not notice that she was growing with him in those days.

Back home in Plains, however, with the two of them jointly immersed in a common pursuit—earning money—he found her delightful, well-informed company and a perceptive, almost instinctive capitalist. They discovered in themselves a capacity for reasoned dialogue and debate. Their previous pattern had been simply to argue—with no really beneficial conclusion. They quickly found that as real partners they were able to disagree, discuss without arguing and reach mutually acceptable decisions. The business was making it possible for them to deal with each other more candidly, more openly than at any time since their marriage, and in the process, each of them was finding in the other a variety of admirable traits that had escaped notice before.

Rosalynn, Jimmy learned, was impressively shrewd and had the combined assets of a gambler and a public-relations agent. Jimmy, she found, was often unbelievably clever and had a scientist's sense of innovation. Together, as they mutually ran his father's business, they built a pool of nonnegotiable assets. Together, they learned what made the little community tick. Together, they familiarized themselves with the concepts and the processes of community leadership. They had spent their years in Norfolk and New London and Honolulu and San Diego and Schenectady growing separately. Back home in Plains, they began to grow together. They were in the process of becoming genuine partners, and the primary catalyst for the metamorphosis was Rosalynn's steely determination to survive as something more than Jimmy's wife and Lillian's daughter-in-law.

"I knew she didn't want to come back to Georgia," Lillian said. "She was enjoying it too much in the Navy and I don't blame her now and I didn't blame her then. I probably would have taken to that kind of life myself, and so I never held it against her that she had reservations about Jimmy's decision to come back—and you know, she was so sweet about it. She never said one word. Never complained one time. Never even mentioned that maybe she was a bit perturbed about living in Plains. She went right to work at the business and she never quit, and from that day on she was Jimmy's partner. Of course, her name wasn't on the legal papers, you know—Jimmy and I bought the business from the other children—but Rosalynn and Jimmy were partners. There was never any doubt about that. And she always has been his partner ever since."

But it was tough—as tough as anything Jimmy and Rosalynn would ever experience. He read with bittersweet eagerness of the launching of the *Nautilus* in January 1954, and their first growing season coincided with one of the worst droughts in Georgia's history. Despite his backbreaking persistence and the sale of more than two thousand tons of fertilizer, their net profit that first year—1954—was $187. "We weren't exactly General Motors, were we?" he chuckled years later, remembering that even their tiny public-housing project apartment cost them more than their profit that year.

One day, in early May 1954, soon after the planting had begun, Jimmy skimmed over a story in the *Columbus Enquirer* about the fall of a French post in Vietnam called Dien Bien Phu, and just a few days later he read with considerable more attention to detail a lengthy account of the Supreme Court's decision in the case of Oliver Brown's suit against the board of education in Topeka, Kansas. Years and years later, he would write that it "concerned racial integration of public schools." It was curiously imprecise language for a usually precise man. The Court's decision in that spring of 1954—rather than merely "concerning" itself with racial integration—flatly outlawed segregated public education, the bulwark of Southern society. An era of revolutionary change was about to begin in the people and the places around Jimmy Carter.

Although the world had been turned inside out in the decade since he had left home for the Naval Academy, the Plains to which he had returned was essentially unchanged. He and his fellow white citizens lived on the north side of the Seaboard Coast Line railroad tracks and the black people of Plains lived on the south side. It was a symbolic separation of residence that extended itself into every other facet of life in the village—as it did in all communities in the South, big and small. As Ensign Carter and Lieutenant Carter, Jimmy's racial sensitivity had been raised by acquaintances and working relationships with black enlisted men and their families (Annapolis did not produce a black graduate until three years after Jimmy had left there), and his duty in Hawaii had allowed him at least a brief exposure to an integrated, interracial society.

Still, when he came home, he became Mistuh Jimmy to his father's tenants and the rest of the local black population. The housing project in which he chose to live was all white. The blacks had their own housing project—across the tracks. He settled back into a segregated life with no visible signs of a painful adjustment. The system was by then so deeply embedded in the very genes of the Southerners— black and white—that about the only time they sensed that there was actually a system was when there was a deviation from it. It had been there so long, so long, and it seemed a good bet that it would always be there.

For three decades after the end of the Civil War, most of the Southern states, for one reason or another, had diligently avoided the passage of laws specifically dictating the separation of blacks and whites in the society. Such separation existed, of course, but for the most part it was simply the extension of antebellum custom, not a legalized segregation. There were avid and energetic efforts to codify the South's traditional way of life, but resistance had been sturdy and, in a few isolated cases, enlightened. The erosion of the opposition, however, was steady. The course toward legalized segregation seemed inexorable. In South Carolina, for instance, where such laws had been defeated year after year in the state legislature, the statutory segregationists by 1898 were on the eve of passing a bill which ordered blacks and whites to ride in separate passenger cars on all trains. The *Charleston News & Courier,* the oldest paper in the region,

had been an eloquent, outspoken foe of such legislation,
and, in an eleventh-hour effort to defeat it, provided its
readers with an editorial designed to poke enough fun at its
advocates so that the bill would appear absurd:

"As we have got on fairly well for a third of a century,
including a long period of reconstruction, without such a
measure, we can probably get on as well hereafter without
it," the editorial began. "Certainly, so extreme a measure
should not be adopted and enforced without added and ur-
gent cause. If there must be Jim Crow cars on the railroad,
there should be Jim Crow cars on the street railways, and
also on all passenger boats. If there are to be Jim Crow cars,
moreover, there should be Jim Crow waiting saloons at all
stations, and Jim Crow eating houses, Jim Crow sections of
the jury box and a separate Jim Crow dock and witness
stand in every court—and a Jim Crow Bible for colored witnesses to kiss. It would be advisable also to have a Jim Crow
section in county auditors' and treasures' offices for the accommodation of colored taxpayers. The two races are dread-
fully mixed in these offices for weeks every year, especially
about Christmas. There should be a Jim Crow department
for making returns and paying for the privileges and bless-
ings of citizenship. Perhaps, the best plan would be, after
all, to take the short cut to the general end . . . by establishing two or three Jim Crow counties at once, and turning
them over to our colored citizens for their special and exclusive accommodation."

The editor was unintentionally prescient. His attempt to
ridicule by drawing an absurd picture of the logical extension of segregated railroad cars was an accurate portrait of
the future South. By the turn of the century, every Southern
state had passed a similar law dictating segregated passenger trains. The next step was political disenfranchisement of
black Southerners, as effective as any military campaign, including Sherman's March to the Sea. In Louisiana, for example, there were 130,000 black voters in 1896. Eight years
later, there were 1300. The attitude was contagious.

Blacks were subjected to years of terror and harassment

all over the region, a vendetta fed by politicians of both Democratic and Republican persuasion. By 1906, even the *Charleston News & Courier* had changed its mind. "The 'problem' is worse now than it was ten years ago," an editorial in the paper began, moving quickly to an ardent advocacy not merely of segregation but of mass deportation of blacks. "Separation of the races is the only radical solution of the negro problem in this country. There is no room for them here." Segregation marched in seven-league boots through the legislatures, producing segregated employment, segregated hospitals, segregated prisons, segregated orphanages, segregated amusement parks, segregated circuses and sideshows, segregated fraternal orders and societies, segregated neighborhoods (entire communities were built on the basis of strict apartheid), segregated telephone booths and drinking fountains, segregated prostitution, segregated churches—and finally in Atlanta, the local courts conveniently provided segregated Bibles for black witnesses to kiss.

There were few instances of moderation and almost no examples of resistance to the trend. For half a century, through law, and even longer, through custom, the black Southerners in Jimmy Carter's South had been systematically and thoroughly repressed. It was not merely a matter of having shown the black Southerner his place, of establishing a particular rank or caste for the black Southerner, it was a ruthless insistence on an almost total exclusion of the black Southerner from Southern life—from its economics, from its education, from its religion and from its politics. White Southerners who raised even the mildest question about the propriety of such a system faced a lonely life wherever they happened to be. In 1947, for example, U.S. District Judge J. Waties Waring, a Roosevelt appointee and a member of an old and respected Charleston family, invalidated South Carolina's so-called "white primary," one more in a long line of efforts to disenfranchise black citizens completely. Undaunted, the Democrats of South Carolina devised a mandatory oath for all those who would vote in the party's primary elections, an oath to abide by and support the concept of racial segregation. Judge Waring was enraged. He ruled again. "It is important that once and for all, the members of this party be made to understand—and that is the purpose of this opinion—that they will be required to obey and carry out the orders of this court, not only in the technical respects but in the true spirit and meaning of the same."

Waring struck down the primary oath just as he had struck down the previous attempts to create the exclusionary primary—and U.S. District Judge J. Waties Waring became a pariah in Charleston for the rest of his life. Literally no one except those on his staff and lawyers appearing before him in court would so much as speak to him. His home was regularly stoned by young toughs driving by and speeding off into the darkness. It was bombed twice. For years there were regular, anonymous threatening phone calls, and all because it was Judge Waring's considered opinion that all elections should be open. The judge, it was deemed, was a traitor to the sacred traditions of the region. In a short time, his name was known all across the South as an example of extreme perfidy, and three decades later, in the city of Charleston, it is still spoken with a sneer by most of the people in town.

The price for any resistance in Jimmy Carter's South was high. Few even considered paying it. Judge Waring, after all, was but one Federal official. The Supreme Court, after all, had endorsed a "separate but equal" doctrine in 1896, and in the years since, the Federal government had all but ignored the South's repression of black Americans. The Southern states, essentially feudal systems run by whites, had been giving steady electoral approval for years only to politicians who vowed eternal fealty to the old ways.

Even after the Supreme Court's historic and unanimous condemnation of segregated public education in that May of Jimmy's first year back in Plains, there was little stir in the

South. After all, there were nearly twelve thousand separate school districts in the region where segregation was the law, and the Court's decision initially applied only to five. It was unquestionably a momentous writ, focused directly on the concept of social equality between the races rather than the mechanical separation of black from white in Jim Crow cars on trains. Still, most white Southerners were blithely unconcerned. History had shown that simply because something was declared to be unconstitutional, it did not immediately cease to exist.

The Supreme Court delayed an implementation order for a year, during which white Southerners who were concerned about the ruling prepared their weapons. When the order came, it referred quite sympathetically to the "solution of varied local school problems . . . in reasonable time." It was an order much to the liking of Southern whites. It provided the basis for the delays that would drag on and on for years. Ernest Vandiver, Georgia's lieutenant governor at the time and later a friend and political supporter of Jimmy Carter, sighed with relief when the Supreme Court dropped its other shoe. "They are steeped in the same traditions that I am," he exhaled. "A 'reasonable time' can be construed as one year or two hundred. Thank God, we've got good Federal judges."

Still, others were not quite so sure. The White Citizens Councils began proliferating from their roots in central Mississippi into Florida and Texas and Arkansas and Alabama and Georgia, a mean and ugly movement furtively but badly concealed as a quasi-chamber of commerce, concerned only with civic pride and betterment, but deeply involved in violence and intimidation and walking hand in hand with a revitalized Ku Klux Klan.

Jimmy, meanwhile, was still single-mindedly working on the restoration of his father's sagging legacy. He was the sole employee for over a year after his return—not counting Rosalynn, of course—personally loading the hundred-pound and two-hundred-pound sacks and bags of fertilizer for his growing list of clients. He was still an avid student, and went so far as to enroll in night agricultural courses at an experimental farming station in nearby Tifton. "I learned rapidly," he recalled, but the health of his enterprise improved slowly, almost imperceptibly, and when he finally raised sufficient courage to present himself at the local bank for a loan in late 1954, he was refused.

Rosalynn was tired but happy. During the harvest that year—that hot and even drier than usual season that seemed to smother the flat terrain that was both her old and new environment—she worked eighteen-hour days, from six o'clock in the morning until midnight. She was, after all, the front office of the operation. Jimmy clawed at the land. She handled the accounting and the critical contact point with the customers—that moment of "settling up" when the check was written by the Carter warehouse to the farmer for his crop. In the harvest season, the work seemed never to stop. A steady stream of customers moved through her life and through the film of red dust that saturated it. Sometimes, Rosalynn prayed for rain. "I know rain didn't do the farmers any good at that time of the year," she said, "but I prayed for it anyway, just to give us a chance to catch up for a day or so."

Rosalynn did not have to work after a while. She did it to survive and to find some self-satisfaction and to create an atmosphere in which she could be secure, in which she would be needed. Lillian occasionally criticized her for neglecting the three little boys, but she paid no attention. She was determined that she would never find herself ensnared in the noose that fell around her mother when Edgar Smith died the year before the war began. She would never be discarded as a person with no marketable skills.

There were other women of similar fortitude in the American South, and on December 1, 1955—about two years after

Jimmy and Rosalynn had come back to Plains—one such woman boarded a city bus in Montgomery, Alabama, and headed toward the house she and her husband owned in the segregated outskirts of Alabama's capital city. Her name was Rosa Parks. She was very tired. She had spent the morning sewing for white customers and the afternoon shopping on the meager budget her work provided. The bus was crowded. There were no seats left after a few stops. A white man boarded. The Jim Crow rule still applied in 1955. Blacks rode in the rear of the bus, but if there were not enough seats to go around for white people in the front, then black riders had to vacate their seats and stand while white passengers sat. "Give that man your seat," the bus driver ordered. Mrs. Parks looked away from his voice. She stared straight ahead, pretending not to hear. "Get up from there, woman," the driver insisted. She shook her head, silently but with increasing vigor. She was tired. She decided she would just sit for a while. She was arrested, jailed, tried and convicted. It was the final straw for many black citizens of Montgomery. A boycott of the bus system began under the aegis of an organization that called itself the Montgomery Civic Improvement Association. At its first meeting, the little group elected as its first president the young pastor of the Dexter Avenue Baptist Church, the red brick place of worship just down the broad boulevard from the gleaming white, white capitol. The young pastor's name was Martin Luther King, Jr. One door had opened and another had closed on Southern history.

"There was strong concern and excitement in Georgia about the Supreme Court rulings and the prospective passage of laws in Congress to eliminate the legal aspects of segregation," Jimmy Carter wrote years later. "I was quite concerned about this problem myself. My views on the subject were sometimes at odds with those of most of my neighbors." There is no evidence, however, that he effectively espoused such contradictory perspectives. As he and his father had maintained their mutual vow of silence on racial matters, he continued his silence as a neophyte businessman in Plains. His passion was for his business and little else. He seemed driven by his own guilt or his father's ghost or both to emulate Earl Carter's life. He began teaching Sunday school at the Plains Baptist Church. He was elected as one of its deacons. He joined local clubs and agreed to serve on the library board for the county and the hospital board as well. He became a scoutmaster—and all the while, the long days that stretched into the soft Georgia evenings were beginning to pay off.

He became a walking encyclopedia on peanuts. (Even during his presidential campaign, when impatient reporters wanted to discuss other matters, he would filibuster with lengthy, impromptu treatises on the relative virtues of various varieties of the plant.) He turned his attention and his expanding expertise to growing and selling certified seed peanuts to local farmers. Using such certified seed, whose fertility was guaranteed by Carter, the farmers planted their crops, which Jimmy then bought and resold. The business expanded, and as it became more lucrative, Rosalynn's role became more important.

"The whole thing got so complicated so fast," she remembered. "We had four different sets of books we had to keep—I mean, for me to keep—and then we had one master set that was an accumulation of the others." She checked out accounting texts from the local library and spent what spare time she had increasing her skills. Then she decided to take a correspondence course to enhance them even further. "I really worked at it," she said. "I never did get the chance, of course, but I think if I had ever taken the CPA exam, I would have passed it easily." Moreover, she was exhilarated by the success of their business, the money it was beginning to produce and the significant role she knew she was playing in their good fortune. "I just loved it, really. It was, well, it was great fun, even if it was work—making all those books come out right on the penny. I guess I enjoyed it more than almost anything I've ever done."

At the end of each season, her husband—the newest seed-peanut mogul in Georgia—would discuss their financial condition with her. No major decisions on capital expansions were made without her advice and consent. "He would come to me to see what was happening in the business," she remembered, "and he would ask if we should continue doing this or that and he would listen to me—he would listen to what I had to say about it because I was the one who knew whether he could or couldn't or should or shouldn't. I never really thought I could do that, but I did, and I think that out of that there came a mutual respect and understanding between Jimmy and me that we might never have had otherwise. I discovered that we were not only building a business. We were really building our marriage, too."

In the late autumn of 1942, soon after Jimmy had begun his sophomore year in college—his first at Georgia Tech—a young, incurably idealistic Baptist minister from nearby Talbot County had founded an experimental Christian commune about seven miles from Plains on land purchased with funds from a group that believed such a project was workable. His name was Clarence Jordan. He was a large man with a broad-gauge, quick mind, and he was persuaded that the life of Jesus, as depicted in the New Testament, offered the sole example for worthwhile Christian commitment. His farm would be a place where love would be the rule, not the exception, he said. The individual needs of those who would live and work there would be met by the community, he said. There would be sharing and caring, he envisioned, and there would be no discrimination of any kind. Those who came to the community would be accepted, regardless of race. There would be but one requirement: a willingness to apply genuine Christian ethics to daily life situations. It would be uncomplicated, he said, and it would be more than simply a noble experiment. It would be a realistic portrait of Jesus' examples. The farm would be called Koinonia, an English translation of a Greek noun meaning community or fellowship.

Like Jimmy Carter more than ten years later, Jordan drove into Sumter County with very little knowledge of farming and very few agricultural skills; but over the next two decades, with hard work and perseverance, Koinonia grew and prospered. But by 1950, the commune's views on racial conciliation and pacifism (Jordan counseled frequently with conscientious objectors) prompted subtle forms of resistance in the community around it, from Plains to Americus, the county seat. At the Plains Baptist Church, where Earl Carter was still a deacon and a pillar, they were told they were not wanted. "Earl thought that was the right thing to do," Lillian said. "He'd heard about what all was going on out there—there was always a lot of talk about that bunch—and Earl, well, he just didn't want any trouble in the church. That's all. Earl didn't want the church upset and those people seemed to have a way of upsetting things. Of course, Earl was particularly against mixing the races and he'd heard that there were colored and whites out there living together and all. He just didn't want any of that in his church."

By 1956, the impact of the Supreme Court's ban on segregated public education had finally reached Georgia's state college system and two young black students who wanted to enroll in the previously all-white Georgia State College of Business in Atlanta asked Jordan to assist them. All applications, including those from white students, had to be accompanied by the signatures of two alumni of the state system, and since Jordan was a graduate of the University of Georgia, he agreed to provide one of the necessary endorsements. The Georgia Board of Regents, however, ruled that Jordan was ineligible to sponsor the students since he had graduated from an institution other than the one to which they were applying. So, Jordan came back to Sumter County from Atlanta without having put his name on their applications.

Nevertheless, the next day, the headlines of the *Americus Times Recorder* signaled in bold type that Jordan had signed the applications of two black students trying to integrate a white college. Sumter County, long dormant in the blossoming struggle for and against the civil rights of black Americans, finally stood up and was counted. What followed over the next three years was one of the ugliest paragraphs in the annals of human relationships in the South, and it took place practically on Jimmy Carter's back porch.

For nearly thirty months, the men and women and children who lived on Jordan's Koinonia Farm were subjected to a siege of violence and economic pressures whose intensity and unceasing constancy amazed even the most hardened of local residents.

By late February 1957, Koinonia was as unpopular a word in Sumter County as the name Waring had been in Charleston. A cross was burned on the front lawn of the farm, and on the last Sunday evening in February, the Knights of the Ku Klux Klan held a rally in Americus, a gathering of about 150 men and women from across southern Georgia. In their white robes and peaked hoods, they ranted and raved for several hours about what was wrong with the country, namely niggers and race-mixing whites and Earl Warren and the Commies and the National Council of Churches. Their meeting over, they took off their hoods, formed a long motorcade and drove out to the Koinonia Farm.

It was the beginning of another intensified round of attacks. Fences were cut, fires were set and more rifle slugs tore through the windows and walls of the residences. A grand jury investigated all the violence. It returned no indictments, but in its final report it accused Clarence Jordan and his friends of almost everything from perjury and fraud to disturbing the peace and suspicion of conspiracy. In nearly three years of bombings, shootings and other mayhem—property damage at the farm was estimated at close to $150,000—no one was ever arrested, except members of the farm itself on trumped-up motor vehicle charges. From the county commissioners to the sheriff to the wonderful solicitor general, Sumter officialdom was of one mind: the Koinonia Farm had to be destroyed. It was contrary to the way things were and always had been in the community—and because of its alien nature, it had to be destroyed.

Obviously, it was not an easy environment in which to practice the principles of Christian brotherhood, as Clarence Jordan and his compatriots on the farm discovered—and as Jimmy Carter soon found out for himself. He had accepted an appointment to the Sumter County Board of Education in late 1955, and he had watched with some astonishment as the others on the board talked openly of how a white agency of government could successfully avoid obeying the law of the land. Occasionally, and only occasionally—according to two of those who served with him on the board—did he ever hint to his colleagues that perhaps there was something amiss in the direction of their deliberations. In September 1957, President Eisenhower had ordered federal troops into Little Rock to enforce a court order for the integration of Central High School. The White Citizens Councils blossomed even more abundantly across the South. There was work for them to do, although they actually contributed very little to the resistance movement over the whole course of the civil rights era.

By 1958, the disease had spread to Plains and several of the leading lights of the community, including a part-time minister and the chief of the little police force, had formed a local Citizens Council. The recruitment of members had been rather simple. After all, it was a white Southerner's duty to oppose the mongrelization of his race, and those who found the Klan a little low-brow for their tastes were quickly drawn to the better class of people in the councils. The police chief and the preacher dropped by the Carter

warehouse one morning to add another name to their growing list of members, but Jimmy politely informed them that
he did not wish to belong. They were a bit confused at first
by his refusal, and took some pains to describe the wonderful work the Citizens Councils were doing all across the
South. Again, Jimmy respectfully declined the honor. They
left, muttering to themselves, and a couple of days later they
returned and announced that Jimmy was the only white
male in Plains who had not yet joined their group. It was
strong propaganda. After all, they argued, what was five dollars to an up-and-coming young businessman like Earl
Carter's son? Jimmy told them he really had not changed his
mind about joining and once again they left.

About a week passed while they shored up their strategy,
and Jimmy looked up from his work at the warehouse one
morning and spotted the chief, the preacher and several of
his own customers and close friends headed his way. This
was the heavy artillery. "They pointed out that it would
damage my reputation and my success as a businessman in
the community if I proved to be the only hold-out," he
wrote years later, "and because of their genuine concern
about my welfare, they were willing to pay the dues for
me."

Whatever instincts were operating in the thirty-three-year-
old member of the school board at that moment, he was to
his credit adamant in his refusal to join. Moreover, he
seemed genuinely angry—a kind of inner fury that he managed scarcely to contain before answering them quietly but
coldly. No, he said, he had absolutely no intention of becoming a part of their organization; if that meant that he
would be hurt financially, well, then, he said, he was willing
to just pack up and leave Plains. He had moved before, he
said, and he could move again. The five dollars, he pointed
out, was nothing to him. It had nothing to do with anything.
He would take the five dollars and flush it down the toilet,
he vowed, before he would give it to the White Citizens
Councils of America—and, he finished, more passionately

than he had spoken ever before in his life, he would not change his mind about it. The preacher and the police chief and the rest of them need not darken his door again, he said, if all they wanted to discuss was his membership in their group.

That evening, over supper, he mentioned the incident to Rosalynn, She winced. They had been in business only four years, and as the company bookkeeper she knew they were not yet in a financial condition that would allow them to survive a boycott. "I was really worried," she said, "but I was also very proud of Jimmy. Those people were ugly. They were all wrapped up in small, mean things and I was so proud that he had stood up to them; I think Jimmy was proud of himself, too." It was not a painless gesture. The local council organized a boycott against Jimmy's and Rosalynn's business, and the Carter enterprises lost a considerable amount of money as a result. "But, he wouldn't give in," Rosalynn recalled. The boycott eventually petered out "because many of my white customers resented being pressured into paying dues into the coffers of a non-functioning organization," he wrote.

The friction between him and the red-neck organizers of the council was but one tiny millisecond in the long and bitter and murderous saga of the ongoing Southern revolution. It amounted to not much more than a match struck against the darkness of the universal night—but it was something, and because it was at least something, it was significant in the life of James Earl Carter, Jr., the son of the man who had decided that for the peace of the Plains Baptist Church, it was better simply to keep the Koinonia members out. Jimmy Carter was, by no stretch of anyone's imagination, a liberal maverick ensconced in the wilds of Sumter County. His roots in the traditional racial construction of his community ran deep and curled themselves around the customs of segregationists who had made Georgia their home for nearly two centuries. Nevertheless, given a clearly delineated choice between the idiocy of the Citizens Councils,

with their empty posturing and their swaggering xenopho-
bia, and a costly rejection of their Neanderthal values,
Jimmy Carter, for whatever his reasons, had done the right
thing. He was, perhaps, in the process of becoming again—
in the process of becoming a citizen of a different South
than he or his parents had ever known.

By 1959, just about five years after he left the Navy and
returned to Georgia, Mistuh Jimmy was well on his way to
prosperity. The specter of the old Carter lands being divided and sold off to put food on his family's table was
gone. It had been unthinkable from the very beginning. The
Carters had not been enormously wealthy people during
Earl's life, but the land was to them what a portfolio of
stocks and bonds might be to another clan. It was capital, of
course, not currency, and Jimmy went to great lengths not to
disturb it. Except for a few acres here and there, put on the
market strategically, none of the land his father had left was
sold. Instead, as soon as he could swing it, Jimmy began to
add to his inheritance in small and carefully purchased increments.

With Rosalynn's assistance, he shrewdly husbanded the
assets of the business, adding pieces of new equipment and
new employees as he went along, using the land as collateral for loans, getting management counseling from the
Small Business Administration, developing his reputation as
a supplier of high-quality seed peanuts, slowly but steadily
expanding his holdings and gradually winning the respect of
his neighbors not only as a worthy successor to the role his
father had played in the community but as a likable young
man with deeply rooted personal integrity and considerable
business acumen as well.

"Jimmy was the sort of fellow who always gave you the
impression that he knew what he was doing," his Cousin
Hugh Carter recalled. "I suspect that sometimes he didn't—

but he never let on in public and he worked hard enough to make up for whatever gaps there were in his understanding of the business."

In addition to his active role in the church, he threw himself with similar energies into the local Lions Club, the only civic organization in Plains, and eventually became a district governor of the group. Because he had switched the focus of his farming operation to the growth and sale of seed peanuts, he became active in the Georgia Certified Seed Association and eventually became its president. He was appointed to the Sumter County Planning Commission. He gave his public trusts the same zeal he gave his personal business. Whether it was the library board or the hospital board or the school board, he did not miss meetings and he did not dismiss any facet of his responsibilities lightly. He found time to study whatever subject was at hand, and in the view of many of his colleagues from those days, he took great pains to act evenhandedly on every decision. "He became the sort of fellow people just naturally believed they could trust," Alton Carter remembered. "I mean, a lot of folks around here got to the point where if they had something they needed done, they'd automatically think of Jimmy Carter." The years at the academy and in the Navy were still working in him in his civilian disciplines. He was still regarded as a man who was capable of getting the job done.

That was not always true, of course. As a school board member, he pushed for a radical realignment of the system. He was never regarded in the county as a dreaded "integrationist," but his endorsement of the realignment—actually, a consolidation of the system based on economic considerations—placed him in a distinct minority of Sumter Countians. The truth was that while he worked hard for the reorganization of the schools and explained his advocacy of it in terms of the money the taxpayers could save, he was also attempting to set the stage for an easier transition to integrated public schools. He did not say that, of course. He would never have said that at that point in his life, but he could see the inevitability of court orders and ultimate integration and he had conceived of the consolidation approach as a means of allowing that change to take place with less of the pain he knew would ensue.

His experience with the Citizens Council was a seed in his psyche. He was proud of his resistance. He knew he had done the right thing, and that was what he wanted to do. Still, when he began studying the school system, it pained him when he realized that it had taken all those years for him to understand the basic inequities inherent in providing free and public transportation to school for white children without doing the same for the black students. He became the consolidation proposal's most ardent spokesman, and he traveled around the county asking people to vote for it in the referendum. But most Sumter Countians were way ahead of Jimmy. If he would not say it, and if they did not know that he realized it, they suspected that any diddling with the school system then was in some way related to what the Supreme Court had ordered in 1954. All change was suspect in Sumter County, but changes in the schools were particularly suspect. The new plan involved the loss of one of the schools in Plains, but Jimmy actively supported the consolidation anyway. The referendum lost by fewer than a hundred votes. In Plains, the vote against it was overwhelming. "The failure of my effort was a stinging disappointment," he wrote, but the excitement of what had amounted to electoral politics had fascinated him. He had been baptized and bitten. He had lost, but he had found in himself an eager excitement and enthusiasm for the combat of politics. He was surprised—pleasantly so.

He was not politically naive. Earl had always encouraged him to take an interest in the politics of the town and the region, even as a young boy, and he had often taken him along to campaign rallies of the various candidates. Jimmy's systematic efforts to win an appointment to Annapolis had further involved him in the give-and-take of the system, and during his military tenure under Admiral Rickover, he had spent quite a bit of time in Washington, watching the Congress deal with military appropriations and getting to know, at least casually, Senators Richard B. Russell and Walter F. George, his fellow Georgians. (Russell, in fact, helped ease the way for his resignation from the Navy when he finally decided to go home in 1953.) Still, his contact with and interest in politics had been rather minimal before his experience with the school-consolidation referendum. He had found it a deeply satisfying cup of tea and discovered in himself an itch he could not scratch. He was once again in the process of becoming.

Lillian thought she noticed something different about her older son after the school-board experience. "He seemed bored with business," she remembered. "Oh, he worked just as hard as he ever had, but it just didn't seem quite so exciting to him as before. Besides, he and Rosalynn had done such a good job on it that it was beginning to almost take care of itself, you know. I could tell he was getting bored." She was right. He and Rosalynn, having been more or less liberated from the grindings of their earliest efforts by the financial success of their mutual work, decided to build a new house. It amounted to something of a mansion against the relative values of Plains and was one of only a few houses in the area designed by an architect. They also enjoyed a fairly active social life; they went dancing quite often at the American Legion club in Americus, spent a great deal of time with Mr. and Mrs. John Pope, their closest friends in the county and residents of Americus (John owned a casket manufacturing business), took weekend trips to stock-car races—a new passion for Jimmy only tolerated by Rosalynn—and watched their three sons begin to move through the grades at Miss Julia Coleman's school. Jimmy, as a leader of the Lions Club of Plains, spearheaded a public swimming pool project, and, like Tom Sawyer whitewashing the fence, soon had almost every man in town involved. When it was built, just around the corner from his new home, it was segregated. He said nothing.

In 1961, soon after John F. Kennedy's inauguration as the

thirty-fifth President of the United States, a lengthy court battle over equal representation in the Georgia legislature climaxed with a Federal court order for its reapportionment. Until that time, the state House and Senate were nothing more than temporary, part-time bodies. Sumter County, for instance, was represented in the State Senate as part of a three-county combination; every two years, the state senator would be chosen from a different county. It was not a particularly attractive seat, especially for Jimmy Carter, but the court's reapportionment order changed all that. "For the first time," he wrote later, it "would have a permanent membership with substantive and continuing responsibilities." He remembered the excitement he had felt several years before when he had led the fight for the school consolidation. The urge was strong. The instinct was irresistible. He decided to become a candidate for the Democratic nomination to the Georgia State Senate. The man who was his principal opponent was an entrenched Establishment figure, having already held the seat once under the old revolving system.

Jimmy wrote: "My family, my close friends and I mounted an amateurish, whirlwind campaign," within the new district, an area that under the terms of the reapportionment had come to embrace seven counties and more than eighty thousand people. "He had the established politicians for him. My supporters were mostly young, and newcomers to politics." He was nearly thirty-eight years old on the day of the Democratic primary election that August of 1962—and he and Rosalynn and John Pope and his wife and Warren Fortson, a young lawyer from Americus, and all the others who had helped him in his campaign were confident of victory. After all, he knew he had worked harder than the other fellow. He had been in every one of the precincts in all seven counties in the district. He had shaken thousands and thousands of hands and handed out brochures at every meeting. He had spent several thousand dollars of his own money—but above all, he had devoted himself completely to the campaign. It was one of those pursuits that he, like

Rickover, believed was possible given sufficient commitment. They were both wrong, it seemed. He lost. In his autobiography, he explains how it happened:

"On election day, I visited as many of the polling places as possible, and everything seemed to be in order until I arrived in Georgetown, a small town on the Chattahoochee River in the extreme western part of the district. It was the only village in Quitman County. There were no voting booths in the courthouse, and all voters were marking their ballots on a table in full view of the voting officials. The local state legislator and dominant political boss of the county was supervising the election—apparently with great interest. Campaign cards of my opponent were on the voting table, and the supervisor would point to the cards and say to each voter, 'This is a good man, and my friend.' He would watch the ballot being marked and then dropped into a large hole in the top of a pasteboard box, and on several occasions he reached into the box and extracted a few ballots to be examined.

"It was an unbelievable scene. He completely ignored my protests. All the other poll workers seemed to obey his orders.

"I rode to a cafe and telephoned the newspaper office in the nearby city of Columbus to describe what was occurring. They promised to send a reporter. When I returned after a couple of hours from a visit to another county, the reporter and the political boss were chatting on the steps of the courthouse. It was obvious that they were old friends, and the reporter was not interested in writing any story critical of election procedures in Quitman County. It turned out that the local big shot was an influential employee of the State Agriculture Department, had complete control over the Democratic Party Election Board, and that his wife ran the County Welfare System.

"I called John Pope, . . . explained what was happening, and asked him to come to Quitman County as an observer. The rest of my day was spent traveling around the district

JAMES WOOTEN

helping my campaign workers get voters to the polls in the
other six counties. We obtained the election results by telephone that night at my warehouse offices in Plains, and finally I was leading by about 70 votes with the Georgetown
box not reported.

"We knew that about 300 people had voted there, and that
the obvious voting irregularities had continued throughout
the day. John and several of my Quitman County supporters
observed the votes being counted. There were 433 ballots in
the box, and according to the names listed, 126 of them
voted alphabetically! When the ballots were unfolded, there
were sometimes four to eight of them folded together. It was
obvious that the box had been stuffed, and I had lost the
election by a few votes."

Jimmy called Fortson, the young lawyer in Americus, and
the two of them drove to Georgetown late that night and
began taking statements from local residents about the voting procedures. They discovered that what had happened
that day had been going on on election days as long as most
people could remember. Carter, bitterly disappointed by
what had happened, steeled himself for what he knew
would be a grim struggle—but he believed he had won the
election and he was damned if he would quit trying to prove
it, just because it was a tough proposition. He had worked so
hard to win. He knew he deserved to win, if for no other
reason than the diligence with which he had campaigned.
Moreover, he was persuaded that a legal election would
have given him the Democratic nomination by a large margin. He thought it was the people's wish that he go to the
State Senate.

The local Democratic machinery laughed at his efforts to
reverse the decision. The election, after all, was over. Carter
had lost. There was nothing he could do. He was just some
little crybaby from Plains, some businessman who knew
nothing about the exigencies of politics. But they did not
reckon on Carter's stubborn, dogged determination, fueled
by his seething anger. No one had made Jimmy Carter sing

"Marching Through Georgia" at the Naval Academy and no one was going to cheat Jimmy Carter out of an election, not if it took him years and every dime he had to correct the wrong.

His opponents soon discovered that Carter was a man to be dealt with seriously. As he and Fortson and Pope continued their interviews of local people, they were followed by local lieutenants of the organization. There were threatening phone calls to the warehouse and to their homes. Occasionally, the lieutenants stood by and listened to the interviews conducted by Carter and Fortson and Pope, taking notes from a discreet but visible distance. "At first," Jimmy wrote, "the people were quite timid and reluctant to talk. But we attempted to question everyone who was alleged to have voted. Many of the 'voters' were dead, in prison, or had long ago moved away and voted in other communities. Some of the Quitman County citizens were evasive when questioned, and others signed affidavits stating that they had not voted. Our support within the county slowly grew as it became obvious that we were going through with the challenge. But we were not making any progress with the outside world. The nearby Columbus newspapers pictured me as a politically naive sorehead and a poor loser. State party officials proved to be aloof or downright hostile. The local judge and district attorney had strong ties in the county." Eventually, Jimmy and his campaign friends presented their case to the state Democratic convention meeting in Macon. "It was ignored," he recalled. "My opponent was declared to be the winner, and the official Democratic nominee for the State Senate. We could hardly believe it!"

Still, Carter refused to quit. He called John Pennington, a quiet, studious but dogged young investigative reporter for the *Atlanta Journal*, and persuaded him that there was a substantive story in the voting irregularities in Quitman County. Pennington retraced much of what Jimmy and his friends had already established with their interviews and his subsequent stories focused new attention on the scandal outside the local area. The defeated candidate and Fortson, meanwhile, were working day and night, building a case against the man who had already been officially declared the winner. "I almost memorized the Georgia Election Code," Carter said. "It seemed obvious that almost every section of it had been violated. We learned about many other illegal activities within the community involving moonshine liquor, previous vote frauds, thefts of land, extortion, and other crimes. The threats continued, and so did our investigation."

Time was running out for Jimmy. The general election was imminent. If his opponent was on that ballot and won— and every Democrat in southwest Georgia perpetually did in those days—that would effectively seal Jimmy's fate as a loser. In desperation, he began looking for the best lawyer he could get and his older cousin, Donald Carter, a newspaper publisher in Macon, gave him the name of an old college classmate of his named Charles Kirbo. The recommendation was heartily endorsed by Griffin Bell, another friend of Jimmy who was practicing law in Americus. Both men spoke so glowingly of this Charles Kirbo that Carter decided immediately that he would hire him as his attorney. With the time growing perilously short, he arose very early one morning in late September and drove the 150 miles to Atlanta to see Kirbo.

"Oh, yeah, I remember that," Kirbo said years later, "remember it well, as a matter of fact. He came in—of course, he'd already called and said he was coming—and he sat down and I recollect that he looked mighty tanned, very young and he seemed a friendly sort of fellow, the kind you'd probably like right off; but I remember that he was what you might call timid, maybe bashful or shy—I don't know. At any rate, he asked if I was going to help him or not. Now, I didn't really know much about the case, but coming from that part of Georgia myself, I figured that if somebody wanted to bet that an election down there was honest, it'd be a dandy bet to take, and maybe even borrow a little to put down if you happened to be short of cash. So, I told him I was fixing to see what we could do."

It was a significant day in the life of Jimmy Carter, the beginning of a friendship that would ultimately produce the stimulus and the strategy for a successful presidential campaign. It was clear from that day in September 1962 that they would be friends. The years would only deepen the relationship. They would have a significant impact on each other's lives; they would come to have enormous respect for each other's opinions, and they would learn not only to talk to each other but to listen as well. "Going to see Charlie Kirbo that day was probably one of the smartest things I ever did in my life," Carter recalled.

Still, the lawyer he hired that day was not an immediately impressive man. It was difficult to imagine him in a courtroom bending a judge or a jury. It was evident that he had a good mind and that he knew the law, but he spoke at the syrupy tempo of sorghum molasses escaping from a chilled Mason jar, and the words that finally emerged—finally, finally emerged—built with painful country-boy reticence into rural homilies, down-home sayings, straw-in-the-teeth aphorisms and aw-shucks disclaimers that effectively concealed whatever skills he might have had as a barrister. He was seven years older than Carter—born in 1917 in Bainbridge, Georgia, a little town south of Plains. He was the sixth of eight children in a pious home that placed a high premium on honesty, hard work, honorable deeds and lofty ambition. Though neither of his parents was formally educated past the third grade, both placed great trust in education. Like Rosalynn's father, they saw college as their children's opportunity to avoid the rigors of their own lives. One by one, through the Depression years, the older Kirbo children helped the younger ones with their studies. All the while, their father was diligently dividing his time between their little farm on the outskirts of Bainbridge, his job as a bookkeeper for a local lumber mill and his nocturnal devotion to his law books.

Finally, after years of study, Kirbo's father passed the
Georgia bar examination; instead of going into a law practice, however, he became the clerk of the local court, a position of no small prominence in the legal circles of the community. It was in and around the county courthouse in
Bainbridge that Charles Kirbo grew up, watching his father
dealing with the dockets, listening to the lawyers, observing
the politicians. It seemed only natural, then, that when it
came time for him to go to college—as his older brothers
and sisters had done—he chose to study law, finishing his
degree at the University of Georgia in 1939. When World
War Two began, he enlisted in the Navy, but was dropped
six months later from its aviation school because of inner-ear
problems. He became an infantry officer instead and commanded an Army company that saw combat from Normandy
on D day all the way into Germany and the end of the war.

Back home in Bainbridge, Kirbo opened a law office,
saved his money, made some good investments in local
land, helped send a younger brother to law school and got
married. In 1960, with his practice running smoothly and
lucratively, he accepted a generous offer of a partnership in
King and Spalding, one of Atlanta's oldest, biggest and most
influential law firms. He was wanted there because, despite
its size and reputation, King and Spalding felt naked without a courtroom lawyer like Kirbo on their staff. He was,
they had discovered, one of the best around. He had an innate sense of justice that juries seemed to catch immediately. His uncomplicated style simplified complex cases. He
spoke so slowly, so simply, so directly to the heart of the
matter that he fairly seemed to exude the country virtues.
He seldom lost a case. King and Spalding were delighted.
They had gotten a jewel. In the two years he had worked
there before the morning he met Jimmy Carter, he had not
disappointed his new colleagues. He would not disappoint
Carter either.

He quickly won a hearing of Jimmy's case before a judge
from outside the new Senate district and forced the Quitman

County election officials to bring the disputed Georgetown box into court. Using the investigative work already done by Carter, Pope and Fortson, as well as the new leads turned up by Pennington's consistently dogged and occasionally brilliant reporting, Kirbo concluded that the crux of the case was in the election box itself. He already had more than thirty affidavits taken by Carter and the others from people whose votes were registered on the Georgetown rolls but who said they had not voted that day at all. Further, the investigation had shown conclusively that when it had appeared that Carter might actually win, the local political leader had rather ineptly loaded the scales. "Actually, he wasn't all that smart," Kirbo remembered. "He forgot to take out the real ballots, so there were a hundred or so too many ballots for the precinct." Still, when the hearing began, Kirbo and Carter were in for yet another surprise. The box was opened before the judge. There were no ballots in it at all—no genuine ballots, no fraudulent ballots, no ballots at all. The courtroom was stunned, silent. An old clock ticked loudly from the back of the chamber.

"Where do you think these ballots are?" the judge asked the Quitman County official.

"Well, Judge, I don't have the slightest idea," he replied. "I believe there is something mighty mysterious about this."

Kirbo took the floor. The judge listened intently, looking away from Carter's new attorney occasionally to direct a stream of rich, brown tobacco juice into a spittoon hidden behind the bench. Kirbo drawled a few facts and then began a long rural story about some chicken thieves who tried to cover up their tracks but could not conceal the fact that the chickens were missing. The afternoon wore along, hot and heavily humid. Finally, the judge had heard all he wanted to hear. He leaned over, deposited another dark plunk into the spittoon and said he would announce his ruling in a few days. Jimmy waited, nearly in terror. He had given so much of himself to this project, he thought. He deserved to win, he knew, but there was no assurance that he would, not even with Kirbo at his side.

The judge's decision came about a week later. He said the Georgetown box was so thoroughly tainted by vote fraud that there was absolutely no way to determine what had been the voters' original and genuine intent in the Democratic primary election for the State Senate nomination. So, he said, the election would be decided by the returns from all the other precincts. Jimmy was jubilant. He was finally the winner, he thought. He was wrong. "A technicality was discovered," he wrote years afterward. "It permitted an appeal of the judge's decision back to the local Democratic Executive Committee, dominated, of course, by the county political boss!" His opponent made the appeal and, not surprisingly, won it. He was declared the victor. Carter was once again the loser. "Our time was running out. The general election was at hand, and our only hope was a rapid appeal to the State Democratic Party officials, beginning with the Party secretary. He was nowhere to be found. Eventually we discovered that he was on a long weekend vacation trip with my opponent's campaign manager!"

Their only other hope on that last weekend before the election was to make their appeal to the state party chairman, J. B. Fuqua, an industrialist and a newcomer to state politics who happened to be on a hunting trip to Canada. He could not be reached, his secretary told Kirbo. Nonsense, he said. Kirbo went to Canada and found him. He presented Carter's case and persuaded him that there was a great injustice to be dealt with. Fuqua agreed and declared Carter to be the Democratic nominee. The Georgia secretary of state ordered the county officials in the State Senate district to put Jimmy's name back on the general election ballots. On the Sunday before the Tuesday voting, Carter, Fortson, Pope and others on his campaign team went all over the seven counties, hand-stamping the ballots with his name; but on Monday, his opponent went back into court, and late that evening, only a few hours before the polls opened the next morning, a judge ordered that all names be stricken from the ballot, turning it into a write-in election. In two of the counties, the order was ignored—but as the day proceeded, Carter and his opponent drove themselves madly, trying to offer the voters a clear examination of what was happening, passing out thousands of handbills and buying thousands of dollars worth of radio time. That night, when the counting was finished, Jimmy had won by fifteen hundred votes.

The Quitman County man who had distorted the first election was subsequently convicted of vote fraud charges stemming from a previous Congressional election. He was given a suspended sentence, but later went to jail on illegal liquor charges. In 1964, the Georgia legislature, with Carter in the State Senate, approved a comprehensive election-code reform. During the debate on the measure, "someone suggested as a compromise that no one be allowed to vote who had been dead more than three years," Carter wrote.

After the votes were counted, Carter went to bed "sick and exhausted." But he also went to bed that night in November 1962 as the state senator-elect. He was thirty-eight years old and he had spent that span of his life in a series of major transformations—from farm boy to military cadet to naval officer to nuclear engineer to agribusinessman to small-town civic leader and finally to politician. In just fifteen more years, he would extend that process of political becoming to its limits.

In 1960, John Kennedy had carried Georgia by a greater majority than he received in his home state of Massachusetts. The solid South was solidly Democratic one more time; but by 1964, the civil rights movement in the South and Lyndon Johnson's flood of social legislation in Washington had substantially altered Democratic possibilities from Baton Rouge to Charleston. Martin Luther King, Jr., had moved from the successful bus boycott in Montgomery (a Federal court ordered the end of Jim Crow seating in all public vehicles) to head a new organization called the Southern Christian Leadership Conference. He had led some of the most momentous campaigns of the era—St. Augustine, Birmingham, an extended period of demonstrations in Albany, Georgia (pronounced al-BEN-ee), only about twenty-five miles southeast of Plains, and, in conjunction with a group called the Student Non-Violent Coordinating Committee, in Americus itself.

They were bloody days all over the South, tense beyond quick or easy relief. All of the meanness and madness stored up for so many years—all of the latent hostility toward racial change and those who espoused it—was vented in one long, rolling wave of shootings and beatings and bombings that served only to fortify the determination and the courage of the hundreds of blacks and whites who locked arms all over the region and went singing together down its country roads, "We shall overcome—someday."

But there were thousands of white Southerners who were just as determined that they would not overcome, and many of them believed their cause was worthy of any price, even murder and mayhem. The Klan and the Citizens Councils began to flex their muscles, spreading their venom from county to county, from the Mississippi Delta to the steeples and statues of Richmond. Only a few days before Carter's victory in the State Senate election in Georgia, James Meredith had enrolled at the University of Mississippi, surrounded by Federal marshals dispatched by President Kennedy, precipitating a murderous riot that was finally put down by federalized National Guard troops; and on the same Tuesday in November when Carter finally won his seat in the Georgia legislature, George Wallace was elected governor of Alabama. It was his second attempt to win the office. He had been defeated in 1958 because, he said, he was "outniggered," and he had vowed that such a deficiency would never again hamper one of his campaigns. He was sworn into office in early January 1963, and, in his fiery inaugural address, he shouted his triumphant vow to maintain "segregation today, segregation tomorrow, segregation forever."

One of his first official acts was to free from prison three men who had been tried and convicted of castrating a black man. In June he made his stand against the integration of the University of Alabama in Tuscaloosa. The Birmingham demonstrations, led by Dr. King, came later that year and were the work of Communists, Wallace raged—outside agitators who would not allow decent-thinking Southerners who cared about their part of the country to work out their own problems. Wallace, once again raising that familiar piece of idiocy, suggested that the bombing of the Birmingham church where four little black girls died was the work of the black demonstrators themselves, "just trying to drum up sympathy."

Wallace knew what he was doing. He sensed that it would be years before any substantial changes would occur in Southern attitudes, and he had no intention of even hinting that he was in any camp other than the maddened white majority's. He became a god, worshiped across the region for his fealty to segregation, and in his state, he was a virtual dictator robed in racism. The fault for all the problems the South was having in those days, said Wallace, was Washington in general and Lyndon Johnson in particular. Johnson, he vowed, would play hell getting any white Southern votes in 1964. He was a race-mixing traitor to his Texas heritage, and he and King would bear the brunt of Wallace's and every other white Southerner's hatred for the change that crept on and on. Despite the South's long tradition of voting Democratic in presidential elections, the Republican nomination of Senator Barry Goldwater of Arizona as its 1964 candidate ensured a radical break with the Southern political past.

It seemed appropriate. So much had happened to change

the world and the country in the years since Lieutenant
Carter had moved from nuclear submarines through his
business apprenticeship and into the Georgia Senate that
one more alteration in the way things were seemed almost
inconsequential. By 1964, the once solidly Democratic
South was scrambling all over itself to vote either for Wallace, who had imported his special brand of racism successfully to the Democratic primary elections in Maryland and
Indiana and Wisconsin that spring, or Goldwater, who,
though not a blatant advocate of racism, offered a significant
conservative counterpoint to the image of Lyndon Johnson
in the South.

But the family of State Senator James Earl Carter, Jr.,
would have none of it. The blood of the Gordys was thick in
their veins and even though "it was a bad time for Democrats in southwest Georgia," as he wrote years later, Lillian
volunteered to run the Johnson headquarters in Americus
and the rest of the family, including fourteen-year-old Chip,
began sporting LBJ buttons. Jimmy's mother was subjected
to the same sort of harassment and intimidation the members of Koinonia Farm had endured several years before.
Her car was damaged several times by vandals, there were
threatening phone calls in the dead of night and obscene
scribblings on the door of her house and the windows of the
little storefront headquarters she was running. "Didn't
bother me a damned bit," she recalled, "not one damned
bit. Stupidity is something I grew up with. I mean it was all
around me all those years. I wasn't surprised and I wasn't
scared. I'm not afraid at all of people who are so afraid themselves of the truth of their actions that they do whatever it is
they do at night or whenever and wherever other people
can't see them."

Chip's experiences left him unsettled, though, and with
somewhat less resolve than his grandmother about partisan
politics. He was most interested in the campaign of 1964
and excited about helping the local loyalist Democrats however he could, but he found that his classmates were not

fond of his expressions of support for President Johnson. His pocket, on which he sported the LBJ button, was ripped from his shirt several times. He was as stubborn as his father, though, and continued to wear it. He would get up every morning that autumn and carefully pin the button to his shirt and march off to school. That afternoon he would come home with the shirt in tatters and the button in his hand. Finally, a gang of larger and older boys roughed him up so badly on the floor of one of the classrooms that he came home in tears. "Put the button back on," his father advised him.

"What if they tear it off again?" asked Chip.

"Put it on again," said Jimmy.

"Then, they'll just tear it off again," Chip argued.

"Then, you just put it back on again," said his father, "if you want to wear it. Do what you want to do—and learn to box."

As expected, and despite Lillian's stubborn efforts, Senator Goldwater won handily in Sumter County and in Georgia and in the tier of Southern states from Louisiana to South Carolina, carrying with him a scattering of Republican Congressional candidates, including the winner in Carter's own district, Howard H. (Bo) Callaway, the heir to a textile fortune whose election to Congress made him the titular head of the state's Republican party. He was the first Republican Congressman from Georgia since the Civil War. Carter was not particularly fond of him, recognizing in him a rival of stature and some similarity.

Callaway had graduated from the United States Military Academy at West Point at about the same time Carter had finished at Annapolis, and both men had turned their backs on military careers to come home and build on their fathers' legacies. Callaway was a millionaire, though, and Carter came to resent the ease of his success. As a state senator in 1963, Carter had tried to expand Georgia Southwestern from a junior college to a four-year school. Callaway, a member of the state Board of Regents, had tried to block the move—and although the expansion was successful, Carter could not quickly forget Callaway's role. "When we were around each other, both of us were somewhat tense," he wrote. Still, with Goldwater's victories in the South, Callaway, seen by Carter as a direct competitor among the state's rising young politicians, had ascended far above a State Senate seat and was serving in Congress.

"I began . . . to make quiet plans to run" against him in 1966, said Carter. Gradually, politics had become the whole of his life. He had begun by then that endless cycle of holding one office while making preparations for running for another when the term for the first expired. All that was required was that there simply be another office available for which to run. For the existential politician, caught up in the process of always becoming something else, the next election was always the most important.

Carter carefully spent his days as a state senator doing all that was expected of him and more. He was seldom absent from the three-month and four-month sessions up in Atlanta. He took a speed-reading course to help him fulfill a campaign promise to read every bill that reached the floor (there were usually more than a thousand in any session), and gained a reputation in the Senate as a nitpicker who would not automatically and with no questions asked endorse the dozens of special-interest bills introduced by so many of his colleagues. He took a particular interest in public education and served on a statewide commission for the study of new school financing systems. He developed a keen and healthy dislike for lobbyists. He served on the Senate's appropriations committee where he became something of an in-house expert on taxes and a critic of the slipshod, unbusinesslike manner in which the government of Georgia was managed. He helped pass the repeal of Georgia's infamous "thirty questions," a voting eligibility test designed to keep blacks from the ballot.

Yet, he was careful and cautious about public involvement that might damage his 1966 race for Callaway's

Congressional seat, and even though racial tensions were
high in Sumter and neighboring counties during the four
years he was in the State Senate, his visibility on such matters—as it had been when he was first a member and then
chairman of the county school board—was comfortably low.
He offered only quick profiles of himself on racial issues,
much like the rapid-fire silhouettes of the ships and planes
that flashed on the screen before him during his days as a
naval cadet. His specialty was taxes, not race, waste in government, not voting rights, the abuse of privilege by state
officials, not the abuse of black citizens in his senatorial district.

Still, Georgia's problems with race seemed small when
compared with the running fires in Mississippi and Alabama. Carl Sanders, the incumbent governor, was perceived
as a moderate who took a chamber-of-commerce approach to
the question of integration. That technique was premised on
the fear of economic loss caused by prolonged demonstrations by protesting black groups. The best thing to do in
most cases, Sanders counseled the besieged local leaders
who came to him for help in staving off the awful revolution,
was to sit down and talk with these folks, make a few
concessions and wait. In no case was there to be violent resistance, he said, because that would only drive Northern
and Eastern investors right out of the state—and that was
something Grorgia could ill afford. After all, Sanders was
presiding over the biggest spurt of new money into the region in more than half a century. Ivan Allen, Atlanta's mayor
and a fair-minded man, was taking the same course. Both
men presented outward images of respectability, caution,
reason and fairness. Both men were actually to the right of
the political center on almost every issue. but in contrast to
such characters as Wallace and Birmingham's Bull Connor,
they seemed to be liberal.

Carter was quick to notice that, in politics, it is often just
as important to be perceived as something as actually to
be that something and, as a matter of fact, that one not need

be anything ideologically at all. Wallace, for instance, who had made such a point of vowing heatedly that there would never be any integration in his state as long as there was life and breath in his compact little body, had actually presided during his term over more integration than Alabama had ever seen before. The Birmingham demonstrations, moreover, had been the major stimulus for the passage of the Civil Rights Bill of 1964, and Wallace's stupidly brutal handling of the Selma voting-rights drive in early 1965—with the thousands of blacks and whites marching from Selma to Montgomery on Highway 80, the opposite direction taken by Carter's little Studebaker on his drive to California and his first submarine duty—had guaranteed the passage of the Voting Rights Act.

Still, despite Wallace's ineffectiveness as a guardian of the old ways and despite the fact that as a general of segregation he was a miserable failure, he was still perceived as a champion, as a man in whom much white Southern faith could be placed. It did not matter what happened. It mattered, though, what seemed to have happened. Sanders did little to enhance the lives of black Georgians during his tenure as governor from 1963 to 1967; but compared to Wallace, he seemed no less a liberal than, say, the junior Senator from South Dakota, a former preacher named George McGovern, or, say, the new Senator from New York, Robert F. Kennedy.

When the state legislature adjourned in the spring of 1966, Jimmy Carter announced his candidacy for the Democratic nomination to Congress, and began the sort of campaign that would become his hallmark in later years—the long, long days on the road that stretched deep into the evenings and the nights, the earnest conversations with passersby on street corners, the dusty, choking drives down back-country roads to reach a general store or a backwater church, the hundreds of speeches and the thousands of hands offered and grasped and shaken. "Each night I brought home a list of names and addresses" of the people he had met that day in his campaign, he said, and the next day, while he was off again into the district, Rosalynn and his sister, Gloria, typed individual notes to all the potential supporters he had met the day before. He went at his Congressional campaign with the same stubborn persistence that had been the primary ingredient of all his previous achievements. Still, Callaway seemed to be the odds-on favorite.

Abruptly, in the late spring, with the primary election just ahead in August, Callaway withdrew from the Republican Congressional primary and announced his candidacy for governor. Carter was stunned. He had been given a free ride into the U.S. Congress, it seemed. The Republicans, who had won the seat in the Goldwater fluke anyway, would be unable to find a replacement of Callaway's caliber on such short notice. Besides, the seat was traditionally Democratic. About all Carter had to do to get to Washington that next January was go through the motions of running in his primary. Still, he was dismayed that he would not get a shot at Callaway, the fellow who had been grating on him for some time—the rich guy who had had everything given to him, who had always been lucky, and never really had to work for much of anything. Carter wanted to take him on and now he was backing out and running for governor instead.

All across the state, Democrats were already saying that Callaway was a sure winner. Those who were not making such a concession were feverishly searching for someone— anyone with half sense and one eye—who could provide a semblance of an alternative to the inane rantings and ravings of a little fried-chicken restaurateur named Lester Maddox, already one of the favorites in the Democratic gubernatorial primary. Among those who were looking for someone else to run was Charles Kirbo. Along with other friends in Atlanta, he persuaded Jimmy Carter to give some thought to forsaking the Congressional race and running in the Democratic primary for governor instead. "It was a tough decision for me to make," he said. "It was only three months until the primary and I was almost completely unknown in the state. We felt that the Congressional seat was now mine."

Still, he wanted to have a go at Callaway. Kirbo had

known that. He wanted to face him in any election for any office, and the temptation was just too great. If Callaway would not run against him for Congress, then Carter would run for governor. Callaway would most certainly win his party's primary. Jimmy thought he could win his. He talked it over with Rosalynn, and she realized midway through the conversation that his mind was already made up. She agreed. He announced his candidacy to the laughter of many, the wonderment of most. It was the first time the question "Jimmy Who?" was raised.

As usual, he was undaunted by what seemed to be the impossibility of the task. He and Rosalynn and Lillian and the three boys and Gloria launched a statewide effort that took them all in different directions. If he was in Atlanta speaking to the press club, his wife would be down in Bainbridge appearing at a garden party, while Lillian would be in Macon, passing out "Carter for Governor" brochures at a shopping center. It seemed to be working. He was becoming much less vague in the minds of Georgia's voters, and he was attracting a corps of volunteers from all over the state, including a twenty-year-old boy from nearby Albany who had just graduated that spring from the University of Georgia. His name was Hamilton Jordan. His father was an insurance man who had been born and raised in Talbot County with an older brother who had become an incurably idealistic Baptist minister—so idealistic, in fact, that he had founded a farm called Koinonia not far from Plains.

"You know my uncle?" Hamilton Jordan asked the candidate one day. "My Uncle Clarence?"

Carter shook his head. "I know who he is," he said, "but I don't think I've ever met him."

It was not enough—all those long days in the sun, all those long miles he had traveled up and down the state, all the money he had spent—his own and others', but mostly his own—all the strain and fatigue he had endured, all the hard work everyone in the family had so willingly invested. He lost. With just twenty thousand more votes, he could have been in the runoff, a second primary election pitting the two candidates with the most votes, designed to produce a nominee with a majority rather than a plurality victory. Maddox, still ranting and raving, had made the runoff along with Ellis Arnall, a former governor and a man with genuinely liberal and humanitarian governmental concepts. Given that sort of choice, Georgia responded predictably. Thousands of Republicans, ignoring their own primary where Callaway was a sure winner anyway, crossed over to vote in the Democratic primary and, believing for some mysterious and utterly illogical reason that Arnall would be more difficult for Callaway to beat in the general election in November, voted for Maddox, thereby giving the Democratic nomination for governor of Georgia to a man with fewer credentials for public trust and public service than James Clark, the thick-necked sheriff of Dallas County, Alabama. Still, Arnall decided not to quit and waged a write-in campaign in the November voting. It was just strong enough to cost Callaway the governorship. The Republican had a plurality of the ballots that fall, but lacking a majority, the election was cast into the state legislature. With Jimmy's Cousin Hugh sitting in Jimmy's old seat in the State Senate, the legislature chose Lester Garfield Maddox as the sixty-sixth governor of Georgia. "Praise the Lord," Maddox whooped when the vote was finally recorded. "Praise the Lord and pass the ammunition!"

Carter was thoroughly depressed. Somehow, it had all turned into a black comedy. He had given up a safe seat in the State Senate. He had given up a pretty sure bet on going to Congress—and it had all been for nothing. He had still not engaged Callaway in political combat and the governor of Georgia was a neurotic, balding little tyrant who believed in ghosts and goblins. Carter was deeply in debt. He had lost more than twenty pounds in his feverish, frantic cam-

paign (he was down to 130) and he had nothing to show for
it. "I left everything I cared for—my farm, my family, my
bird dogs—and my wife and I spent sixteen to eighteen
hours a day trying to reach as many Georgia voters as possible," he wrote. Between the two of them, he estimated
that he and Rosalynn had come into personal contact with at
least three hundred thousand voters in the brief span of his
campaign—and still he had nothing to show for it. He was
right back where he had begun in 1962 when he had made
his first decision to run for public office. He held no public
office at all.

Rosalynn urged him to look on the brighter side. After all,
she said, there were those three hundred thousand people
they had met and there were those thousands who had actually worked for him and voted for him. That was considerably more than something, she argued. And what about
those long lists of names she had so religiously, meticulously compiled during their pursuit? she asked, and he
agreed that perhaps there was more to be thankful for than
he had at first perceived. He began to think about it, and
the depression passed. He had momentarily forgotten
Rickover's favorite aphorism—show me a good loser and I'll
show you a loser—and he had, in his disappointment over
losing, ignored one of the oldest tenets in the Southern politician's creed: you run for governor the first time to get noticed and the second time to get elected. Huey Long had
failed his first time out and so had George Wallace.

So, by the time Lester Maddox was being inaugurated as
governor in Atlanta in January 1967, Jimmy Carter was off
and running for governor again, his pale, icy eyes focused
dead ahead on 1970. "I don't intend to lose again," he said.

Anyway, I kept walking and walking up Fifth Avenue without any tie on or anything. Then all of a sudden, something very spooky started happening. Every time I came to the end of a block and stepped off the goddam curb, I had this feeling that I'd never get to the other side of the street. I thought I'd just go down, down, down, and nobody'd ever see me again.

—J.D. Salinger,
THE CATCHER IN THE RYE

ON A STEAMING MORNING in September 1970, a car pulled up in front of an old office building in downtown Augusta, Georgia, and a short, round-faced man waddled across the sidewalk and deposited himself in the backseat, next to Jimmy Carter, the forty-five-year-old gubernatorial candidate whose four years of tireless, grass-roots campaigning had landed him atop a heap of seven Democrats in the primary election a week before. He had been so close to a majority, but finished with a fraction less, and so, in another week, he would face the runner-up, Carl Sanders, in a two-man contest that would produce the Democratic nominee and, for all practical purposes, the next governor of Georgia.

They drove away from the center of the aging town toward the local television station where Carter was scheduled to appear for an interview, a route that took the car through the center of Augusta's black residential and business section, still scarred from a bloody riot that had swept through its streets the previous spring. In one night of terror three black men had been shot and killed by Augusta police (all of their wounds were in the back), and the city's already fragile race relations had deteriorated even further. Even the internationally known Masters Golf Tournament, held annually in Augusta, had done little to take the town's mind off its tensions, despite the sizable economic benefits the prestigious, week-long event always produced for the local white merchants. As in nearly every other facet of life in Augusta, blacks were allowed to participate in the Masters only in subservient roles as caddies, greenskeepers, bartenders, waiters, cooks, maids—but not as players, and that was precisely the way the stumpy little man riding next to Jimmy Carter that September morning preferred it.

His name was Roy Harris and he was something of a legend in the American South, particularly in Georgia. He was a successful lawyer, polemicist, publisher and politician whose influence in an election year had often meant the difference between victory and defeat for a candidate to whom he gave his blessing or his disapproval. Lester Maddox had been his choice in the 1966 governor's race, and Lester Maddox had won the Democratic nomination—and in the subsequent machinations of the legislature after both Maddox and Callaway, the Republican, had failed to win a majority in the general election, Harris had applied his muscle to the problem and Maddox had won again. Maddox had been the sort of candidate and governor Harris had appreciated—a racist of the first magnitude who was proud of his segregationist creed, preached it at every opportunity and practiced it faithfully in every aspect of his life, both public and private. When Maddox, barred from running for governor again, had chosen to run for lieutenant governor instead in 1970, Harris had enthusiastically nodded his approval and bestowed his public endorsement. Maddox had won overwhelmingly again, thus avoiding the necessity of a contest in the runoff election that had brought Jimmy Carter to Augusta that day and to his appointment in the backseat of the car with Roy Harris.

They were a curious couple—Carter and Harris—for in 1966, Harris had not only enthusiastically endorsed Maddox but given the back of his hand to Carter for what he perceived to be his lack of genuine Southernness in his views on race. That year, Carter had campaigned actively among blacks, frequently urged their continued registration, cited his record in the Georgia Senate as evidence of his concern for the voting rights and privileges of a minority, and promised, in his platform spiels, to put an end to the ritualistic deprivation of black Georgians' civil rights. In 1966, Carter was indubitably not a man Harris could endorse. He was, in fact, the sort of candidate Harris could gleefully attack, and did, in his long-distance calls around the state to his network of courthouse politicians and in his weekly tabloid newspaper that had become a veritable bible for serious Southern segregationists. Its columns, often headlined in fiery red ink, consistently praised the superiority of the white man in the history of human civilization while, week after week and year after year, "documenting" the animalistic nature—and, of course, the innate inferiority—of black men and women, consistently called "niggers" in Harris's paper.

Blacks, in Harris's view, were about to put an end to the progress whites had given to the world by perfecting their conspiracy with such godlessly Communistic forces or pawns as the Kennedy family, Lyndon Johnson, Hubert Humphrey, most Catholics and all Jews. Whatever else Roy Harris may or may not have been in the six decades he had spent on earth, he had never been reticent about his opinions on race. "Niggers," he once growled, "are niggers and no amount of crossbreeding is going to help them any. The tiniest drop of nigger blood will spoil a man. History shows that. Everybody knows that, and those who don't know that have probably got some nigger blood in them, that's all."

It was the sort of blatant foolishness that had moved Carter to spurn the attempts of his fellow citizens in Plains to enlist him in the White Citizens Council years before—an organization in which Harris had been and still was a paramount force—yet there Carter was, a week away from the election, riding through Augusta with Harris, keeping an appointment with the man who, as much as any other South-

erner, symbolized the mean recalcitrance of a slave-based
society, challenged by decency and the United States Constitution.

The car arrived at the television station, Carter shook
hands with Harris and disappeared inside, and Harris,
beaming in the late summer sun, announced his verdict.
"On the way, he asked me what I thought he should be
doing and I told him to just keep doing what he was doing,"
said Mr. Segregation. Roy Harris approved of Jimmy
Carter's campaign for governor, and so had a great many
other segregationists in the state. Four years had made an
enormous difference in Carter's campaign technique and
style. Something had happened.

It had not been easy for him to get himself back together
again after losing in 1966, so total was his commitment to his
quick campaign. His mind dwelled on the debts amassed
from his candidacy (the estimates ranged from $100,000 to
$150,000 and upward from there), but his major angst issued
from the simple, undeniable fact of his defeat. It was not
easily dealt with. For the first time in his life of becoming,
the process had left him empty and cold. He had become a
loser and it grated on his soul. For several weeks, he was
almost completely detached from the swirl of life around
him. Then, Rosalynn's doctor in Americus discovered a sizable tumor in her uterus and recommended surgery. That
crisis took his mind off its preoccupation with defeat—at
least, for a while—and the doctor's announcement following
the operation that he saw no reason the Carters could not
have another child seemed finally to clear his psyche. He
and Rosalynn had wanted another baby when they came
back home to Georgia from the Navy in 1953, but she had
not been able to conceive again, and eventually they had
simply given up on the idea. The doctor's pronouncement
after Rosalynn's surgery gave them new hope, although he
had carefully pointed out the risks involved in a pregnancy

at her age. They were both jubilant when she became pregnant in early 1967. Jack was already in college, and Chip and Jeff were rambunctious teenagers by then, and the idea of another baby in the house was deliciously attractive to both of them. They loved children. Jimmy occasionally seemed even more drawn to them than Rosalynn was. They both agreed that their preference would be a girl, and by the time Amy was born in October 1967, most of the darkness in him had disappeared. By then, he was campaigning again.

They were rewarding years for both Jimmy and Rosalynn, despite his frequent absences and his crowded schedule. She enthusiastically supported his second candidacy, although she dreaded the Kennedy-style campaigning—with everybody in the family out on the hustings—that he insisted on. She dreaded spending all that time away from home again, meeting people she didn't know, making speeches that frightened her and kept her awake all through the preceding night, but if Jimmy wanted to run for governor, he would have her complete endorsement and cooperation. Besides, she realized that even as their mutual participation in the peanut business had benefited their marriage, their joint commitment to the 1966 campaign had done the same. It was a new experience for both of them, this strange world of politics, and although it was at times excruciating in its demands, it was allowing them another chance to discover themselves. Their marriage, she said later, was never really in jeopardy at any time, but she was convinced that building their fortune and leaping into politics together were major sources of its continuing strength.

They lived an affluent life, far above the standards of the little village to which they had returned. They had their new house, their income was substantially more than adequate, their family business was growing steadily, their children were hale and hearty, and the healthy new baby was merely the icing on their many-layered cake. She had nice clothes, all she wanted from wherever she chose to buy them, although she was never inclined to devote a great deal of time to such luxuries. She had a maid and any other domestic help when she required it, and her relationships with those whom she had feared most when they had returned to Plains from Schenectady in 1953 were most cordial. Of course, Jimmy's mother had fortuitously spent most of those years outside the little village, first as a housemother for a fraternity at Auburn University in Alabama and then as a resident manager of a nursing home in a nearby southwest Georgia community, and Lillian's absence had served a dual purpose, as far as Rosalynn and Jimmy were concerned. It not only kept her out of their hair—she was not a malevolent woman, but she could work mischief simply by her fey presence—but it also gave her a sense of real worth about her own life.

At the university, she had plenty of time to devote to her still almost constant reading discipline, and her days were spent in the company of young people and the academicians she both respected and despised—respected for their attention to scholarship and despised for their detached, uninvolved attitude toward the local community and the larger world. There was, she said later, "a certain emptiness to life on a campus," a lacking easily disguised by the business and the noise of an existence amid the energetic lives of the young. And so she left in 1963 after seven years at Auburn, and soon afterward took the job in the nursing home owned by a longtime family friend, delaying her first day on the job for a while for a U.S. State Department tour of the Soviet Union with a group of other older Americans. It was grandly exhausting for her, she recalled. All her life she had been reading about the rest of the world and all her life she had been confined to the American South, with only a few journeys outside its vague boundaries. Then, suddenly, she was swept away to England and Eastern Europe and the vast sweep of Russia, and the enormous sense of adventure that had both attracted and befuddled Earl Carter was merely whetted by her experience.

She wanted more—and a great deal more—but, as she recalled long afterward, she was a part of that "vast tribe of

Americans who are unyoung and unbeautiful and therefore unusable," and she fretted and complained and carped to anyone who would listen as she went about her duties at the nursing home, an institution that reminded her daily of the traditional American treatment of the elderly. She reaffirmed her determination that she would never be either a burden to those around her or a woman lacking a sense of personal worth. "I had drummed that into my kids, every one of them, with as much consistency as I could, all through their lives—to be worth something, not only to other people but to themselves," she said. "I believed—and I think they came to see I was right on the money about that—I believed that there was nothing more important than to know inside yourself that you were worth something."

One evening in 1966, while watching television with some of the patients at the nursing home, Lillian saw a public-service announcement in behalf of the Peace Corps, and took its message literally. "It was something like 'You're never too old to help,' or something like that, and it gave an address and a telephone number and so I just wrote them and joined up," she said. She was sixty-seven years old. Her daughter Gloria was delighted. Her daughter Ruth was less ecstatic. Jimmy had the last word. "He said, 'Mother, I think it'll be awful for you and I think you'll love it,'" she said. "As usual, he was right, but it took me awhile to get to the second part." She was dispatched to India in 1966 after learning a useless dialect at the Peace Corps language school in Chicago but putting in valuable time on improving and modernizing her nursing skills. In India, she was at first horrified and repulsed by the filth she found around her, not only in the meager quarters in which she lived but on the never-ending parade of patients she and the others on the Peace Corps team treated every day. She became physically ill. Then she became miserably homesick—and then she adjusted, spending long and what she later called "sadly happy hours" each day on the job, making friends who remember her still.

When she came home in the autumn of 1968, "She looked like a skeleton," Jimmy recalled. He ordered a wheelchair for her from the airline to roll her from the plane to his car at the Atlanta airport. She arrived back in Plains to much hoopla staged by the family, including a welcome-home party, complete with a large banner, at a new house built for her beside the pond that Earl and Jimmy and the black tenants had dug and dammed so many years before. The old "pond house" had burned soon after her husband's death, and the new one was of modern design and construction with a two-story living room and great expanses of glass. She loved it. "After what I'd been living in in India," she said, "the place was like a mansion."

By the time his mother returned from the Peace Corps, Jimmy was well into his 1970 campaign, although he had not settled by then on a single strategic thrust for his pursuit. He was merely preparing the state patiently for later cultivation, and while the Nixon-Humphrey campaign ground noisily on around him, he methodically traveled Georgia, presenting himself, offering his hand, flashing his smile and talking in soft-spoken generalities about the need to reform state government. He was, by then, a moderately wealthy man. Shrewd borrowing and capital investments had expanded the base of the peanut warehouse operations and broadened its profit potential as well. The business was worth more than $500,000 by then, more than half of which was his, and the two thousand acres he owned in Sumter and adjoining Webster County were modestly valued at about $75 an acre, although he knew that, without a great deal of difficulty, he could get as much as $300 per acre, or perhaps more, if he wanted to sell.

With a bit more attention to the business, he could have been a millionaire in no time at all. Peanuts were becoming very important as a crop, with government subsidies and other assistance, and Jimmy Carter had made himself one of the experts in the business. He had worked hard to achieve that level of knowledge, just as he had always worked to master any field in which he found himself. But he had no intention of devoting any more of himself to the peanut business than absolutely necessary. He was running for governor—full time—and someone else would have to take care of that side of the family's investments. He thought he knew just the fellow.

Billy Carter had joined the United States Marine Corps the day after graduating from high school in 1955, less than two years after his older brother had come home to rescue the family's financial fortune. He had been on the first bus out of Americus the next morning, as a matter of fact, so intent was he on shaking the red dust of Plains from his feet. He took a brief leave later that year, returned home with a private's stripe on the sleeve of his dress blues, and married the daughter of a local family that had never really been on good terms with the Carters. Then he was gone again, off to seek his fortune in the military, just like his brother—except, of course, Billy was an enlisted man.

He had always been a tough kid. There was a deep anger residing within him and an apparent resentment for any and all kinds of authority. Like Jimmy, Gloria and Ruth he had developed an early fondness for books and reading, but unlike the others he had—it seemed almost purposeful to Lillian—carved out a rather miserable academic record at Plains High School, finishing next to the bottom in a class of twenty-six young people. There had been no lack of love in his home during his formative years. Lillian had doted on him, and his two sisters had helped her teach him to read. Years later, all three of the other children remembered that although Ruth had been her father's favorite, Billy was his mother's pet. That was one reason Lillian turned down Earl's seat in the state legislature after his death. Billy was then just sixteen, and not the easiest boy in the community to control. He seemed disdainful of the accepted symbols of achievement that seasoned his adolescent life—his father's phlegmatically persistent work habits, his older brother's military success and trumpeted return home on a white horse and in shining armor—and Lillian fought back her tears and smiled gamely when Billy told her of his decision to join the Marines. "It hurt like the dickens," she remembered, "but somehow I thought it would be good for him— and I know now that it was." Indeed, it seems to have been, although it took several more years for Earl's youngest son to realize that he could not spend the rest of his life fighting. His wife, Sybil—a strong, loving, candid woman who was as tough and yet as gentle as Billy's mother—was a steadying influence on him, and as their relationship deepened in the first years of their marriage, so did his sense that the Marines were not precisely what he wanted for them for the rest of their lives.

He came back to Plains in 1960, just in time for Jimmy's successful candidacy for the state senate; but he left after a couple of years and enrolled at Emory University in Atlanta, enjoying the literature courses and sudsy evenings at Manuel's, a wonderful bar and grill run by Manuel Maloof and noted for its freewheeling political debates, over which Manuel garrulously presided. Billy quit school after two years and moved down to Macon to try his hand at managing a paint store there. Finally, in 1964, he moved back to Plains for good and put his hand to the family plow. The next year, he purchased a small interest in the family business and by 1966 was sharing some of the managerial responsibilities with Jimmy, the gubernatorial candidate.

By late 1968, Jimmy was confident that he would have no business conflicts with his campaign now that Billy was home working hard and day by day learning more and more aspects of the ever-growing Carter enterprise. There had been financial problems in 1966, Jimmy remembered, problems caused by his absence and by the lack of an assistant who could take over for him. That would not happen again, he knew. Billy was part of the 1970 campaign, whether he knew it or not.

"I worked with more concentration and commitment than ever before in my life," Jimmy wrote in his autobiography about those years between his gubernatorial candidacies. "I tried to expand my interests in as many different directions as possible, to develop my own seed business into a profitable and stable enterprise, and to evolve a carefully considered political strategy to win the governor's race in 1970."

He seemed to be all over the state. He organized a multi-county planning and development association and then served as its first chairman. Then, he was the prime mover in the formation of a statewide planning commission and, of course, its first president, guiding the ad hoc citizens group into such channels as government reorganization (he had already decided that that would be one of the principal thrusts of his campaign), management and budget reformations in the state bureaucracy (again, already a part of his campaign blueprint), economic development, recreation, transportation, tourism, health and social justice. His 1966 race had given him just enough visibility to make him popular in the charity circles of the state, and he accepted the Georgia chairmanship of the March of Dimes, staying busy all the while in the state's agricultural groups and civic clubs. Eventually, he was named state chairman of the 180 Lions Clubs in Georgia, and that, like his whole range of activities in the interim between 1966 and the official, all-out beginning of his 1970 campaign, was a perfect opportunity to do what Jimmy Carter often did best—better acquaint himself with people he did not know and, in the process, in more cases than not, give them a reason to remember him.

And, he was born again.

It is, of course, critical to the comprehension of any public figure—to the extent that any public figure, particularly the modern politician so devoted to image, can be comprehended—that his religious views be made as clear as possible; in the case of Jimmy Carter's "new birth," it seems of even greater import. While John Kennedy's membership in the Roman Catholic Church made him suspect, Catholicism was not particularly exotic to most voters; Jimmy Carter's down-home, born-again theology was not only an oddity in the arena of contemporary American politics, it was downright peculiar. But the concept of the "new birth" is fundamental to the American evangelical tradition and the Southern Baptist creed.

To be "born again," in that view, is to experience a "conversion" in which one accepts the sinful state of his own existence (based on the fact of "original sin" from the moment of either birth or conception, a question not yet decided in the evangelical circles) and simultaneously accepts Jesus as more than the historical centerpiece of the New Testament, endorsing him as the true, divinely provided Son of God and "personal savior" whose crucifixion served as an act of atonement in behalf of all human sins, including, of course, those of the individual in the process of being "born again." Thus, to be "born again" is to be "saved" from the inevitable consequence of an inevitably sinful life—eternal damnation and punishment—a salvation that, in the fundamentalist's view, issues only from the process of the "new birth." It was the very crux of the religious thinking that permeated the early life of Jimmy Carter and still survives in the minds of millions of Americans, Southerners and otherwise, rural and urban. It is the descendant of the fiery-furnace, old-time revivalism that accompanied the settlement of the American South in the nineteenth century, an approach to evangelism that combined Chautauqua, circus and indefatigable oratory in its efforts to bring salvation to the world.

In the story in the gospels, when Nicodemus, a Jew of wealth and position, visits with Jesus, the question is raised as to how Nicodemus shall "be saved." Jesus answers that he "must be born again"—and that became the battle cry raised by hundreds of preachers for several generations in the South, especially that battalion of fire-breathers known specifically in the trade as "evangelists." From early spring, into late summer, they worked their special gifts across the entire region, offering themselves as paid consultants to local congregations, organizing and conducting what were known as "revivals." They became mandatory events in the life of every Southern evangelical flock, regardless of the denomination. The Episcopalians held very few revivals, their theology being structured so as not to require much spiritual replenishment. Needless to say, there were not that many Episcopalians in the South.

Among the Southern Baptists, however, and the Freewill Baptists and the Primitive Baptists and the Church of God and the Church of Christ and the Christian Church and the Methodists and the Presbyterians and the Cumberland Presbyterians and the Nazarenes and the Assembly of God and all the rest of the dozens of less visible churchly sects, the "revival" was an important, annual event in the life of the community. It was a time for concentrated doses of preaching and praying and singing. For as long as two or three weeks running, the evangelists—the consultants—would rise to the very heights of their calling, their voices the voice of the Lord, their arms flailing, their fingers pointing, their eyes rolling back into their heads at the mention of the eternal perdition due everyone beyond the reach of Jesus, their fists pounding on the pulpits as they raised the grim specter of spending an eternity with old Satan himself, caught somewhere in the flaming bowels of as literal a hell as their imaginations and the use of holy writ could concoct. "Ye must be born again," they would demand—and every spring and summer, thousands would respond, making their sinful way down the aisles to the altars of the little country churches, publicly accepting the atonement of Jesus for their sins.

It was very strong medicine, especially for children and adolescents, the group on which most evangelists focused, and Jimmy Carter had answered the call and been "saved" in the summer of 1935 when he was eleven years old. He had been baptized in the large vat behind the pulpit of the Plains Baptist Church. Lillian and Earl had spruced him up in a white shirt and tie for the occasion and the pastor had placed a white handkerchief over his nose just before forcing him beneath the water "in the name of the Father, the Son and the Holy Ghost." Whatever had been the extent of Jimmy's original sin, not to mention those assessed to him during the first eleven years of his life and those that would, no doubt, be recorded against his name in the coming years, they were all immediately accounted for. Should he die, he was safely on his way to eternal reward in heaven, a spiritual enclave with streets paved in real gold, just beyond an entrance guarded by pearly gates.

In the years since his baptism, Jimmy had come to a more sophisticated world view. That theology was no longer the light of his spiritual life. He had read a great deal of the work of modern theologians whose emphases were on the social and ethical impact of the gospel—the sort of thing Clarence Jordan had been trying to practice out at the Koinonia Farm. The pressures must have been enormous. Jimmy was a well-traveled, well-read, well-educated man with an engineer's precise mind and a taste for logic. Yet his family and his roots and his position in the community demanded that he pay homage to a theology that did not make sense to him, that did not match any of his experiences. He kept silent, though. One did not always have to say everything one was thinking, particularly when it went against the grain of most of one's neighbors. He had practiced that sort of discipline before. He was really rather adept at it by then.

But for Jimmy, the period immediately following his defeat in 1966 had been devastatingly depressing. He had lost after having followed his magic formula for winning—do the best you can with what you have. He had done precisely that and still he had lost. "I was going through a state in my life then that was a very difficult one," he said later. Nothing he did brought him any pleasure. "When I succeeded in something, it was a horrible experience for me—and I thought I was a good Christian. I was chairman of the board of deacons. I was the head of the Brotherhood [a laymen's group] in all the thirty-four churches in my district, and head of the finance committee, and a Sunday-school teacher, just about all my life. I thought I was really a great Christian."

His sister, Ruth, however, was not so certain. She had endured her share of heart-stopping revivals at the Plains Baptist Church and a few more at the Methodist Church, with her friend, Rosalynn, and then she had grown up and become a beautiful young woman and met and married a veterinarian and moved off to North Carolina where she began raising her family and building an affluent life as an upper-middle-class housewife. Then, it had all turned sour for her, she remembered. Like Jimmy, she discovered that almost nothing she did brought her much joy or satisfaction. She solved it by becoming involved in the charismatic movement just blossoming in modern American Christianity and by becoming a lay evangelist herself, developing a technique for bringing inner peace, or a reasonable facsimile thereof, to others through amateur psychology and nondirective counseling. Like all the Carters, she was bright, quick and broad of mind, and she threw herself into her new calling like an insurance salesman. She saw potential clients everywhere, especially in her own family, and although Lillian summarily dismissed her efforts as "ridiculous," she began to talk with Jimmy during visits home about his "real relationship with the Lord." He conceded that it was not what it might be, despite the outward appearances of piety and religious devotion; moreover, he admitted, it did not seem quite as relevant to his personal pursuits as he wanted it to be. It had been of no comfort to him at all, for instance, when he had lost in 1966. "You've got to commit yourself completely to Jesus," his sister advised. "There's no half-

way position, if you expect your religion to be of any value
to you or anybody else, including the Lord."

Not long after their conversation, the pastor of the Plains
Baptist Church offered his little flock a Sunday morning sermon he called "If You Were Arrested for Being a Christian,
Would There Be Any Evidence to Convict You?" Years
later, Jimmy would remember only the title, nothing else,
but he would also recall that the sermon had had a substantial impact on him. "My answer by the time it was over was
'No,' " he said. "I had never really committed myself totally
to God. My Christian beliefs were superficial, based primar-
ily on pride, and I'd never done much for other people. I
was always thinking about myself." That was the beginning
of his second "conversion experience." There were no bolts
of lightning from heaven and no shining visions of angels in
glorious raiment. There was simply a decision to alter the
nature of his relationship with the Deity he worshiped. He
had calculated it carefully. The way things were with him,
his religion was almost useless, not much more valuable
than his membership in the Georgia Certified Seed Association. He wanted something more for his spiritual investment, and he concluded that he could not get it without a
deeper investment of himself. He decided to make it.

"I formed a much more intimate relationship with
Christ," he said, "and since then, I've had just about like a
new life." His participation in the little white church took
on more importance for him. He began to take part in missionary efforts to towns and cities in Georgia and elsewhere
in the country, including Philadelphia and Boston. His new
faith, he found, was functional. He discovered a warm comfort in taking a rather fatalistic view that allowed "God's will
to be done" on earth and in his life. "All things work together for good for those who love the Lord," the Scriptures
suggested, and that, Jimmy eventually concluded, might explain any number of otherwise inexplicable events, including an unsuccessful political campaign to which he had devoted himself so completely.

But a second failure was far from Jimmy Carter's mind. He was busy laying the groundwork for that campaign, and his life took on predictable rhythms. "On a typical day, I would go to the warehouse or the farm very early and work until sometime in the afternoon," he said. "Then, I would drive somewhere in Georgia to make a speech and return home late at night. Names, information about the community and speech notes were all dictated into a small tape recorder in the automobile. The next day, Rosalynn wrote thank-you notes on an automatic typewriter which also recorded names, addresses and code descriptions of the persons I had met."

This campaign would not be the hurry-up, catch-up amateur hour that his 1966 effort had been. He spent hours and hours studying issues and preparing speeches, "sometimes spending several days and reading three or four books to prepare an original one on environment or health and crime control or criminal justice or certain aspects of education," he said. He also utilized the remnants of his corps of volunteers from 1966. Hamilton Jordan had left Georgia in the interim to spend two years in Vietnam with a civilian aid organization, but there were still dozens of young people who had worked for him before who were willing to work for him again, and he assigned many of them to the task of preparing a detailed analysis of every Georgia election over the previous twenty years.

"For each of the 139 Georgia counties, we prepared colored charts and graphs showing how the people there had voted in state and Federal elections for all different kinds of candidates, emphasizing all kinds of issues," he wrote. "Since we knew the candidates and the issues, it was instructive for us to compare the relative strengths of the candidates from one election to another. After a little study, the general impression of voter motivations in the individual counties began to form."

He may not have realized it at the time, but he was attaching himself to a political thesis that had become the key to

George Wallace's success. By 1967, the year after Carter's
defeat, Wallace, barred from succeeding himself as governor
of Alabama, had succeeded in ensconcing his wife, Lurleen,
in the office. She signed the bills and the executive orders,
but Wallace still ran the politics and the government of the
state while biding his time for the 1968 presidential election. His basic technique had always been to discover what
most of the voters were thinking and tell them that was what
he thought too. He had never been a genuine ideologue,
even in his younger days, although he had shown certain
liberal tendencies during his tenure in the state legislature
in Montgomery and had run a relatively liberal-to-moderate
gubernatorial compaign in 1958, losing the election but winning the endorsement of the Alabama chapter of the National Association for the Advancement of Colored People.
But Wallace reasoned that his opponent had won precisely
because he had spoken the words voters wanted to hear and
he never forgot that lesson. "Leadership," he would pomp-
ously intone years later, "derives from the people to the politician, not the other way around."

By 1968, with his county-by-county survey of past elections and their overriding issues, Jimmy Carter was coming
to understand the Wallace thesis. He discovered something
he had not quite grasped in 1966. Georgians, on almost
every single issue, were either slightly or substantially more
conservative than he. He knew that was important to keep
in mind as 1970 approached.

The speaking invitations had continued to arrive, many of
them arranged for him by friends he had made in his 1966
campaign and his subsequent activities in his various clubs,
committees and organizations—and his wide-ranging travels
around Georgia as a Southern Baptist lay speaker. He had
accepted as many as possible, wedged them into his schedule and spent most of his time on the road, traipsing back

and forth from north to south, from the Florida line to the Tennessee border, trying out new speech themes, testing the water for certain issues or certain approaches to certain issues. The years 1967–1969 had passed so quickly for him—a flittering of images in his mind. In 1967, the three American astronauts had died in a fire at Cape Kennedy. Israeli troops had crushed Arab forces in a persuasive, six-day show of their skills and courage. The government of Mao Tse-tung had exploded its first hydrogen bomb. Cassius Clay had been stripped of his heavyweight boxing title after his conviction for draft evasion. There had been riots in Detroit, Harlem, Rochester, New Britain, Connecticut, and even Birmingham, Alabama. Christiaan Barnard had performed the first successful human heart transplant in South Africa.

In 1968, the North Koreans, who had built a little navy since Jimmy had come home to Plains, had seized the *Pueblo* and its eighty-three men. Lyndon Johnson had declared that he would not seek reelection that year. Martin Luther King, Jr., had been murdered. Robert Kennedy had been murdered. Richard Nixon and Spiro Agnew, the governor of Maryland, had been elected and inaugurated and had asked the country to lower its voice. Nixon had promised peace with honor in Vietnam. In 1969, two Americans had walked on the moon. James Earl Ray had pleaded guilty to King's murder and Senator Edward M. Kennedy had pleaded guilty to leaving the scene of a fatal accident at Chappaquiddick, Massachusetts. As 1970 began, James Earl Carter, Jr., stepped up the pace of his campaign, still unsure of its basic thrust, still searching for the voice that would be heard and the words that would persuade.

Like Jimmy Carter, Joseph Lester Powell, Jr., was the product of rural, southwest Georgia. He had spent his boyhood as an affable, obedient, hardworking son of a moderately prosperous farmer who was respected in the community as honest, diligent and generous. His mother, a teacher in the Dooly County educational system, kept the boy well supplied with books and taught him to read at an early age. It was a skill he avidly embraced, and he read almost everything he could get his hands on. Like Carter, he was given a diminutive nickname to distinguish him from his father. He was called Jody—and he too lived a Huck Finn life, growing up near Vienna (pronounced Vyannuh), as a post-World War Two child. It was a warm, vital Southern home. The Powells—Joe, June, Jody and his sister—were great talkers and dinner-table debaters, and the boy grew up with the impression that an idea broached was an idea to be discussed. A gifted, natural athlete, he starred in most of his high school's sports, but studied no more diligently than necessary. Still, he earned superior grades and set his sights on one of the military academies.

He was graduated from high school in 1961 and headed directly for the new Air Force Academy in Colorado. It was to be expected of him. His town—the scene of a black man's lynching several years before—was suffocating from its own lack of energy and ideas, and his parents were elated that he was leaving for a place where ideas and education and discipline were primary virtues. But on Christmas Day of 1964, he drove back into Dooly County, drained, dejected, depressed and ashamed. He had been caught cheating on a history examination and summarily dismissed from the academy. He had stood fifth in his class in history and he had not really needed to cheat, he remembered years later, but he confessed to his parents that it was true that he had cheated and that he had deserved to be removed for violating the academy's honor code.

For the next five years of his life, he was as unsettled as the times themselves. He moved up to Atlanta and finished his undergraduate degree at Georgia State. He went to work for Life of Georgia, the biggest insurance company in the South, and then met and married a pretty, intelligent young schoolteacher named Nan Jared. He hated his work, loathed it. "Some mornings, if he got to the expressway and the entrance ramp happened to be a little congested, he would just turn around and come back home and call in sick," his wife recalled. So, he quit and went back to books and ideas, a milieu in which he seemed to find some pleasure and satisfaction. He took graduate courses in political science at Emory University, also an Atlanta school, and began work on a long doctoral thesis on populism in the South. He came to know as much and perhaps more about old, weird Tom Watson as Lillian's father ever had, and he also came to grips with one of the region's chronic weaknesses—the apparently incurable tendency to respond to rural candidates who played racist themes.

In the course of his research, Jody analyzed the results of the 1966 Democratic primary in Georgia, dug a little deeper into the subject and discovered that this fellow named Carter who had almost made the runoff had run a fairly liberal campaign. A liberal, nonracist campaign from a southwest Georgia peanut farmer? It was a bit more than Powell could swallow. He decided to inquire further. If this Carter was what he seemed to be, he just might be the sort of man Georgia could use as governor. He wrote Carter, told him of his thesis and his research and was invited to the house at Plains one weekend to discuss the 1970 campaign with a group of other young volunteers. Powell became Carter's personal assistant, which meant that he drove the car on the long trips and the short ones, bought hamburgers while Jimmy made phone calls, kept a list of names of the people they had met, rode herd on the candidate's schedule—and eventually, after they had spent so many hours together, became Carter's friend and adviser.

Jordan had returned from Vietnam in 1969 and Carter had hired him as his campaign manager. He was twenty-six years old. Powell was twenty-four. Rosalynn mentioned once to Jimmy that she "liked both boys but thought they were awfully young to be handling so much of the important part of a governor's race." Carter quietly informed her of their place in his life. "I don't know of anybody else and I can't imagine that there is anybody else that I'd rather have helping me," he said. While Jordan handled campaign strategy and much of the scheduling, keeping in close touch with Charles Kirbo, Jimmy and Jody began their relentless search for votes across the state. They seldom slept in motels but rather spent their long succession of nights on the road in the homes of their campaign allies. "It was cheaper and it allowed Jimmy to find out more about the community and the people and the issues and how they were thinking on the issues than if we'd holed up in some hotel room every night," Powell remembered. Sometimes, they would make the long drive back to Plains, arriving in the wee hours, and Jimmy would catch a few winks in his own bed and Jody would take the couch in the den or perhaps slip over to Lillian's house to sleep in a real bed, next to a roaring window fan. "Sometimes, I thought the whole place, with me and Miss Lillian in it, was just going to get airborne," he remembered.

Lillian loved having him. She enjoyed guests, but she particularly liked Jody for his zest, his good looks, his respectful courtesy, his down-home wit and his youthful optimism. She had spent a great deal of time with young people in the seventeen years since Earl's death, including her years as a fraternity housemother, and having Jody around was just to her liking. She doted on him, fixing his breakfast the next morning and swapping tales with him about southwest Georgia and Jimmy and her travels and his. "I just can't believe Jody would have ever cheated on anything," she said, suggesting that perhaps some mysterious force had conspired to arrange his expulsion from the Air Force Academy. "I'll bet it was Richard Nixon and his gang that did it," she said. She was joking, of course, but probably only about the alleged conspirators.

Late in 1969, Carter commissioned a statewide poll to determine his standing in Georgia as a candidate for governor.

Its results were not too surprising to him or anyone on his staff. Carl Sanders, who could not succeed himself in 1967, was planning to run again, and the pollster used Sanders's name against Carter's in the sampling of the state. "Both Sanders and Carter were seen as a little more liberal than the electorate," the poll reported, but "this is more true of Sanders than it is of Carter." The research also determined that about twice as many voters were able to rate Sanders as were able to rate Carter, a ratio that suggested Carter had a definite identity problem in Georgia, despite his 1966 race and his heavy schedule of public appearances in the years since. But the poll also raised an interesting point that immediately fascinated Carter.

"Of those voters who are aware of both men," the pollster wrote, "it is that group of populistic staunch segregationists who see both Carter and Sanders as being too liberal. This suggests that neither candidate has made strong inroads into this group which is twelve to fifteen per cent of the electorate." Nevertheless, the report continued, Sanders would have the "bigger problem" with this group because his "past actions were better known." The pollster's figures showed that in September 1969, only 25 percent of the Georgia electorate had ever heard of Jimmy Carter and only eleven out of every twenty Democrats could voice any opinion on him at all. But the pollster, William Hamilton, saw all of that as an asset. "As he begins to become better known over the next twelve months, he can emphasize a moderate conservative tone in his campaign and therefore put himself between Sanders and the bulk of the electorate." Another way of putting it was that Carter merely had to keep Sanders to his left. That became the thesis for the campaign, and Carter, with the astute assistance of a new member of his team—Gerald Rafshoon, a smart, tough, ambitious advertising man in Atlanta—was brilliant in its application. He transformed all of Sanders's supposed assets into liabilities, including his image as an urbane attorney who had already spent four years in the governor's office.

From the very beginning, Carter, Jordan, Kirbo, Rafshoon

and Powell believed in the simplicity of their task. Sanders would be stuck for good with what he was perceived to be. He would be able to do nothing about that, the Carter people knew. In the meantime, with a lot of hard work, a little luck and some slick advertising, the people of Georgia would come to know Jimmy Carter precisely as he wanted them to know him. It seemed simple to justify, too. "There was nothing in those polls that Jimmy couldn't live with," Rafshoon said later. He insisted that there was nothing perfidious about a candidate's adjusting himself to a matrix of ideology and rhetoric judged to be most acceptable among the voters. "He was always Jimmy Carter," Rafshoon argued. "Hell, you wouldn't expect Sears Roebuck to step into a big, multimillion-dollar promotion without having the benefit of consumer research on what people are most interested in purchasing."

Using much of the expertise and the people he had gathered in his four years of campaigning, Carter put together a platform for his candidacy that was both remarkable for its blandness and impressive in its use of the images and symbols that Hamilton's research had shown to be of real significance in the race. "To serve all Georgians, not just a powerful or selfish few," it began. "To make appointments on the basis of qualifications for the job and never for political expediency," it continued. "To strengthen local government and return the control of all aspects of government to the people," it stated. The translation was simple.

Carl Sanders was just the sort of fellow who would turn his back on the little folks of Georgia—the real people—curry up to the powerful, selfish ones, whom he would no doubt appoint to high-paying, influential jobs on the basis of political expediency, and cave in to most of Washington's current social-reform pressures, including the wholesale integration of almost everything, particularly schools. Carter's platform goals for education were more specifically stated: "to establish and maintain the highest standards of quality in the public schools and colleges of Georgia, in spite of any obstacle brought about by integration, court rulings, local apathy or other causes." Again, that portion of the platform raised the specter of alien influences. His aim, Carter said, would be "to return control of our schools to local people, within the framework of the law." The "local control" issue had by then become a familiar code word across the South. It was the era of "freedom of choice."

The Nixon Administration, plying its Southern strategy, had effectively begun putting the brakes on real enforcement of school-desegregation guidelines established both in the Justice Department and the Department of Health, Education, and Welfare. Attorney General John N. Mitchell was only a few months away from actually going into court on the side of segregationist defendants in a Mississippi case and asking that the Federal courts delay implementing a previous order for complete integration of the state's schools. Even George Wallace was no longer shouting the words of his inauguration address. He was for freedom of choice, he said. "Why, if a little black child wants to go to school at some particular school [he had finally learned to say "black" instead of "nigger" or "nigra," and he was quite proud of the achievement]," Wallace drawled in 1970, "well, then, that child ought to go to the school he wants. That's freedom of choice and that's what I believe in. But now, there's no reason, with freedom of choice, why some little white child that don't want to be bused all the way across town to some school he don't want to go to ought to have to do that, you see. Now, that's freedom of choice, too. That's what we're talking about. We're just talking about local folks taking care of their own business and other folks taking care of theirs—and long as you got this freedom of choice, well, then, what you got is just fine, you see."

But with "freedom of choice," which became the Nixon doctrine of civil rights, desegregation simply did not take place. The power of intimidation was still held by the white majority. In many Southern communities, if a black family exercised its freedom of choice to attend the white school, they were then given the freedom to choose to leave town or lose their jobs. "Local control" was never really an issue. It was simply a code word for the absence of Federal court orders implementing the constitutionality of one school system for all the people in a community. "Local control" meant getting the Supreme Court out of the picture as well as the Congress and the entire Federal apparatus—except, of course, in matters of welfare.

Carter pledged not only "to insure that it is never more profitable for able Georgians to stay on welfare than to work" but also "to join our sister states in shifting the burden of welfare payments to the Federal government." Moreover, in his platform, Carter pledged that he would "return the control of the Georgia Democratic party to Georgia Democrats," suggesting, of course, that there was substantial truth to all the accusations by Maddox and others that outside interests were dallying with the right of local people to control their local destinies, particularly their schools.

It was a truly magnificent piece of work, this platform for governor. On paper, it managed to cancel whatever liberal image might have survived from his 1966 campaign—the same sort of appearances that had attracted Powell and angered Ray Harris—and substituted the views of a man quite in step with his fellow white Georgians—the thousands and thousands who felt that outsiders were trampling on their integrity and independence and their right to run their society exactly as they pleased. The aliens were almost always Yankees in the minds of the white Southerners—Yankees from HEW, Yankees from the FBI, Yankees from the NAACP and SNCC and SCLC (black Yankees spending Jewish Yankees' money), Yankees from the Justice Department and the television networks and the Northern newspapers—and the aliens were, in the white Southerner's mind, set on changing everything that was true and right and good and beautiful. Carter's white Georgia constituency, he discovered, feared outsiders, so his platform cleverly showed him to be a man who shared that anxiety.

Still, what was even more impressive about the platform, a document seldom seen, much less read by the majority of Georgia voters, was the consistency with which Carter was able to translate it into the daily rhetoric of his campaign. He had carefully planned the direction it would take, with the pollster's help and Rafshoon's guidance, and once having made that decision, he kept his ship steady on course. The platform was the meticulously drafted chart for his voyage and there were few deviations.

For example. Sanders was a wealthy attorney from Augusta, the base of Roy Harris's segregationist operations, but Sanders was not significantly more affluent than Carter, and when Hamilton concluded his poll for Carter in the autumn of 1969, only about 1 percent of the electorate had responded negatively to Sanders's money, agreeing with one of the cleverly written question-suggestions in the poll that perhaps Sanders had used his years as governor to acquire his wealth. Moreover, only about one in four believed that Sanders—as Hamilton's question put it—had "become too close to the Atlanta bigwigs" and only about one-fifth believed that Sanders had "become too citified, nationally and Atlanta-oriented."

Carter went to work on those figures. By the time the primary rolled around in September 1970, Sanders's wealth, his relationships with Atlanta's influential people and his connections with such national Democrats as Hubert H. Humphrey were critical factors in almost every voter's mind, and they were there because Jimmy Carter put them there—day after day, speech after speech, handshake after handshake, as he and Jody scampered all over the state. Powell was not always pleased with what he saw happening around him: Carter's rhetoric, so softly slanted toward the instincts of the rural people who had so loyally and energetically backed George Wallace's presidential bid in 1968, Carter's loosely supervised headquarters and advertising operation which allowed for every opportunity for the campaign to indulge itself mysteriously in shady enterprises

without the candidate's specific knowledge—but Powell admired Carter, and believed in him as a far superior candidate not only to Sanders but also to anybody he'd heard
about or read about in all of Georgia's long political history.

Moreover, he admired the man's intensity and his pure,
raw skill. He knew exactly what had to be done, and how to
do it.

Integration had spawned a rash of little segregation academies all across the South and Georgia had its share. They
existed for but one purpose, to provide a kind of classroom
(most were so substandard that they did not even reach the
levels of the old substandard black schools the whites had
insisted were equal) for the children of parents who simply
could not stomach the fact that integration was fast becoming a fact of life in the South. The schools were criticized
regularly and roundly by educators and, of course, by liberals who saw them as a drain of money and children from the
public system. Carter saw the whole flap as an opportunity
to make a little political hay. Just a few days before the primary election, he stopped off in Swainsboro, Georgia, and
visited one of the segregation academies, an obvious effort
to reassure the people of that south Georgia town that he
was in their corner when it came to the right to have private
as well as public education. An all-white class of sixth-grad-
ers warmly applauded him when he said they could rest assured that he would do "everything" he could for private
schools. Carter's strategy was clear.

In 1966, according to the charts and graphs his volunteers
had drafted, the strongest Democrat on the scene had been
Lester Maddox and his chief asset had been his image as a
man who opposed the integration of public facilities, including specifically his little fried-chicken restaurant, the Pick-
rick. To defend it against the dreaded black hordes, he had
distributed pick handles to his customers, much like Andy

Jackson handing out muskets just before the Battle of New Orleans. Maddox was a bit touched, some people said, but he was the strongest Democrat around in 1966—and the people who were drawn to him that year were still out there waiting to vote for George Wallace for President two years later in 1968 and they were still out there, with their same instincts, two years later—and Carter meant to have them. They were the largest single bloc in the state, except for black voters, and he was rather passive in his courtship of that particular segment. He spoke to an occasional black group, but he believed he could win "without a single black vote," he said. He might have. He almost won without the traditional runoff. On September 9, 1970, he captured more than 49 percent of the vote and led Sanders by nearly a hundred thousand votes, and in the two weeks before their next battle in the runoff, Carter worked feverishly to solidify his position. It was that pursuit that had brought him on that September morning in 1970 to his backseat ride through Augusta with Roy Harris, the state's most visible, venomous symbol of segregation.

Harris endorsed Carter happily. Others of his ilk would follow. Marvin Griffin, the governor who had answered, "Never, no, never!" to the first signs of integration, announced his support for Jimmy. Griffin had been Wallace's temporary vice presidential running mate in 1964. Ernest Vandiver, the former governor who had reminded Georgians in 1955 that a "reasonable time" for the desegregation of public schools "might be one year or a hundred years," fell in behind Carter as well, and even the lame-duck incumbent, Lester Maddox, made the same choice—but only after talking with Roy Harris. Between Sanders and Carter, said Maddox, "I believe the peanut farmer is the right man." At least, Maddox said, Carter had never been caught fooling around with such people as Hubert Humphrey.

Carter reciprocated. "Lester Maddox," he said, "is the embodiment of the Democratic party." Georgia's liberal community was aghast. Black leaders such as Julian Bond

and Vernon Jordan and Andrew Young and Martin Luther
King, Sr., shook their heads and wondered aloud how long it
would be before an election in their state would be conducted without the shadow of race. Carter was not impressed with their criticism. He said he would invite
George Wallace to Georgia to discuss "mutual" problems if
he were elected and he predicted that the Federal government would soon see the error of its swarm of guidelines
and regulations and permit a return to freedom-of-choice desegregation plans, and he pointed out that most of the black
leaders he had spoken with really wanted that. He was
against busing, he said and most right thinking black people
were too.

"I was frozen in," Sanders said. "Everybody knew what I
was and what I stood for. I couldn't get out there on the
streets and start waving my arms and saying, 'Hooray for
George Wallace.' People knew me too well for that. It
wouldn't have worked." Sanders was no political Einstein,
but at least he knew what hit him: the Maddox-Wallace
vote, skillfully transformed into a Carter mandate.

Carter won the runoff going away. He called it a "good
and decent campaign, focused on the issues the people
raised," and then easily disposed of his Republican opponent, Hal Suit, a television anchorman from Atlanta. By midnight on November 2, 1970—seventeen years to the week
after he and Rosalynn and the three boys had driven into
Plains to start a new life as Georgians rather than Navy people—Jimmy Carter was the governor-elect of the state.

He had come that distance partially because of fate but
more because he had never quite been able to find satisfaction in what he was doing along the way. He had come
home to Plains in response to duty and in response to guilt
but mostly in response to his mother who had said simply
that she needed his help to preserve the family estate. Once
that seemed assured, he seemed also to have dismissed his
fealty to the business—to have, as Rosalynn sensed and later
said, "come to a point of boredom" with peanuts. From the

moment he became involved in the school-consolidation referendum, there was no turning back for him. Politics became his new submarine, and although there would be many ports over the next few years, his vessel would always be moored with its bow pointed seaward, ready for the next cruise to the next destination.

"The night he won," Hamilton Jordan remembered, "I said, 'Well, Jimmy, I guess it's about time to start calling you governor,' and he just shrugged and said, 'Well, whatever you want.' He didn't seem the least bit excited about it."

Perhaps that was because he was exhausted. He had lost considerable weight again. He and Rosalynn estimated that in the previous eleven months alone, they had made personal contact with more than five hundred thousand individual Georgians, and they were down to their last reserves of energy and patience. Powell, Jordan and Kirbo thought Jimmy seemed jittery, edgy. They reasoned that it was merely postpartum depression. His labor had been so long and hard, and now that he had given birth to victory, he did not know quite what to do with himself; but other close friends recalled that Jimmy confided to them that he was distraught by the campaign he had run and by some of the things that had happened during its course. Sanders had been smeared a couple of times, including one occasion when thousands of copies of a photograph were distributed showing him and several black members of the Atlanta Hawks, a professional basketball team, celebrating a play-off victory with a mutual champagne dousing. Carter had nothing to do with that, but his campaign did, according to the best evidence—including the recollections of some who worked in it—and in the postelection period, Carter's friends believed he was worried about the quality of his campaign. An associate of Sanders said Carter called his defeated Democratic opponent and apologized. In 1976, Carter

denied that had taken place. Rosalynn remembered, nevertheless, that he told her he would never go through such a
campaign again, and black leaders said later that he told
them it was a regrettable approach to politics, but necessary
at the time and in the place. "You're going to like me as
governor," he promised.

It was a clear day, but the wind was sharply bitter as it
came sweeping across the crowded lawn of the golden-
domed Georgia capitol, chilling the bronze statue of Thomas
Watson with its fist raised toward the north, and sending
shivers through the several thousand people gathered there
that cold morning in January 1971 to witness the inauguration of the state's sixty-seventh governor, James Earl Carter,
Jr.

Rosalynn stood beside him on the raised platform and beside her, Amy fidgeted like the three-year-old she was. The
Navy choir from Annapolis sang, a few clergymen (including
Carter's pastor from the Plains Baptist Church) offered
prayers, and on the other side of the lectern, adorned with
the state seal recommending "Wisdom, Justice and Moderation," Lester Maddox stood triumphantly, wetting his lips
with his tongue. He was a very happy man. As the new lieutenant governor, he would be in a position to fulfill his destiny in life—to maintain his guardianship over the morals of
his fellow Georgians. As governor, Maddox had been especially mindful of that responsibility. He had issued a decree
banning all short skirts on the women in state offices. There
were people who laughed at him, he knew, and there were
some who thought he was probably a little insane—he enjoyed riding a bicycle at public gatherings, backward—but,
for the most part, he was seen simply as an aberrant product
of an exotic moment in Georgia politics: the 1966 rising of
Howard H. Callaway and the Republicans and the write-in
campaign of Ellis Arnall. The legislature, in the meantime,

had repealed the statute which called for its selection of a governor in the absence of a general-election majority, and Maddox had happily signed the revision into law. After all, he had nothing to lose by then. What had happened in 1966 was an exception to the Southern political tradition. The Republicans had added a few more Congressional seats across the region, but the party was still little more than a shadow.

Maddox had not seemed to have damaged the state irreparably, it was thought, although he had not always brought it honor and glory. There were even those among the liberal camp who gritted their teeth and said he hadn't been as bad as they had expected. For one thing, Maddox was disarmingly candid. He often blurted out whatever happened to cross his mind. He was occasionally rude, but frequently amusing. The previous spring, for instance, at his last appearance at the Southern Governors Conference in stately Williamsburg, Virginia, he had been given a bicycle by Winthrop Rockefeller, the millionaire governor of Arkansas. "Ah b'leve ah'd druther had a airplane," Maddox had whined in accepting the gift. Carter disliked him intensely, even though the two men had run strikingly similar campaigns. Maddox, he said later, represented all that he believed was wrong in Georgia politics for so long; still, Carter could not argue with one innovation Maddox had introduced. It was called "Little People's Day."

Every two weeks, during Maddox's term, the doors to the governor's office were opened to anyone and everyone who wanted to line up in single file and shuffle through the large lobby, through the tall oak door, shake the governor's hand and perhaps say a few words. The first time Maddox tried it, a group of black prisoners who had escaped from a road gang the previous day had walked up to him and surrendered. "That," said Maddox to reporters, "is not exactly what we had in mind." On another occasion, a tiny black woman with piercing eyes and a wild countenance came into the governor's office carrying a small package wrapped in a copy of the *Atlanta Constitution*. The state police sergeant standing just behind Maddox eyed the woman suspiciously.

"What's that you got there, honey?" Maddox asked. "You bring me some fish?"

The old woman shook her head. "No, sir," she drawled, staring hard at Maddox, "it's a real gift for you."

Maddox noted the look on her face and glanced nervously at the sergeant. The woman continued to stare at him. "I been watching you, the way you treat the little people, and I just wanted to give you a little something in return," she said. "It's a big surprise for you. I fixed it up all by myself."

Maddox was nervous. "Well, honey, you just give it to the sergeant here," he said. "He's officially in charge of all gifts to the governor, and I thank you very much." The woman seemed reluctant to hand over the package to anyone but the governor, but the sergeant plucked it from her hand and walked hurriedly from the large, high-ceilinged office. A pair of explosives experts began unwrapping the *Atlanta Constitution* and found a small fruitcake inside and a scribbled note to Maddox which said: "Dear Governor. Thank you for Little People's Day." It was signed, "One of the little people." That night, in the kitchen of the ramshackle old Victorian mansion that was the governor's official residence, Maddox told his wife about the gift. "You know, honey," he mused, "sometimes I guess it's just hard for me to believe that the niggers love me too."

That wasn't hard to understand. He had become in a short span of time a sort of second-string George Wallace on the all-American racist squad. He loved "nigger" jokes, defended segregation on a Biblical basis as a divinely ordained social structure and portrayed himself as a humble man of God, burning with Christian love and devotion. When Martin King was murdered in Memphis in April 1968, and thousands of Americans, black and white, came to Atlanta to mourn his death and march in his miles-long funeral cortege, Maddox barricaded himself in his office and surrounded the state capitol with a cordon of state troopers. He was, one assistant disclosed later, "scared nearly to death." He envisoned "hordes of coloreds storming the capitol and lynching him."

But on that chilly morning in January 1971, there was no sign of fear at all on the face of the balding little man standing just a few feet away from Jimmy Carter—just an occasional licking of the lips to keep them moist in the cold dry wind. He felt loved. After all, Georgians had thought enough of the way he had run the governor's office to choose him resoundingly as lieutenant governor. They liked Lester Maddox, he knew, and apparently they liked the way he campaigned because they had just elected a man who had gone after the office in much the same way he had. It would be interesting, he had said earlier that day, to see just how close to Lester Maddox this Jimmy Carter could really come.

Moments later, he found out. Having taken the oath of office, Governor Jimmy Carter stood behind the lectern with the state seal, addressed himself formally to Maddox and his fellow Georgians and began his four-year term. "It is a long way from Plains to Atlanta," he said. "I started the trip four and a half years ago, and with a four-year detour, I finally made it. I thank you all for making it possible for me to be here on what is certainly the greatest day of my life. But now, the election is over, and I realize that the test of a leader is not how well he campaigned but how effectively he meets the challenges and responsibilities of the office." They were rather curious words: ". . . the test of a man is not how well he campaigned." Perhaps they were nothing more than a rhetorical preface for his affirmation of the need to fulfill those "challenges and responsibilities"; yet Carter's formal oratory was traditionally sparse. There were few wasted words and almost no ornamentation. It was as though he was asking Georgia, in the only way he could

manage to ask it, to understand that he had found it absolutely necessary to wage the sort of campaign he had. It was
as though he was admitting that it had not been the best of
him. It was as though he was trying to tell them more than
he was willing to say that cold morning at the capitol.

If that was the case, he decided to show them in other
words that he was not precisely the sort of fellow they had
come to know during the campaign. He broke it to them
slowly, gently:

"This is a time for truth and frankness. The next four years
will not be easy ones. The problems we face will not solve
themselves. They demand the utmost in dedication and un-
selfishness from each of us. But this is also a time for greatness. Our people are determined to overcome the handicaps
of the past and to meet the opportunities of the future with
confidence and with courage.

"Our people are our most precious possession and we
cannot afford to waste the talents and abilities given by God
to one single Georgian. Every adult illiterate, every school
dropout, every untrained retarded child is an indictment of
us all. Our state pays a terrible and continuing human and
financial price for these failures. It is time to end this waste.
If Switzerland and Israel and other people can eliminate illiteracy, then so can we. The responsibility is our own, and
as Governor, I will not shirk this reponsibility.

"At the end of a long campaign, I believe I know our people as well as anyone," Carter said. He had reached his
theme by then, and his voice was firm as he continued.

"Based on this knowledge of Georgians—north and south,
rural and urban, liberal and conservative—I say to you quite
frankly that the time for racial discrimination is over," he
said.

Maddox looked up at him from his nearby seat and
stopped wetting his lips. Rosalynn stared straight ahead.
Carter continued: "Our people have already made this major and difficult decision, but we cannot underestimate the
challenge of hundreds of minor decisions yet to be made.

Our inherent human charity and our religious beliefs will be taxed to the limit.

"No poor, rural, weak, or black person should ever again have to bear the additional burden of being deprived of the opportunity for an education, a job, or simple justice. We Georgians are fully capable of making our own judgments and managing our own affairs. We who are strong or in positions of leadership must realize that the responsibility for making correct decisions in the future is ours. As Governor, I will not shirk this responsibility."

Moments later, at the end of his remarks, he quoted William Jennings Bryan on the subject of destiny. It "is not a matter of change," he said, "it is a matter of choice. Destiny is not a thing to be waited for. It is a thing to be achieved."

Although it lasted less than nine minutes, it was probably the most important speech in Jimmy Carter's political career.

He was on page one of *The New York Times* the next day and on the cover of *Time* magazine a few weeks later as one of the South's "new" voices. There were others being raised in those days, of course—Governors Reubin Askew and Dale Bumpers of Florida and Arkansas—and they were duly noted; but it was Jimmy Carter who became the grinning symbol of the changing region. Apparently, neither *The Times* nor *Time* had been listening to that same voice during its campaign against Sanders the previous year. The entire pseudosegregationist and states' rights thrust of that race had been quickly buried beneath a sizable drift of fluffy rhetoric about the liberality of his inaugural address, an indication, perhaps, of the degree to which Neanderthaloid tendencies had been justifiably taken for granted in past appraisals of Southern politicians. Given the history of the South in the previous decade, it was no wonder that Yankees found Carter's declaration that the time had come to end discrimination both striking and promising; but it was also a means of separating himself from his questionable 1970 campaign. It was lovely. In a few deft strokes on that January morning in 1971, he had, for all practical purposes, purged the 1970 campaign from the public perception of him and replaced it at once with a new image, precisely the image he had fostered in the unsuccessful 1966 campaign.

He had become, in the mind of the media at least, a reflection of the "new" South, a concept as old as his mother, but a role in which he would become quite as comfortable and expert as in any of his previous adaptations.

If symbols were to be the new currency of American politics, Jimmy Carter could adjust.

"I wish you wouldn't keep appearing and vanishing so suddenly," said Alice. "You make one quite giddy."

"All right," said the Cat, and this time it vanished quite slowly, beginning with the end of the tail and ending with the grin, which remained some time after the rest of it had gone.

"Well! I've often seen a cat without a grin," thought Alice, "but a grin without a cat! It's the most curious thing I ever saw in all my life!"

Lewis Carroll,

ALICE'S ADVENTURES IN WONDERLAND

BY MONDAY of the last week of the summer of 1977, the Secret Service and the servants at the White House had grown quite accustomed to the new President's unswerving devotion to a farmer's hours. So, on that particular morning, none of them was surprised when, just before six o'clock, he tiptoed from his bedroom on the second floor of the old Georgian mansion, leaving his wife still sleeping in their bed, and walked across the broad hall to an elevator that whisked him quickly to the basement. He headed outside into the grayness of the predawn, striding briskly along a colonnade past the carefully manicured Rose Garden, turning left past the Cabinet Room and finally entering the Oval Office—the focal point of elected power in America—through its tall French doors.

Once inside, however, he seemed hardly to notice the elegance of the spacious room or the history that fairly seeped from its curving, off-white walls, but walked directly across the thick blue-and-white carpet—emblazoned with an enormous Presidential seal—through a small alcove used by his personal secretary and into a cozy little study that had become the working core of his Presidency in the 242 days of his Administration. The Oval Office was reserved for more ceremonial appointments—greeting visiting dignitaries, posing for pictures with politicians and clergymen and the poster children for charity drives, lunching with his wife or the Vice President, making a nationally televised speech—and although he had retrieved John F. Kennedy's old desk from storage and installed it there before the first week of his term was over, he spent little time at all behind it, preferring instead the adjacent study where Richard Nixon had often retired for afternoon naps in the crumbling days of his tenure in the White House.

But, as the agents and the servants and his staff and most of the American public had quickly discovered, the new President was not a man for siestas. He began most of his days before the sun rose over Washington and worked long and hard and late on a crowded schedule that made little provision for leisure—and the essence of his labors was reading, reading, reading. In eight months, he had spent literally hundreds of hours behind the desk in the little study, wearing the dark-rimmed glasses the public seldom saw, poring over the ceaseless flow of paper generated by the vast governmental machinery he had been so narrowly elected to lead, and in the process ("an education every day," he called it), he had come to know a world far, far different from the one he had perceived before and during his rapid rise to power. There were so few simple questions, he had learned, and even those less complicated demanded difficult answers not always politically palatable or diplomatically deft.

He insisted the job was a joy to him and his wife said she had never seen him happier, but in eight months he had aged considerably, adding new wrinkles and deepening old ones, increasing the basic undercoating of gray in his hair. It was no wonder. In eight months on the job, he had carved himself a place in White House history as one of the hardest-working Presidents ever to shoulder the responsibilities of the office. Even those who were less than fond of his stewardship there were quick to concede that his energy and industry were remarkable. Whatever else the American electorate had wrought the previous November, it had produced a President who worked like a farmer in the final days of harvest. If traditional White House office hours were insufficient for the tasks he set for himself, he simply stretched the day by beginning early and ending late.

It was slightly past six o'clock that morning when he settled himself once again in the big chair behind the desk in the little study, getting another head start on another long day. A steward wearing a blue blazer with the Presidential seal sewn on the breast pocket poured coffee for him as he glanced quickly at the headlines on the newspapers that were waiting for him. There was a soft rapping on the hallway door.

"Come on in," he said.

"Good morning, Mr. President," said the large man ambling across the study toward him.

"You get any rest?"

"Oh, three, four hours, I guess," the big man answered.

"You see this?" the new President asked, handing him a copy of the final edition of the *Washington Post*.

"Yeah," the fellow muttered, glancing at the headline and returning the newspaper. "It was waiting for me on my doorstep. I read it in the car."

The newspaper lay across a corner of the desk, its main headline still visible to both men: RIBICOFF, PERCY STILL THINK LANCE OUGHT TO RESIGN. The study was quiet except for the rattle of the fine china cups on the steward's silver tray.

"Pour Mr. Lance some coffee, too, please," the new President told the steward.

It was not a new experience for either of them, this predawn tête-à-tête between James Earl Carter, Jr., the elected executive, and Thomas Bertram Lance, Jr., the appointed technician. They had talked dozens of times before in the little White House study before Washington came awake, but they had begun their morning meetings seven years before when Carter, as the new governor of Georgia, had brought Lance, a freewheeling banker from the northwest regions of the state, into his fledgling state administration and appointed him head of the Department of Transportation. It had been a cesspool of scandal and graft for years and had come to be known as the "department of politics and paving." But Lance had quickly worked a variety of what were regarded as major miracles there—reducing the budget and the staff while simultaneously increasing services, lending an air of honesty and respectability to the agency that it had never before enjoyed or deserved—and he had played a significant role in building the centerpieces of Carter's governorship, bureaucratic reorganization and zero-based budgeting, a complex fiscal arrangement in which each governmental agency must annually justify its budget requests and "prioritize" (a word that came to have great usage in the Carter presidential campaign and White House) them in its presentations. Over the months, Lance had not only become an important part of the governor's inner circle, he had also become his closest personal friend.

They had a great deal in common. Both had grown up in rural communities, hard to find on a Georgia map, and both had worked hard at expanding small-town businesses beyond the wildest dreams of their founders. Both had come a long way in a brief time, both were deeply religious, and both had a robust sense of family and roots. Still, they were always a rather odd pair, the planter from Plains and the banker from Calhoun: Carter, so slightly built, almost fragile, and Lance, a hulking bear of a man, six feet four inches and 250 pounds, thick-necked and ham-handed; Carter, so impeccably dressed, so immaculately groomed, and Lance, incurably rumpled, inveterately careless about his attire; Carter, so reticent and reserved, nearly shy, and Lance, backslappingly gregarious, a hail-fellow-well-met who could have taught Norman Vincent Peale a thing or two about positive thinking; Carter, so meticulously passionate about the tiniest of details, and Lance, a big-picture man quickly bored by nuts and bolts. Lance was the sort of man Carter had never known in all his years of becoming—a personality type rarely found in the officer corps of the U.S. Navy and scarce in the rolling hills of southwest Georgia, a man whose elastic mind readily embraced and understood prodigious quantities of money as some men's minds comprehend the high and low temperatures of the day, a high-rolling entrepreneur and risk-taker whose love for the good life might have been expected to offend the more ascetic governor.

Still, they became boon companions in the first few months of his term as governor, playing tennis, plotting end runs around the recalcitrant legislature, joking with each other and laughing at each other's faults and foibles—Carter chuckled, of course, but Lance was more inclined to guffaw. Those who knew them both in those days were relieved that at last the governor had made a friend who was, at least, something of a contemporary. Unlike Charles Kirbo, who was not only a few years older than Carter, but also of an entirely different generation in terms of personality, temperament and outlook, Lance was more of Carter's time; and unlike Jody Powell and Hamilton Jordan, Lance was mature, a man with a family and a citizen of some standing and substance in his community.

Lance had been born in north Georgia in 1931, the son of a hardworking but relatively poor president of a little church-related college. He found his parents' lack of ready cash an unacceptable life-style and set forth as an adolescent to guarantee that he would never face such ignominious shortages. His were the purest of American instincts, the urges spawned by the system itself and a hundred rags-to-riches stories he had read and memorized by the time he was twelve years old. There were two ways to live, he deduced—with or without ready cash or credit—and by working diligently at a series of odd jobs, he went away to college in Atlanta with money in his pocket. It wasn't a fortune, but he was never without funds or the realistic prospect thereof. Not a particularly brilliant student in his college years just after World War Two, he was quite well liked by his classmates for his heart-on-his-sleeve candor and his love for good jokes and parties and bull sessions that lasted well into the wee hours. His academic problems, though not grave, did not bother him. He was in love. The object of his youthful affections was LaBelle David, the fragile, pretty daughter of the leading banker in Calhoun, their hometown. When they were married in 1951, he still had every intention of getting his degree. After all, his father was a college president and almost everyone he knew was planning on finishing college. LaBelle wanted that for him, too, but when she became pregnant and the prospect of feeding three instead of two sank in on them, they faced the question of whether Bert should accept money from her—her family, actually—or try to finish on his own, thereby lowering the standard of living they had enjoyed together.

He dropped out of college and took his wealthy wife back to Calhoun where her father hired him as a $90-a-month teller in the Calhoun National Bank. He discovered, much to his surprise, that his father-in-law did not actually "own" the bank, as he had always surmised, but rather that a Chattanooga banking family held controlling interest. Lance also discovered that holding power in a bank was not unlike holding four of a kind in any poker game. It had distinct, if not unbeatable, advantages. The Davids, he observed, lived a life unfettered by the need for ready cash or credit. Their checks, regardless of their balances, were honored. Their loans, regardless of collateral, were granted. Lance noted this, as he plied his teller's trade, and being no fool, deduced that it required no special intelligence, foresight or courage. That, he decided, was precisely where he wanted to be—and by 1961, after several years of diligence behind the counter, he had become president of the Calhoun National Bank.

It was like giving Isaac Stern a violin. Soon afterward, along with a small consortium of LaBelle's relations and local businessmen, he raised the money—very little of which was actually his—to purchase the controlling interest in the bank. The David family was exuberant. The local community was equally elated. "A Hometown Bank for Hometown Folks," the bank's local advertising soon read. Never again would Bert Lance have cash-flow problems. He was living the great American dream—living in a big house, driving a big car, spending big money on big favors to good friends, changing the very nature of the bank's approach to business, granting big loans and, when it was necessary, writing big overdrafts on his account. Like those of his father-in-law and other members of the David family, they were honored.

Big profits require big investments, and Bert never lacked for capital. Before anyone realized what had happened, his aggressive banking techniques had actually transformed the local landscape. The carpet industry was just beginning to blossom in the area. The Calhoun National Bank became a standard benefactor. There were new jobs with new carpet factories and new jobs with old companies whose expansions were bankrolled by Bert's largess. The assets of the bank doubled and then tripled and then quadrupled, and everybody said that Bert was a savior of the regional economy.

When Jimmy Carter came to north Georgia in 1970 looking for prominent allies, the name of Thomas Bertram Lance, Jr., was at the top of his list. They liked each other almost immediately, although neither had any idea of what the other was like—and it came as no surprise to anyone that Jimmy Carter, after defeating Carl Sanders in the primary and walking away from the Republican in the 1970 general election in Georgia, would tap Bert Lance to take over one of the most important facets of the state bureaucracy.

And so began their early-morning conferences in the high-ceilinged governor's office deep in the bowels of the Georgia capitol, far beneath its soaring, gold-flecked dome, and Lance, who was as shrewd as he was quixotic, as much a dreamer as a hard-nosed money changer, came back from a Chicago trip one afternoon with a copy of James David Barber's book, *The Presidential Character: Predicting Performance in the White House.* He signed the flyleaf with an appropriately affectionate inscription for Carter and asked him to note the concluding lines of the book which he had dutifully underlined. "For the rest, there is laughter," Dr. Barber had concluded in the last paragraph of his writing. "Americans do a lot of that—at themselves, at politicians, at all the pomposities and cynicisms that stand in the way of genuine experience. We have yet to be immobilized by irony. A Presidential character who can see beyond tomorrow—and smile—might yet lead us out of the wilderness."

No one knows just when the idea of running for President planted itself in Jimmy Carter's mind. Peter Bourne, an English-born, American-educated physician who helped Rosalynn's drug-abuse programs get off the ground in Georgia, remembers flying back from Washington with the new governor less than four months after his inauguration and raising the question of whether he had ever given any thought to a presidential candidacy. "He just smiled," Bourne recalls. "He took it quite in stride, as though I'd asked him if he'd ever given the least thought to the idea of hunting again. I don't think it was the first time the subject had been raised in his mind." Similarly, Jordan, Powell and Kirbo all insist that when they finally broached the subject to him—in 1972—he seemed merely to acknowledge that it was a possibility to be considered and not a striking, startling proposal that had caught him by surprise. Carter himself is vague on the origins of his impossible dream. "I think it just evolved, probably without my being aware of it at all, until at some point or another I entertained the idea, probably for just a split second and probably without realizing I had, and then it probably occurred again, this time maybe for a little longer than the first, and also probably without my actual conscious realization that it was there, until finally when I acknowledged that it was there, I couldn't remember when it wasn't there," he said. That may be as close to the truth of how the campaign formed in his mind as any explanation he or anyone else will ever offer.

It is an explanation utterly consonant with the existentialist that he had become over the long years since he had made his voyage from Plains and back again. In the process of becoming, it was not always necessary for him to be aware of the changes taking place in him. What was important was for him eventually to recognize that they had taken place. He could never fully explain—to his own satisfaction, at least—the instincts that had driven him or pulled him away from the land his father had tilled so long, and he could never fully explain—to his own satisfaction, at least—the willingness to come back again, particularly in view of the fact that he had thoroughly separated himself from his father and the village of his roots. It was a process of becoming, generated as much by boredom as by ambition, with a dollop of snobbism included in the mixture. It was such a mottled blend that he was never quite able to rationalize his rather precipitous plunge into politics and its continuing hold on him as he moved from office to office, always vertically: the Georgia Senate, the race for Congress, the Georgia governorship and then, the Presidency. They were ideas, it seemed, that simply evolved within his psyche into concepts and then into possibilities and then into pursuits. That is his retrospective theory, but a perspective that omits his natural, competitive bent.

From his days in Miss Julia Coleman's classroom, he had found more pleasure in personal rivalry than in any other form of physical or intellectual pursuit. It had not been easy to stay ahead of Eloise Ratliff in Plains High School, particularly after he noticed how pretty she was, but he had managed it because he did not want to finish second to someone he knew. At Annapolis, he was selectively aggressive in his

studies because he was unchallenged by personal acquaintances. He made few friends there on the banks of the Severn River, and those friends that he did make finished below
him in the final academic ratings of his class. It was curious
that he was one of a small minority of midshipmen there
who took flying lessons at the naval base across the river.
They were not mandatory and he had no real interest in naval aviation. They seemed simply to be the result of his rec-
ognition that flying an airplane was quite a difficult, complicated task, that others had nevertheless mastered it—
including at least three midshipmen he knew well—that he
was surely as competent and as capable as they. Ergo, he
would learn to fly an airplane too. After he had, he lost interest in it. He never flew again.

When he returned to Plains to take over the business his
father had almost lost, his most successful and most visible
competitor was a warehouse concern run by a third-genera-
tion of the Williams family. By the time he decided to leap
into politics by running for the State Senate seven years
later, the Carter operations were equal to the Williams's and
growing even faster. Similarly, one of the basic motivations
for his Congressional race in 1966 was the gnawing reality
of Howard Callaway's success in the same field. In the process of becoming, he had become a selective competitor.

Carter concedes that such a theory was in operation during his tenure as governor when he entertained several of
the country's more illustrious politicians in the new mansion the state had built in the last year of Lester Maddox's
term. He met Richard Nixon and Spiro Agnew, but the visits
that had the most impact on him were those of the men who
were most prominent in his own party, men who in one
fashion or another had come to be known by the media and
the public as weighing in at the presidential level. Muskie
came and Kennedy and McGovern and Humphrey, and
Carter came to feel that none of them was smarter than he—
a conclusion that did not require the wisdom of Solomon nor
the sensitivity of Isaiah—and all of them were considerably

much less disciplined. He noticed, in particular, their drinking habits. All of them, he saw, seemed inclined to have just a little more liquor than was good for them, just enough, and occasionally a great deal more than enough, to render them careless, to divide their attention, to take their minds off what they were doing—and what most of them were doing, to one degree or another, was running for President.

Alcohol had never been a problem for Carter at all. Excessive drinking was frowned on in the Navy, and, besides, he had never actually cared for it that much. Now, a good wine—that was a different matter. He enjoyed quality wine, but it had never interested him enough for him to become a connoisseur, and he had never allowed it to captivate him so as to intoxicate him beyond a pleasant sense of relaxation. Temperance was a supreme virtue for Carter, perhaps because abstinence was the supreme virtue in the Southern Baptist milieu in which he had lived. Earl and Lillian had always enjoyed moderate amounts of liquor (she still has what she calls "my wonderful Fresca" each night—the crystal-clear soft drink stained walnut by a generous lacing of bourbon), but because their church's official position on alcohol was abstinence, they were both careful to keep it a part of their private lives. Their bridge guests over the years were generally those who shared their rejection of the church's drinking views, and the old pond house was never a citadel of prohibition. Drinking, in Earl Carter's household, was not perceived as wrong, but neither was it embraced as unquestionably right—a moral dilemma that spawned both caution and care.

At forty-six years old, the new governor of Georgia could tell one friend—who believed him—that he had never been drunk in his life; but the recognizable names in the Democratic party who were guests at the mansion during the early period of his residence there could say no such thing, and a couple of them could not even make that claim about their visits to the mansion. Carter watched them. He genuinely enjoyed their company, enjoyed their stories about running a national campaign, about the Senate, about Washington. He particularly enjoyed Humphrey's visit, but he watched them all and he wondered to himself about their stature in the party and around the country. Rosalynn was watching, too, and it was, perhaps, after one of those evenings with a guest that she said to him, as she recalled later, "The boys and I think you'd be just as good a President as the Senator, and probably much better." He laughed, but then reticently agreed. "You and the boys are probably right," she remembered him saying, "but we'll have to get Amy's opinion, too."

However it got there—and he cannot or does not say—the idea of something more politically significant than being governor of Georgia had implanted itself in his mind before the end of his first year in Atlanta.

Whatever else may be accurately said of Jody Powell and Hamilton Jordan, it cannot be said of them that they were ever bashful. They worked hard at their jobs as the new governor's top aides but they were not of his ilk after hours. They drank and caroused and enjoyed themselves, much in the fashion of other Southern men in their mid-twenties, and in a brief period established themselves in Atlanta as the equal of any roué or rascal in the contemporary political establishment. There were stories aplenty about the new governor's "rover boys," including one that emerged from the 1971 Southern Governors Conference at The Greenbrier, a posh, if stuffy, golfing resort in White Sulphur Springs, West Virginia. They arrived a day before their boss to make preparations for his participation in the largely ceremonial gathering of the Old Confederacy's chief executives, and when the sun slipped past the yardarm, they slipped quickly from the prim elegance of the old resort and headed for the less inhibited side of town. Finding a roadside tavern just on the outskirts, they settled in for a sudsy evening of

stories and companionship, making new friends of both gen-
ders but, in the process, managing to offend the sensibilities of a rather sizable group of rather sizable young men.
They were invited outside to negotiate the legitimacy of
their presence there. Jordan, ever the astute politician,
disappeared, leaving Powell behind to take on the local
champion.

"For the first time in my life, I felt like a Christian," Powell remembered. "I never knew there were so many Romans
in West Virginia." When he stumbled into the lobby of the
hotel later that night, his clothes ripped and filthy, the flesh
beneath his left eye rapidly turning royal purple, he was refused his room key; the next morning, as he stood waiting
for the governor's plane at the local airport, he dreaded his
boss's reaction to his appearance. "But he didn't say anything," Powell recalled. "He just sort of grinned like he was
relieved it was nothing worse than a black eye."

Carter had known Jordan for five years by then and Powell for nearly two, and if there was a singular mark of their
relationship, it was his tolerance for their occasionally erratic behavior. Jordan was incurably rumpled and given to
wearing work shoes and sweat shirts in his office adjacent to
the governor's. There were complaints from around the
Georgia capitol that such attire was not appropriate for the
governor's executive secretary, and Carter occasionally reported the griping to Jordan; but nothing changed. Powell,
who had never worked in journalism, had become the new
governor's press secretary "in the same way that people
grow older," he said. "He asked me, after we won, what I
wanted to do for him as governor and I said I didn't know,
and so he said, 'You want to try press secretary?' and I said,
'Why the hell not?' How's that for careful deliberation?"

Still, both young men proved themselves as political aides
and counselors as the months moved along in Carter's first
year as governor. He dealt with them, in most instances, as
equals, not as substitute sons, and seldom rebuked them for
their occasional nonconformity. "But, I'll tell you something

we learned about him in those days," Powell said. "Just about the only time he ever said anything at all was when he was displeased with our work. We found out that if he didn't say anything, that meant he was probably happy with what we were doing. But if he was unhappy enough, he could and did eat us out royally. Fortunately for us, he never did that in front of anybody." Rickover's stinginess with personal praise had found a second-generation repository in the new governor, adjusted only to the extent that he tried to avoid embarrassing his subordinates in the presence of others. He was quite capable of embarrassing political adversaries, and occasionally reporters—then and later—but never his friends, and his relationship with Powell and Jordan, his fellow southwest Georgians who had worked so hard in his victorious campaign, was precisely that: a friendship, deep and constant, laced with loyalty.

Consequently, there was in their relationship an almost instinctive mutual trust. Strategy and tactics, as proposed by any of the three, could be questioned and argued, perhaps heatedly, but the motives were never an issue in their discussion. It was merely assumed that each was interested in and concerned with the well-being of the others and that any suggestion would express that interest and concern, however unacceptable the suggestion might eventually be judged. For instance, in the spring of 1972, Jordan mentioned that possibly Carter should present himself to Senator McGovern—the apparent Democratic presidential nominee—as a vice presidential candidate who would be able to help the party and the ticket in the South. Carter showed a tentative interest, but Powell said it was a ludicrous idea. After all, Carter had tried—and quite vigorously, at that—to sandbag McGovern's candidacy through most of the year after assessing him as a potential disaster in a contest with the incumbent Nixon; but, ultimately, Carter came to agree with Jordan that it was an idea whose time had come, and he instructed his two young aides to have at it. Powell, who was thoroughly persuaded that it was a fool's errand and

might prove to be counterproductive, nevertheless partici-
pated vigorously in the venture, once the decision had been
made.

As it turned out, Powell was right. McGovern sniffed dis-
dainfully at the presentation and suggested that if he wanted
a Southern governor as his running mate, it would certainly
not be Carter. It might be someone like Askew of Florida or
Bumpers of Arkansas—the other voices of the "new" South
who had judiciously, but to no avail, avoided making pre-
convention judgments on McGovern—but it most indubitably would not be someone who had overtly tried to keep
him from getting the nomination. It was precisely as Powell
had envisioned it—a fool's errand—and they had been embarrassed by it as well.

Still, the 1972 Democratic Convention provided some sa-
lient information about their boss. He had been the governor of Georgia for less than eighteen months, and he was
already restless. Even the Vice Presidency, known for its
traditional invisibility, did not look all that bad to him. Besides, Powell and Jordan, in their first dip into the larger
pond of national politics, had discovered that no one they
had met seemed any more divinely ordained to swim in that
water than they.

They came back from Miami—Carter, Powell, Jordan and
Rafshoon—convinced that McGovern, the nominee of the
party, was hopeless. Of course, they were personally
piqued that the South Dakota Senator had rejected their
rather brazen efforts to offer Carter as vice presidential nominee, but their doubts ran much deeper. McGovern did not
seem to any of them to be the sort of man who could play
the hardball politics a presidential candidacy required. His
people seemed to be rank amateurs, with the notable exception of Gary Hart, the future Senator from Colorado. There
was a kid named Caddell, for instance: Patrick Caddell, a

Harvard brain who had become the darling of the liberal
press for his polling procedures during the primary season
and his willingness to talk about them to reporters. Jordan
had met Caddell and come away very much unimpressed.
"Hell, he's younger than I am," he said.

There was another thing about McGovern that bothered
Carter and his boys. He took such a hard stand against the
war that it was difficult even to discuss it with him. They
were of a different tradition, and their roots were in a society in which military service was the expected if not the
mandatory avocation of every young man. Carter himself
had been dejected about missing a chance actually to fire
some torpedoes in anger, and some of Powell's best friends
at the Air Force Academy were by then flying missions over
North Vietnam, including one who was shot down, captured, escaped, captured again and died in a Hanoi cell. Jordan, rejected from military service for reasons of health, had
spent two years in Vietnam anyway before coming back to
run Carter's 1970 campaign in Georgia. If they had personal
doubts about the propriety of the war—and it is extremely
doubtful that they did—they kept them to themselves.
Theirs was a creed that essentially agreed with Robert E.
Lee's suggestion that "the call of one's country is a high
one, and the call of one's country to war is the highest."

Besides, they all agreed, it was an impossible position to
sell politically. They knew that with hundreds of thousands
of Americans involved personally in the war—those who
were fighting there, those who had been there, those who
were on their way and all their fathers and mothers and
grandfathers and grandmothers and aunts and uncles and
nephews and nieces and cousins and sweethearts and wives
and children and brothers and sisters—there was an underlying suspicion of anyone who doubted that it was an honorable war. To say that it was not, and to say that publicly and
to say that in the midst of a presidential campaign against an
incumbent President who constantly issued broad hints that
he had a secret solution that would bring peace and honor

for the country, was a perilous proposition at best. "I'd sure as hell hate to have to try to peddle that," Rafshoon sighed, and the rest of them agreed. George McGovern wouldn't carry a single state in the country, Carter predicted. "At least, I'd carry Georgia," the governor laughed—and the rest of them glanced at each other, realizing that what had been on their minds for some time was on his mind as well.

Jordan went to work writing a lengthy and, in places, a brilliant memo about just what would have to happen for Carter to win the Democratic nomination in 1976. He submitted it to the governor. Not an eyebrow was raised. He was running. It was four years away, but that was nothing new to him. He was running. From that autumn on, it would consume him—the planning, the plotting, the speeches, the travel—and although he would complain about it occasionally to Rosalynn, she said she never saw him happier.

He was absorbed in his favorite process again—the process of becoming.

In a sense, Carter took with him into a presidential campaign one of his major advantages over Sanders in the 1970 governor's race. He was an unknown quantity in Georgia and he would be an unknown quantity in the country. If others thought running from Washington as a Senator or a Representative—as someone with a record in Federal office—was an asset, he sensed once again that it was a liability. People didn't trust people who had had a chance to foul things up, he reasoned, and the antagonism toward the Federal government was deep and strong. As a matter of fact, it had not taken more than a few months for his own popularity as a state politician to fade once he had actually come into office. There were decisions to be made, positions to be taken, bills to sign or veto, programs to propose and defend, policies to promulgate, appointments to make. If any politician honestly attempted to use his office as a means for substantive change, the odds were fairly great that he would lose rather than gain in popularity among his constitutents.

So, the fact that he had never held Federal office before didn't bother Carter. He would have nothing to explain, nothing for which he had to apologize, nothing for which he could be blamed and no record at all to defend—except his record as governor. That might be a problem, Jordan predicted. Not that he had taken positions for which he should be ashamed in the twenty months since he had taken office, but rather that any governor's record would be automatically looked upon as irrelevant to a presidential campaign. He would need something, Jordan said, to show that he was a little further along than the Georgia Certified Seed Association's board of directors. His record as governor, Jordan suggested, could become a significant part of a presidential campaign if it could always be explained in terms of its relationship to his goals as a presidential candidate. Keep that in mind, Jordan advised. Carter would not forget.

When Lance left the little study on that Monday of the last week in the summer of 1977, the new President had less than an hour in which to make his initial assault on the large stack of papers waiting for him before his next appointment, his regular morning briefing from the man he had chosen as his national security adviser, Zbigniew Brzezinski, a pre-World War Two immigrant from Poland whom Carter had plucked from the faculty of Columbia University and brought to the top-secret dungeons of the White House basement to serve in the same capacity as Henry Kissinger in the early years of Richard Nixon.

A dapper, aristocratic fellow, Dr. Brzezinski prided himself on his syntax—he tended to speak in distinctively organized paragraphs, replete with complex sentences and subordinate clauses—and his punctuality, and at precisely seven forty-five, he appeared at the door to the little study, a sheaf of cables in his hand, the overnight diary of a nervous world. For eight months, the two of them had been conducting their morning conferences, and for eight months, Dr. Brzezinski had been carefully instructing the new President in the intricacies of his own approach to foreign policy. It was fueled principally by Brzezinski's rather fervent urgings to distinguish himself from Kissinger, the colossal bench mark in American diplomacy against which much of the new Administration's foreign initiatives would be measured. The two men had been rivals for some time, having clashed in the esoteric circles of the academic world years before, with Kissinger, under Nelson Rockefeller's aegis, moving quickly from the campus to the inner circles of the Nixon White House and eventually to the position he had wanted all along—Secretary of State.

Brzezinski, said those who knew him, had watched that ascension with a jealous eye, realizing that it might have been his own career path, given the proper turn or two, and although his own *Weltanschauung* was the product of years of intense study, it was nevertheless colored by the fact of Kissinger's success. After all, they were both foreign-born, naturalized Americans for whom a life of teaching and a role in the nether fringes of the nation's foreign-policy community had become a warm and comfortable home. Brzezinski, given the same opportunities as Kissinger to influence the direction of the country, was determined that his contributions would be discernible from Kissinger's, as distinctly different as safely possible. He divided the broad spectrum of international relationships into a series of regional clusters and persuaded Carter to focus his attention and foreign-policy energies on the smaller categories rather than the three or four major alliances Kissinger had nursed during his tenure at the White House and at the State Department, and Carter warmed to the idea. Like all American Presidents, particularly those who succeed a man of a different party, he wanted to make a personal mark on the shape and structure of the world. Besides, during his campaign, he had criti-

cized Kissinger on several counts, not the least of which was
his alleged neglect of the nation's "traditional" ties with less
powerful but natural American allies. Brzezinski had found
a willing student in the new President, and Carter's trust in
and dependence on the man he called "Zbig" grew as the
months of his Administration passed.

They were not strangers by any means when their White
House residency began in January 1977. They had known
each other for quite some time, in fact, ever since they had
been brought together as members of something called the
Trilateral Commission, an ad hoc gathering of citizens of
prominence and stature from Japan, Western Europe and
North America. The commission was the brainchild of
David Rockefeller, the chairman of the Chase Manhattan
Bank. Organized in 1973, its specific purpose was to influence the foreign policy of all the countries represented in its
membership and to prevent a further deterioration in the
economic relationships between the United States, Japan
and the industrial nations of non-Communist Europe. The
commission was conceived as part of the unstated notion
that whatever was beneficial for David Rockefeller's bank—
and the American economic establishment at that level—
was eventually beneficial to the country. With national foreign policy focused so relentlessly in those days on the day-
to-day details of detente with the Soviet Union and the People's Republic of China, there was little attention on the
more economically significant relationships with nations
competing in the American market, an omission that, in
Rockefeller's and Brzezinski's mind at least, had created a
dangerously competitive and pitifully unproductive relationship among the regions.

At Rockefeller's request, Brzezinski became the chairman
of the commission and began adding to its rolls the cream of
the out-of-power foreign-policy establishment, as well as
bright newcomers with some access to power—such as the
scrubbed and shining voice of the "new" South, James Earl
Carter, Jr. The governor did not hesitate when asked. It was

one more means of gathering credentials above and beyond the Georgia Certified Seed Association. Through the commission, Carter found opportunities to mix and mingle with economic- and foreign-policy nabobs from England and West Germany and the Netherlands and Scandinavia and Japan and Canada, not to mention Brzezinski and David Rockefeller and Cyrus Vance and the senior Senator from Minnesota, Walter F. Mondale, and the chief executive officer of the Bendix Corp., W. Michael Blumenthal. The commission's membership was an impressive list of the leading lights in the industrial world on both sides of the Atlantic and Pacific, including corporate financiers, academic experts, industrialists, politicians—in and out of office and power—and powerful media executives. It was, Carter wrote in his autobiography, "a splendid learning opportunity."

It was no wonder, then, that, with his Southern roots and his exposure to the essentially conservative instincts of those brought to the Trilateral Commission, he would take a distinctly establishmentarian view on the single most important issue in the country during his tenure as the Georgia governor. In 1973, he went to Wisconsin to attend the annual meeting of the National Governors Conference, and there, using Powell and Jordan as operatives within the group, aggressively lobbied for a resolution from the conference that would have recommended against raising the Vietnam War as an issue in any of the upcoming gubernatorial or Congressional elections. It would be devisive, he argued, and not in the best interests of the country to debate a war in which American troops were still actively engaged. Later, as a candidate who called it a "racist war," he would say that his opposition to it preceded his interest in that resolution. Clearly, it did not—or if it did, his political machinations at the Governors Conference were merely that, political machinations unrelated to his views on the war. It was evident by then that Jimmy Carter was not the liberal *Time* magazine had perceived. On the two substantial issues of his lifetime—civil rights and the Vietnam War—he had gone with the flow of his environment, and like George Wallace, he had changed his mind only long after many of his neighbors had done the same.

Still, even after he decided to launch a serious but secret presidential campaign, he had been a good governor, by all the contemporary standards. He had made plenty of enemies, of course, who would rail against him then and now for what they regarded as policies and programs not in the best interests of the state. But there is ample evidence that his stewardship of the office was exemplary, and particularly so when seen against the backdrop of other recent Southern governors—John Bell Williams and Ross Barnett and Paul Johnson of Mississippi, Orval Faubus of Arkansas, and, of course, Wallace in Alabama and Griffin, Vandiver and Maddox in Georgia. For one thing, Carter invested himself almost completely in the job. He applied to the governorship all the diligence and early-rising dedication that had produced such satisfactory rewards for him in his past pursuits. Indeed, it was his rigorous yet efficient schedule that had first attracted Dr. Bourne to him and motivated the doctor to devote such great amounts of time—at first voluntarily, later as a member of the staff—to his Administration. "I'd never seen anybody, much less a politician, who was so very much alive, so vital," Bourne remembers.

The new governor was thoughtful, innovative and in some respects rather revolutionary—for a Southern governor, at least, for he seemed intent on bringing substantive change to an ancient bureaucracy whose paralysis he viewed as detrimental to the welfare of the people it was supposed to be serving. He focused a great deal of time and energy on the reorganization of the state agencies, calling on Bert Lance to help him attract the brightest young men they could find in Georgia business circles for a task force that would design the new shape and structure of the state government. He did the same, with Lance's assistance, again when he began to install his cherished system of zero-based budgeting. It was different, of course, and different to the degree that the legislature of Georgia, a body generally devoted over the years to the preservation of its power and the affluence of its patrons, was by and large alienated.

Lance, Kirbo, Jordan and Powell were more inclined to work traditionally with the representatives and senators— more willing to swap and trade, giving a little here, taking a little there—but Carter had little interest in building such relationships. Time after time, he declined to make any compromises until the last minute; his theory was based on the premise that it is only at the eleventh hour that a compromise has any value, since refusing to change one's position until the last moment extends the possibility that a compromise may not be necessary at all. In some instances he was right. Faced with losing an entire package of programs and policies under Carter's veto, the legislature bowed; but in other cases, Carter's own recalcitrance destroyed legislation he dearly wanted to become law. It was a hard-nosed posture that would hold constant throughout his term as governor. He found it so difficult to negotiate matters that were of any importance to him—and since that was such a striking departure from the manner in which things had always been done in the Georgia capitol—that his adversaries there multiplied like rabbits taking hormone shots.

"Jimmy just hated all that swapping and trading and such stuff as that," Charles Kirbo recalled. "Those people would come into his office and say, 'Governor, if you'll just see your way clear to take care of this little matter'—it might be a road or a little old bridge or some piece of Federal money for their district or something—'well, then, I'd be pleased and happy to support your bill,' and Jimmy would just sit there behind that big desk and listen to them and smile at them and when they were finished, he'd just sit there and shake his head from side to side and they'd get up and leave, madder'n a wet hen."

Kirbo and Carter's allies called it a matter of honor. His

enemies thought he was just plain stubborn. "Like a south Georgia turtle, that's what he's like," said one veteran of the legislative-capitol wars. "He just keeps on moving in the direction he's headed and it doesn't matter what you do to him. You can step on him or hit him with a stick or run over him with a pickup truck, and it doesn't faze him a bit. He just keeps right on going in the way he wants to go."

Carter was easily offended by the legislators' blatant attempts to give and take in matters of public policy. He had never done that when he was in the State Senate, he told Kirbo, and he didn't see why it had to be such a common practice around him while he was governor. "Isn't there some bill, some issue that just stands on its own merits?" he once asked Kirbo in exasperation. "Is everything always a matter of cutting a bit here and trimming a bit there? Why can't people just vote for or against it and let it go at that? If one more legislator walks through that door and asks for some trade-off deal, so help me God, I think I'll throttle him." He was particularly sensitive to any effort to amend a program or a project in which he had taken some interest. Everyone in the capitol soon learned that to tamper with a piece of legislation that had come directly from the governor's office was to invite the Carter wrath. He was certain of himself—very certain—and confident of the quality of his work. He was, after all, a skilled engineer who approached the problems of state government methodically and with great attention to details. He did not, after all, appreciate questions about his solutions from those who had not spent half as much time studying the problem.

It was an attitude that provoked much scorn in many circles of the government in Atlanta. "He was always so right about everything," said one of his adversaries. "Always so goddamned right, and righteous. That's what it was. That's what I didn't like about the little bastard. He was righteous. If you happened to agree with him, he thought you were one of God's chosen tribe—but if you didn't, you were automatically in league with the devil himself, and probably a whoremonger and a child molester to boot. I tried to like him and tried to work with him for a while until I figured out that I'd never be able to disagree with him without him taking out after me like an avenging angel. He was righteous, all right. Too goddamned righteous."

But Carter could also be persuasive, if he considered the prize worthy of his time and effort. "He could charm the lard off a hog," it was said of his efforts in that direction, but not said often about his relationships with the legislature. He came to see its members, for the most part, as venal, incompetent hacks. For some of them he saved his most vituperative—in his way of thinking—label. "They're children," he would say. "They don't take this seriously." He did, of course—seriously enough to see to it that his reorganization legislation made it through the legislature (it was a reverse-veto arrangement; Carter could order reorganizational moves by himself and if the legislature disapproved, it could veto them), and seriously enough to produce an improved structuring of the state bureaucracy. It was the first reorganization of the government in Georgia since Richard Russell's term as governor in the early 1930s, and it would become the pièce de résistance of Carter's tenure in the same office. Wherever he went as a presidential candidate, he talked about what "we did in Georgia"—further proof that he was, as Jordan had said, a little further along than the Seed Association's board of directors.

Similarly, Carter worked hard at other aspects of his responsibilities as governor. He seemed to be taking his commitment to racial equality seriously as well, and black appointments became rather routine. What was even more significant was his insistence that state jobs all up and down the bureaucracy be made available to black citizens. It was more than tokenism, and the black political leaders in Atlanta and the state knew it. By the time he stepped down in January 1975, the number of black state employees had increased from 4850 to 6684. Moreover, Carter was steadily building a solid friendship with the black leaders and politicians around him. He seemed much more amenable to the give-and-take of politics when it was on a black and white basis. Leroy Johnson, the first black legislator in the Georgia General Assembly since Reconstruction, was an ardent Carter ally.

"I think the thing that most black people liked about Carter then was that he played pretty hard-nosed with everybody, and especially with us," Johnson recalled. "I mean by that that if he was willing to swap with us on something, he fully expected us to keep our end of the bargain, even if it was a hard one. He asked for a lot from us, as I recall, and we didn't always deliver because it was probably too much to have promised in the first place—and, by God, he'd let us know he thought we were incompetent. But, by the same token, when he promised us something, he delivered. You could count on it, as he'd say. You could just count on it." One of the things he promised was that he would proclaim Martin Luther King, Jr., Day on January 15, 1973, and in February of 1974, he unveiled a portrait of the dead civil rights leader in the rotunda of the state capitol.

With the weight of his inaugural address and the image it had fostered in the media, his attention to black employment and the homage he had paid to King would fairly well settle any arguments about whether he would be a racist presidential candidate, a valid apprehension on the part of Carter and his advisers. He was a white Southerner and a white Southern planter, and a white Southern planter who, like his segregationist father, had traditionally paid his black employees less than his white employees (a practice that continued until the spring of 1976). Moreover, even a cursory look by anyone interested in the 1970 campaign would produce the sort of suggestions that could be damaging to a man searching for a national constituency. His shoulder rubbing with Roy Harris, for instance, was suspect. His courtship of Vandiver and Griffin and Maddox raised legitimate questions, as did his vigorous endorsement of the segregationist academies in the last days of the race and his casual but rather cleverly placed comments to several reporters that he really saw himself as a "red-neck."

Those things were there in the record of his candidacy, and although he could point to his refusal to join the White Citizens Council as evidence of his opposition to that sort of ignorance, he could not cite any actions as a member of the Sumter County Board of Education that indicated his commitment to equal rights for black children in his community. There was, of course, the time in 1966 when he and Rosalynn had voted against a resolution in the Plains Baptist Church that endorsed the segregation of the congregation. He had not only voted against it, he had spoken against it, and only one other person had voted with the Carters. The resolution had passed and Carter had remained in the church.

It wasn't much of a defense against the charges that might be raised when he started his candidacy. There had to be something more—even more than making a holiday out of King's birthday, and even more than hanging his portrait in the capitol. He and those who were in on his secret knew he needed prominent black men and women to attest to his liberalism. Consequently, by the end of 1973, Jimmy Carter had come full circle again. In 1966, he had sought the help of blacks and liberals in his race against Lester Maddox. In 1970, he had sought the support of white conservatives in his race against Carl Sanders. For 1976, he would be reaching for the blacks and liberals again, and he had not forgotten how.

Jody Powell remembers an afternoon late in 1973 when Carter summoned a small group of black officials and community leaders to his office at the capitol. "It was small potatoes, as I recall," Powell says. Yet, when the meeting ended and the group began to leave, Martin Luther King, Sr., lingered behind. He seemed distraught. There were tears in his eyes. Carter went to him and put his hand on his brawny shoulder and asked what was bothering him. King told the governor that in all of his long life, as a man who had always tried to seek the right things for his people, and as the father of a man who had risen to some prominence and importance in the country, he had never before been invited into the office of the governor of Georgia. "It is quite an honor," the old man said, and Carter looked deep into his eyes and gave his elbow a firm squeeze. Martin King, Sr., was a lifelong registered Republican, as were many black men of his generation. He had not particularly liked John Kennedy at all and had to be persuaded by his son to vote for him in 1960. But in 1976 he was Jimmy Carter's man, even with his strong reservations, and it made a substantial difference in the outcome of the election. "He's the finest politician I've ever met," the old man would say again and again as the presidential campaign progressed. "He's one of the finest men I ever met," he would insist—and from Watts to Harlem to the south side of Chicago, the old preachers would nod their heads and tell their congregations what "Daddy" King had said about this fine, upstanding young gentleman from Georgia.

Still, Carter needed more black support than that of an aging Republican preacher—who still had doubts about him, anyway—and he thought he knew just where to find it. In the summer of 1974, he told Andrew Young his secret, and although it wasn't much of a secret anymore (some state legislators were snickering behind his back and questioning his sanity by then), Young was still amazed at Carter's request for assistance from him.

The two had met in 1970 at the home of a liberal Atlanta architect, Paul Muldauer, when both were running for office, Carter for governor, and Young for Congress against a right-wing Republican conservative, Fletcher Thompson, who held his seat as a result of the same aberrant moment in Georgia politics that had produced Lester Maddox as a man of power. The Fifth District seat in Congress—representing most of metropolitan Atlanta and much of its suburbs—had always been Democratic, but in 1966, when Maddox became the gubernatorial nominee of the Democratic party,

Charles Weltner, the young incumbent, decided that he could not in good conscience run for reelection on the same Democratic ticket with a man who had defied attempts to integrate his restaurant by handing out weapons to customers. Weltner dropped out of the race and Thompson stepped into the seat as a result of the general election. Two years later, Weltner tried to get it back, but he was unsuccessful, and in 1970, Young, then a thirty-eight-year-old neophyte in electoral politics, had won the Democratic nomination. When he met Carter at a fund-raising cocktail party at the Muldauer home that night, he was in trouble. Thompson, the incumbent, was running television advertisements that included a film clip in which Young seemed to be endorsing the militant Black Panther organization and "the destruction of the Western world." He would lose, but he would carry the black precincts solidly and win an impressive number of white votes as well. Carter liked Young. Moreover, Carter needed Young, and he called him and asked him to consider endorsing his presidential candidacy. Young had served for several years as Martin King's right-hand man, a tough negotiator during the string of demonstrations that had helped to change the South. He would be a prize catch for Carter.

But Young was also a very deliberate man. He had learned from experience, long experience, that the words of a man in his position often took on a meaning or an import beyond their original intent. The film clip used against him in 1970 was an example. He had not intended to endorse the destruction of anything, much less the Western world, yet there it was in living color on the television screen. It was all out of context, and he had eventually overcome its impact and won the seat in Congress in 1972, but he had learned to be careful, very careful, about what he said and how he said it. That was not always immediately clear to those who watched him from a distance. He was handsome and at times debonair. He seemed quick with words, occasionally glib—a man who gave the appearance of being perfectly at ease in the midst of loquacious banter from his fellow black clergymen or his peers in the Congress. But beneath it all, he was a very cautious man, measuring what he wanted to say or meant to say, before he said it, against the way in which it could be heard or interpreted—and the decision he was facing after Carter's call was precisely the sort of decision that warranted that kind of cautious deliberation. He would take a long time with this one, he thought. No glib ad-libs, no cracks, no homilies and, above all, no response that could be misinterpreted.

Not that Andrew Young lacked spontaneity. He had not survived the civil rights years with prepared texts and written statements. Once, years before, when he was at the core of yet another racial confrontation, he had climbed to the top of a burned-out car in a run-down section of Charleston, South Carolina, and watched a large group of angry young black men squaring off with an approaching line of local white police, all in riot gear. Bricks, bottles and rocks had already come arching out of the back ranks of the blacks, and a blaring loudspeaker from the other side had already ordered them to disperse or be arrested. It was a summer Saturday in the low country of South Carolina, and the air was sweet with the semitropical blossoms, the smell of the nearby ocean and the heavy odor of impending violence. Young was sure of it. One more rock would do it. He had seen it before, in Selma and St. Augustine and Birmingham and a dozen other ugly battlefields back down the long road he had walked with Dr. King and all the others. He had to try to stop what he knew was about to happen, he decided, and so he had climbed to the top of the old car and raised a battery-operated bullhorn to his lips.

"Now, brothers," he began, shouting, "you all listen to me a minute, will you?" They turned toward him, startled by the new voice of authority on the scene. "You know," he said, "I've been thinking about how we could let the white folks in this town know that all we want to do is join with them in making things right for everybody. Isn't that what we all want?" There was no sign of assent from the crowd, but at least they were listening. Their attention was on him, not the white police. "And you know, I was also thinking about going to church tomorrow," Young continued, struggling to find a theme, to keep them with him and away from the long line of police. "I always go to church on Sunday, don't you?" he said. There were a few chuckles, but not many. The young black men were not particularly interested in some black preacher's church jokes. Still, there was something compelling about the fellow up there on the shell of the burned-out car. "You know, the one thing I don't like about going to church is that us black folks are usually too poor to have air conditioners," he said. "Lord, it gets hot in our churches, doesn't it?" The black men were listening casually. "The ladies get to fanning and the preacher's sitting up there wishing he could take off his coat and the sweat's rolling down him like the River Jordan, but he knows he can't take off his coat because that wouldn't be dignified. You brothers are lucky. You're not preachers and you don't have to be dignified. You can go to church if you want and take off your coats if you want to."

He was still groping, vamping, but the black men had inched toward him a bit and the line of police had retreated the same, minute distance. The gap between the two forces was widening. "So, what I was thinking about was why don't all of us go to church tomorrow morning where it's cool?" he said. "That's what I was thinking about, brothers, and I thought you'd like to know. We'll just all get up in the morning and put on our Sunday clothes and march ourselves right on down to the white folks' churches. They're cool, you know. The white ladies don't fan in those churches. They've got air conditioning in the white folks' churches, and I was just standing here thinking that that's what we all ought to do on the Lord's day, just to show the white folks that we love the Lord just like they do, and all we want to do here in Charleston is help them make things right for everybody. What do you say? You all want to go to church with me in the morning?" The whoop was unanimous. It had worked magnificently. The moment had passed. Non-violence had been preserved, and the next morning, scores of black Charlestonians—and Andrew Young—worshiped in the previously all-white congregations of the old city.

Years later, he would recall how he felt, standing on that old car, watching the beginnings of a riot, and he would laugh easily and say yes, yes, he had been frightened, and yes, yes, he had indeed started to talk before he knew what he meant to say, but no, no, he hadn't really prayed that day. "There just wasn't enough time to pray," he remembered. "I just started rattling on and on and it was so hot that I really did think about having to go to some steaming church the next morning and to tell you the truth I began to dread it—and the rest of it just sort of rolled out without any more cogitation than that."

But there would be no instant, extemporaneous answer for Carter, however. Now, Young was a member of the U.S. House of Representatives, the first of his race to win a seat there from the Deep South in nearly a century. He was a leader, not just in Atlanta or in Georgia, but in the minds of several million black people all over the country who remembered his close association with Dr. King. Now, he was being asked to back a Southern white man for President, a white man whose ancestors had owned slaves and whose own father, just one generation removed, had worked black people as though they still were, steadfastly maintaining the status quo of segregation and tenant farming and sharecropping with them in the time-honored tradition of disproportionate shares. Moreover, this white man whose presidential candidacy he was being asked to endorse had tainted himself, however lightly, with the same stripe that identified most other white politicians in the South. He had run a campaign aimed at the instincts of white people who feared integration. He had worked hard and often on that course without much regard to the language he used or the techniques he applied to attract the support of the people who had been drawn in past elections to the railings of George Wallace and the rantings of Lester Maddox.

Still, it wasn't quite that simple, and Andy Young knew it. This same fellow had been a better governor, racially, than any ever elected in Georgia. He not only had said the right things—after he had won—but he had also worked hard, really quite hard, to create new jobs for black people in state government, and Young thought Carter had tried honestly to assure that, in the administration of the government, the last vestiges of the old ways were being erased. He had made good friends in the black community and he had not been patronizing about it. He had given politically and he had taken politically, and as Leroy Johnson had often said, when he had said he would deliver, he had delivered.

But what in the name of God had possessed him to run for President? He had no chance of winning, none at all, and that bothered Young a great deal. If he climbed in bed with Carter, he would go to sleep with a loser. It would be one more failure, one more useless stand, one more opportunity to have real impact gone with the wind of a foolish dream by this foolish man. Moreover, if he backed Carter, Young knew he stood a good chance of becoming a pariah not only among blacks but among white liberals as well. He was well-known, respected, a man of influence in the foundation boardrooms in New York as well as the back streets of black ghettos. He would almost certainly be asked to give his support to some other candidate, to a liberal he knew with at least a sporting chance for the nomination—and if he fell in with Carter and took a lot of black primary votes with him in the early going, Carter would still ultimately lose, and the liberal he might have supported would lose as well, and that would leave Young with no place to go and no influence to wield or trade. His value to a candidate with a chance to win would be lost.

The white liberals would never forget it. Good, sturdy relationships, carefully crafted over the years, would be blown away, perhaps beyond all retrieval, and if there was one thing Andy Young valued, it was his relationships. Not for himself, though he was fast becoming as skilled a political practitioner as any of his colleagues in the House of Representatives, but basically for the commitment he had made so long ago to racial equity. Of all the men who had walked those dusty and sometimes bloody roads, including Dr. King himself, Young seemed to stand head and shoulders above them—in the depth and the extent of his commitment and his gentle, unswerving faith that right would eventually win. He was, perhaps, the last Christian in the bunch, and politics had not changed him—not that much.

It was a gamble, he knew, but finally, painfully, he decided to go with Carter. It was a negative decision, actually, based on a rare surge of Southern provincialism and the rationalization that perhaps his endorsement would, in some way, be of some help to his constitutents in Atlanta. If Carter lost in the early going—and that seemed utterly certain to Young—it would probably not be too late to go to work for someone else. Udall, perhaps, or Harris or maybe even Julian Bond, although they were no longer as close as they had once been. At any rate, the damage would probably be slight. He could stay with Carter through Florida and perhaps help him trim the margin between him and Wallace in that primary—that would be a significant achievement, he thought. If Carter could hold Wallace down to a narrow victory, things would look better for other liberals down the line. He could compensate later, Young thought. He could overcome. He had always believed that.

Julian Bond had no problem at all deciding how to respond to the request of an intermediary that he endorse Carter's candidacy. "Fuck him," said Bond. "I'm going to run myself."

"We didn't much care," Jordan said. "We had Andy and we had 'Daddy' King. We knew that that meant we'd get Coretta [the younger King's widow]. We didn't much care what the great Senator Bond had to say about things."

By mid-1974, when he was in the last year of his term as governor, his presidential campaign was moving even better than Jordan, in his prescient memorandum, could have dreamed, and one of those unwittingly responsible for its progress was Robert Strauss, the chairman of the Democratic National Committee and, in the absence of anybody else, the titular leader of the party. Through Strauss, Carter became chairman of the 1974 Democratic Campaign Committee, a usually thankless and rather lackluster job that requires a great deal of travel, dozens of fund-raising speeches on behalf of Democratic Congressional candidates and a lot of nights in Holiday Inns. Carter was jubilant, however. There was a small party in his office the night the appointment was announced in Washington by Strauss, and he was equally elated when Strauss bought his idea to bring Jordan to Washington to work at the committee for a while. "He said it'd be good experience for the boy, being as how he didn't know much about national politics and all," Strauss remembered later. "Hell, I didn't think much about it, didn't think much about it at all."

Carter, Powell and Jordan did give it considerable thought. It was manna from heaven. The governor would be out on the road, doing what they had come to believe he did as well or better than anyone—meeting people and giving them a reason to like him and remember him, all the while learning what was going on out there in America and establishing some credit, however minimal, in the larger Democratic community. In the meantime, Jordan would be in Washington, inside the Democratic National Committee. "I didn't know how it all worked," Jordan remembered. "I'm not ashamed of that. I just had never had much of a reason or a chance to know—but it was golden, boy, it was golden."

It was also much akin to an engraved invitation to the local fox, requesting the honor of his presence in the henhouse for an extended stay—all expenses paid.

Soon after Brzezinski left the study on that September morning in 1977, Jordan came in to report briefly on a long meeting the afternoon before with Powell, Charles Kirbo, Vice President Mondale and Frank Moore, the White House director of Congressional liaison. Kirbo had been summoned from Atlanta for the session, for after eight months in office, Jimmy Carter was facing his first crisis, and in times of crisis, he turned as he always had to the small coterie of Georgians on whom he had always depended for sound counsel.

Lance, the affable bear he had chosen to run the Office of Management and Budget, was in deep trouble, not from anything he had done or not done during his brief tenure in Washington, but rather because his ethics as a businessman and his campaign funding as an unsuccessful Georgia politician were being called into question by the press and an important Senate committee, and being investigated by the Office of the Comptroller of the Currency, the Securities and Exchange Commission and the Department of Justice. For almost half the summer, Lance had steadfastly maintained his purity—in interviews with individual journalists and in three days of nationally televised testimony before the Senate Governmental Affairs Committee. He had done reasonably well, but Carter and the group that had met at the White House on Sunday afternoon knew that Bert Lance was capable of destroying—however unintentionally—all that Carter had tried to construct during his long campaign and his brief residence in the Oval Office. Carter had run a frequently brilliant campaign that had taken him through the minefields of the primary season to the Democratic nomination and on to his election in November with little more to offer the voters than the image of high-blown morality and rigid ethical standards he worked hard to construct.

In the months since his inauguration, he had continued that thrust, building layer upon layer of image, offering more symbols than substance, and finding that his status in the American mind had remained fairly constant. People believed they had themselves an honest President and they liked the idea. But day after day all through August, a cascade of stories about Bert Lance's past flowed from the media fountain, and when he appeared before the Senate committee on the last weekend in summer, Carter and his White House intimates knew that the specter of the Watergate hearings had been raised in the minds of thousands and thousands of viewers. Still, Lance would not resign and Carter would not ask him to leave. He was remembering, perhaps, the hours they had spent together in Atlanta and the large chunk of Lance's life that had been spent in his behalf in those long-ago days, remembering, perhaps, the early-morning meeting they had had in early 1973 when Lance had told him he hated to leave the Carter Administration but would have to since he planned to run for governor himself the following year.

Carter couldn't have been happier, and he told him so that morning, and the two of them knelt in the governor's office and prayed together concerning Bert's future. Then Lance went home to Calhoun to plan his campaign. Of all the candidates who would eventually join the race, Lance would be the one with least financial problems. His campaign finances were unique. First, he gave the Calhoun bank—of which he was a principal stockholder and former president—a letter and a check for $5000. The money was to be used to offset any expenses incurred by the bank in behalf of his campaign. Moreover, he signed over a savings certificate for slightly more than $100,000. Then, he opened two campaign accounts—and went out to run for governor. The $5000 was quickly gone, but no additional funds followed. The bank was billed for and paid a variety of Lance's campaign expenses. At the end of each month, the bank billed one of the campaign accounts. Sometimes, the campaign organization would pay the bill promptly and legitimately, but frequently its checks would be for more than the account contained. The bank honored the checks, nevertheless.

It was an interesting arrangement. It was also illegal. It was also no different from the manner in which Lance had been operating for years, well within the grand traditions of his wife's family whose overdrafts had never been questioned nor penalized by service charges or interest fees. Since banking regulations prohibited loans of more than $5000 to officers or board members—except for mortgages or educational loans—the big investment dreams Lance nurtured over the years were nourished by overdrafts, interest free. They were gratis lines of credit, and they were richly productive for him. By the winter of 1973–1974, when he formally announced his gubernatorial campaign and publicly disclosed his net worth, he was a millionaire. He was worth $3.4 million, to be exact, he said—and that, as much as anything else, made him a loser.

Still, Lance did not seem to mind, not the way Carter's loss in 1966 had driven Jimmy into a deep depression. He laughed about it with Carter and went up to New York and borrowed $2.6 million from the Manufacturers Hanover Trust Company and came back to Atlanta and, with two partners, purchased controlling interest in the National Bank of Georgia, the fifth largest bank in the state. He became its chief executive officer, promptly sold it his own airplane at a profit and began building its image and its assets, just as he had at the Calhoun bank. He appeared in the bank's television commercials and radio spots, smiling lopsidedly and drawling, and he opened branch offices and combed the South for new business and in 1975 he personally approved a $3.9 million line of credit to his old friend, Jimmy Carter, who was expanding his peanut business down in Plains as well as running for President of the United States, and when he was elected the next year, his very first appointment was Thomas Bertram Lance, Jr., as director of the Federal budget.

After all, Carter had promised over and over again during his campaign that he would bring order and sensibility to the government's money-handling, and that he would eventually balance the budget. Who else but Bert would he want in the job most significant for those two objectives? Lance said yes, immediately. "Listen," he said, "if Jimmy Carter wants me to come to Washington to be his chauffeur, I'll just go out and buy me a uniform and a little cap." Carter asked him to get rid of his National Bank of Georgia stock since it might present the appearance of a conflict of interest in his new job—and Carter had solemnly told the voters that he not only would avoid actual conflicts but even their appearance should he become President.

Lance had known that the sale of the stock would cost him considerable money since the mandatory nature of the transfer would make it a buyer's market. But, he said, "I think I can work that out." That was his creed. He had always worked things out and Carter believed he could. But the stock went down and no buyers could be found and the National Bank of Georgia failed to pay a dividend and Lance found himself going rapidly broke. He asked the President to extend his deadline for selling the stock, hoping that, like the South, it would rise again, and when the President took his request to the Senate committee that had approved the arrangement in the first place, Carter's first crisis began.

For weeks, there were stories about Lance's peculiar campaign financing and about an agreement between the Calhoun bank and the Comptroller's office to correct its lenient overdraft policies and about a Justice Department investigation of the campaign overdrafts that had been closed the day before Carter had nominated Lance and about the cancellation of the Comptroller's agreement soon after Lance learned in mid-November that he would be a part of the new Administration. And there were more. In dribs and drabs, but damaging dribs and drabs, it became clear that Lance had tacitly made the New York bank understand that after he got his $2.6 million loan and purchased his stock in the Atlanta bank, he would certainly be favorably disposed to placing large amounts of the Atlanta bank's funds in the New York bank—a correspondent account, it was called. Interest free, of course. It also became known that Lance had reneged on his pledge to the New York bank to pass on any stock dividends his Atlanta stock might produce as additional collateral for the $2.6 million loan. It was a standard agreement in any loan of that size secured by stock. Instead, Lance used the fourteen thousand shares paid to him in late 1975 as a dividend by the Atlanta bank as collateral for a $150,000 loan from another New York institution, the Chemical Bank of New York. When Manufacturers Hanover Trust Co. insisted on having the additional shares, he stalled them. Finally, he went to the First National Bank of Chicago and borrowed more than $3 million. He then paid off the New York banks but was still substantially in debt to banks in Atlanta and Knoxville, Tennessee.

That was the way things were done in the banking world, Lance explained before the committee. His conscience was clear, he drawled, but the committee pressed him and the network cameras focused in on his pudgy face and his small eyes. He had hired Clark Clifford, the gray eminence of Washington attorneys, an inside man in several administrations and a former Secretary of Defense under Lyndon Johnson—and although Clifford gave his defense a certain air of elegant respectability, the questions continued.

Had he not used the airplane to fly people to New Orleans and to University of Georgia football games? Yes, yes, he had, but that was business. Had he not used the airplane for purely personal reasons—getting back and forth between his enormous Atlanta mansion and his sprawling summer home on Georgia's Atlantic coast, taking his children back and forth to college—and had he not allowed Jimmy Carter to use it when he was campaigning for President back in 1975? Yes, said Lance, that was all true, but what of it?

But there was more to it than could be dealt with by simply saying that business was conducted best in that way. The questions were honing in on the White House by then. What did the President know and when did the President know it? Was the President involved in the cancellation of the agreement between the Comptroller's Office and the Calhoun bank? Was the President aware of the fact that the Justice Department investigation was closed on the eve of his public nomination of Lance? Didn't the President perceive at least the appearance of some conflicts in Lance's behavior, and had he not promised that he would not tolerate that in his Administration? Was the President maintaining one standard for other appointees and a different one for Lance?

There was much too much damage wrought by that last weekend of the summer of 1977 to be repaired easily, the group that met on Sunday afternoon at the White House decided. The question of the propriety or legality of Bert's banking and campaign techniques seemed no longer to be relevant, they agreed. Most of them had known that for quite some time, but when the President arrived that evening from Camp David, there was still no certainty that the problem had been solved. It was still the President's decision and Jimmy Carter showed no signs of relenting on his decision to stand behind Lance all the way. They were friends, and none of this fit any of the blueprints he had drawn for his Presidency. Carter was a methodical man, and he did not appreciate surprises. Nor did he respond well to them.

Informally, the Carter presidential campaign brain trust had figured the most opportune time for him to announce his candidacy would be in mid-1975, or perhaps a bit earlier, depending on what other candidates were doing. He would leave the governorship in January 1975, and that would give him plenty of time that year to break the news and hit the road. But in early August 1974, the chart was amended. Nixon resigned, Ford became President, and the day after Ford was booed at the little church outside Washington, a handsome young Alabamian named Morris Dees called on the governor of Georgia. His name was not on the public schedule of Carter's activities that day. Carter had asked his secretary not to record it.

Morris Dees was not a man with any interest in Georgia

state government. He was an iconoclastic liberal millionaire from Montgomery who had put together the highly productive fund-raising effort of George McGovern in 1972. Carter had called him the previous Friday, the day after Nixon's resignation, and asked him to come to Atlanta to talk about "some items of mutual interest," Dees later recalled. "I didn't know if he could win or not," he said, remembering the meeting, "but I didn't know anybody else who could either, so when he asked me if I wanted to come aboard and raise funds for him, I said I would. Besides, I was glad to see a Southerner besides George Wallace get into it."

Still, as deeply into the campaign as he was by then, Carter was having some difficulty deciding actually to announce his candidacy. "I remember he kept saying he was going to feel awfully funny getting up and telling folks he was fixing to run for President," Kirbo said. "Now, he wanted to run. He'd already made up his mind to that, but he was worried about folks making fun of him—he can't stand to be laughed at in that way—and he just kept jiggling with the timing of his announcement. So, one day, I remember, we were talking about it, and he started in again on how high-heeled it was going to look when he actually did it, and I said, 'Jimmy, one of these days you're just going to have to raise up on your hind legs and tell them you're fixing to run.' Well, he said, he knew that was right, and I said something like, 'Well, then, why don't you just go on and do it?'—and I believe it wasn't long after that that he did. Just raised up and did it."

The membership of the National Press Club in Washington, like the rest of the American journalism establishment, prides itself on its cynicism, and Carter's formal announcement there on December 12, 1974, prompted yawns and a few chuckles, but little more. It was not even the first hat in the ring; Morris Udall had beaten him to it. But Carter's

speech that day was notable in that it became, as his campaign platform in 1970 had, the matrix for his presidential
campaign rhetoric. It set the tone and pointed the way, and
he seldom changed it in the twenty-three months of travel
and handshaking and speaking that followed.

There was a crisis in public confidence, he said, and that
was what was wrong with the country. It was a malaise that
could only be cured by the election of a man in whom the
people could once again believe. "I'll never lie to you," he
promised. That was it. Tax reform and welfare reform and a
strong national defense and a more open government with
greater privacy for the individual—all of that was included,
but it was included as a product of the basic premise, the
need for a President the people could believe. "It is now
time to stop and to ask ourselves the question which my last
commanding officer, Admiral Hyman Rickover, asked me
and every other young naval officer who serves or has
served in an atomic submarine," Carter said quietly, paus-
ing just before his final sentence. "For our nation, for all of
us, that question is: 'Why not the best?' "

In months to come, there would be scholarly essays on the
"evolution" of Carter's campaign strategy. There was never
much of an evolution after his campaign began. It was all
there in his first speech, and from that day forward, his run
for the White House was merely a reiteration—a constant,
dogged, day-to-day, week-to-week, interview-to-interview
reiteration—of all that he had proposed before the National
Press Club in the last month of 1974. There were adjustments to the rhetoric (Rafshoon called it "fine tuning"), and
there were new elements injected by exterior force, but
Carter's campaign for the Presidency, like his successful
campaign for governor, was the product of a reasoned, calculated analysis of the electorate—of what positions on what
issues would strike the most responsive chords among the
voters, an application, again, of the approach that Wallace
had perfected—and once that judgment had been made,
Carter seldom strayed far from the blueprint it produced. He

was back on the *K-1* again, following the program perfected
ashore, making adjustments only when absolutely necessary. On the surface, his campaign would appear to be homi-
letic, populistic, but beneath it all lay the logic and the precision of the nuclear engineer.

His two candidacies in 1966—first for Congress and then
for governor—were the last occasions on which Jimmy
Carter would present himself purely to voters. In 1970 and
again in 1976, his campaigns would present a candidate tai-
lor-made for the occasion. He was doing the best he could
with what he had, and what he had was a block of evidence
that indicated strongly to him that the best candidate is the
candidate who adapts himself to the instincts of the voters
within the specific context of the campaign moment. Having
dismissed a distinctive ideology as excess baggage, he
brought to his presidential pursuit from its very conception
the credentials of flexibility. He would not argue many issues, he decided, but he would project personality. He
would not espouse many specific positions, he decided, but
he would wholeheartedly embrace universally approved
possibilities. On almost all matters of substance—just the
sort of thing that could suddenly abort a presidential candidacy—he would offer broadly phrased opinions, replete
with disclaimers and open to broad and, if necessary, argu-
able interpretation.

Later, after his campaign was under way, he would try to
explain his strategy in terms that left him some dignity. "In
1968, and in 1972, there was a really strong division among
the supporters of the different candidates, all depending of
course on whatever positions they took on whatever issues
they were interested in or involved in—for or against abortion, for example, or for or against gun control, or for or
against the war, or for or against amnesty, for example—but
I don't believe that's the case in 1976 at all. I think our people have been hurt and scarred so badly by Vietnam, Cambodia, Watergate, the CIA revelations, that they're just simply looking for somebody they can trust—just somebody

they believe they can believe. I'm not saying that nobody cares anymore about this issue or that issue, but I don't think that's what most people are thinking about when they vote," he said.

As part of Jordan's spring-training regimen, Carter began in late 1972 to travel abroad, using what he often called "my own state department," the Coca-Cola Co., as his travel agent, his embassy in the country he was visiting and as often as not as his means of transportation. His membership in the Trilateral Commission also afforded him the opportunity to travel and eventually, again at Jordan's suggestion, he established trade missions for Georgia in West Germany, Brazil and Japan. On every visit to every foreign capital, he paid attention to names and to rank, and when he began his presidential campaign he would speak fondly of his "good friend," Golda Meir, or of the "long conversations" he had had with Japan's Takeo Fukuda. It did not matter that his relationship with foreign officials was, in reality, just slightly casual; this was the whole of his foreign-policy experience, and he was determined to make the most of it—to present it in the best possible light. He was never timid about allowing it to stand as the extent of his background in diplomacy, arguing, with a thesis that sounded much like Wallace's know-nothingism, that those who had had so much experience in running American foreign policy had not really done so well.

Besides, as he pointed out, he was persuaded that that was one of those issues in which voters might very well be interested but which would not play a primary role in their ultimate decision on whom to support. "I don't give a damn about abortion or amnesty or right-to-work laws," he once told a reporter. "They're impossible political issues. In fifty years, people will still be arguing about them and they won't be any closer to resolving them than they are now. I can't possibly help anyone—including myself—if I'm out on the edge of such volatile things, and I don't intend to be. It would be foolish. If I'm going to lose, it's not going to be because I staked my whole candidacy on a ban on abortions or the right to have them."

It was a thesis that would run true throughout his campaign. It would be shown through a letter unearthed from the State Archives in Atlanta that Carter, as a candidate in 1970 and as governor, had opposed any repeal of the Georgia law which allows nonunion shops to operate. Compared with his 1976 position that he would not oppose such a repeal on the Federal books, it seemed to have been a substantial reversal of opinion. Yet Carter simply shrugged the whole thing off. "Look," he said, "if labor can get such a repeal through Congress, I'll sign it—but I'm not going to work for it. That's what I meant back in 1970 and that's what I meant when the letter was written." Once again, it was a matter of intent and once again, he explained, his intent was pure and blameless. In his first year as governor, for instance, he had proclaimed "American Fighting Man's Day" soon after the conviction of Lieutenant William Calley for the murder of Vietnamese civilians. The trial had taken place at Fort Benning, near Columbus, Georgia, and less than an hour's drive from Plains, and the guilty verdict had stirred a great deal of protest, especially in that part of southwest Georgia. Carter, who had never taken an antiwar position either as a private citizen, candidate or governor, asked that the citizens of Georgia show their pride for American soldiers by driving with their lights on that day. It was widely interpreted as a means of expressing his own support for Calley, but when he was asked about it four years later on "Face the Nation," the CBS television panel program, he said, of course, that was not the case at all. "I don't think that was said in support of or in opposition to the conviction of Lieutenant Calley. As you know, the Calley conviction took place in Georgia; it was a very highly emotional thing, and rather than focusing the attention of Georgia people on the Calley case itself, I tried to hold down violence and to take the sharp edge off the Calley conviction, which was a very vivid issue in Georgia at that time, by saying 'Let's think about all of our fighting men that did perform well.' But I have never been a supporter of Calley nor have I ever deplored his conviction nor have I ever in any way supported what he did. I think it was abominable, what he did."

So, in retrospect, one thing became another, and Jimmy Carter's intentions remained above reproach. In all of the give-and-take between himself and the public and the press throughout the long campaign, Carter projected himself as a candidate who had not made mistakes. On only two occasions did he look back with some measure of publicly stated apology. He said that "perhaps" he had not been quick enough to grant his black neighbors in Plains their rights as citizens and that "perhaps" he had not been quick enough to recognize the sins of the Vietnam War. (Rosalynn explained her husband's silence on the latter issue as simply a matter of not having a forum in which to speak. "He was just a governor, you know," she said.)

Later during the campaign, Carter was badgered by his staff and by Young into apologizing for his "ethnic purity" remarks, a commentary on the sanctity of neighborhoods that almost cost him the support not only of Young but of Coretta King and the skeptical Martin Luther King, Sr. He had responded to a reporter who had asked him about the feasibility of distributing low-income housing in the suburbs by saying that he saw "nothing wrong with ethnic purity being maintained. I would not force the racial integration of a neighborhood by government action, but I would not permit discrimination against a family moving into the neighborhood."

The storm raged around him for several days, costing him valuable time and momentum in his campaign. Powell insisted that he had made a mistake and ought to apologize for it and forget it as much as he could and go on to the next step in his campaign. Carter, however, would hear nothing of apologies. He was adamant. Young called to say that if he didn't apologize, he would leave his campaign. Carter apologized and quickly, then flew down to Atlanta for a reunion and a bear hug from the easily persuaded "Daddy" King. The portrait at the capitol, the birthday holiday and the invitation to the governor's office had paid off. It was like watching the first few sprouts of corn come popping through the top soil. Carter was both relieved and jubilant that a major crisis had passed without serious injury, but behind his apology lay an even more significant insight. As he told friends, he still didn't see what he had to apologize for. "The only thing I'm really sorry about is that the whole thing was misinterpreted," he said. "I meant every word I said. People just misunderstood me."

Essentially, though, what had happened to Carter during what came to be known as "the ethnic purity episode" was that he had departed from his script. He had taken a position on an issue and he had quickly discovered that he had been right all along. It was something he just couldn't afford to do, and something he did less and less as the campaign moved along.

There was a chronic tendency on Carter's part, adopted by some of his aides, to complain about being misunderstood. If some Iowans thought they had heard him say that he opposed a constitutional amendment banning abortion and others thought they heard him support such a move, it was only because he was misunderstood. If one reporter believed he had heard him say in the morning that he would dismiss Clarence Kelley as director of the Federal Bureau of Investigation and then say in the afternoon he was uncertain what to do about Kelley should he become President, he had been misunderstood again. If hundreds of voters thought they heard him say he would include the home-mortgage interest deductions in his package of "loopholes" to be eliminated in the name of tax reform, that was another misunderstanding.

Since the essence of his candidacy was the projection of

an honest, straightforward, candid man, the very suggestion of equivocation was blasphemy; but since the most effective rhetoric of his campaign was the rhetoric that could appeal to all the voters—or as many as he could stretch his thesis to include—equivocation was mandatory. "The problem," Carter explained one day during his campaign, "is that reporters like to take little snippets of what I say and then compare them to little snippets of what I've said before and make something of it. We're discussing large, complex, complicated issues in this campaign and it isn't fair to me or to the voters to treat them in little snippets like that."

The problem, in reality, went a bit deeper than his appraisal indicated. The problem was that Jimmy Carter wanted to have it both ways. He wanted all the votes, not a 90 percent majority, and he had already proved to himself that, although it seemed an impossible task, he was quite capable of trying—and so in many cases, he tried to have it both ways: to attract both liberals and conservatives to him on the same issue, to please segregationists and integrationists, farmers and Wall Street bankers, Eastern sophisticates and Oklahoma yahoos. One of his closest aides in the campaign thought it was a compulsive trait. "I don't believe he can help it," he said. "I think he really believes that without compromising himself, he can walk from one room where he's met with the Conference of Catholic Bishops and convinced them that he's against abortion and walk right into another room and persuade a caucus from the National Organization of Women that he's with them on abortion; and if you talked to him then and asked him about it, he'd say that both groups had agreed with him on abortion."

Carter had had his first sip of victory in January 1976. It had been only a minute droplet—a plurality of the votes in the sparsely populated Iowa caucuses—but it had been more than enough to provide the momentum necessary to carry him into the wintry bitterness of a New Hampshire primary, the first in the skein of thirty that he would contest to one degree or another during the campaign year. He had won in Iowa because he had applied the principles of his 1970 gubernatorial campaign to that state—day after day of personal, face-to-face electioneering, with Powell always close by taking names and addresses for the thank-you notes and the follow-up efforts—and he proposed to do the same thing in New Hampshire. "I don't really believe this, of course," he said one day in February, "but I like to think that if I could shake the hand of every voter and just sit down and talk with them all a little bit, I'd get every damned vote—every single one of them."

That was what he was trying to do on another February morning when he flew into the teeth of a snowstorm (and damned near into one of the White Mountains) on his way to keep a day of campaign appointments in Berlin, New Hampshire, a tiny, industrial, Democratic enclave in the far northern reaches of the state. Inexplicably, he found himself scheduled to visit a Catholic elementary school, and shortly past noon, while the storm raged white outside the wire-protected windows of the little gymnasium, he stood on the free-throw line amid a sizable assembly of small children. He seemed perfectly at ease, despite the snickering of several reporters who wondered why a presidential candidate who needed every vote he could get was spending his valuable time in the company of youngsters who wouldn't be eligible until future elections. Smoothly, Carter began talking to the children. Abruptly, those listening realized that he was offering them the same, standard, "stump speech" he gave his adult audiences.

"Our country's been hurt," he said. "It's been hurt by Watergate and the CIA revelations and Vietnam and Cambodia. But our system of government hasn't been hurt. We've still got a strong system of government, haven't we?" The children all nodded gravely, and Carter continued—softly, evenly, smiling that ingratiating smile that includes just a slight, almost imperceptible nod of the head and tilt of the face. "No," he said, "Watergate hasn't hurt our system of government. It's still strong. Watergate hasn't hurt our basic economic assets. They're still strong—but most important, Watergate hasn't hurt the spirit of the American people. They're still strong, too." The children were entranced. They gazed up at him and they listened and they heard exactly what he had been telling their parents and everybody else who would listen for over a year. "You know," he concluded, "if we could just have a government as good and as honest and as decent and as competent and as compassionate and as filled with love as are the American people, that would be wonderful thing—and I believe we can, don't you?"

The kids agreed. The gymnasium erupted into enthusiastic applause, wild and happy shrieks and excited screams. They thronged him, grabbing his ankles and his legs, clutching at his coat, reaching for his hand. "It was unbelievable," he said later that day. It was also the basic force of his campaign, reduced and compressed into a single moment. The strength he brought to his campaign was the strength of a man with one simple message: you can trust me. The children did, almost instinctively, and for the next ten months more and more of their parents and their parents' counterparts followed their lead.

Fred Harris was saying that "privilege" was the issue. Morris Udall was framing his efforts with appeals for specific, ideological loyalties. Henry Jackson was droning on and on about his experience. Birch Bayh was saying he was proud to be a politician. Sargent Shriver was invoking the memories of his dead brothers-in-law—but Jimmy Carter was asking people not only to vote for him but to trust him as well. "If I ever lie to you, if I ever mislead you, if I ever avoid a controversial issue, then don't vote for me," he said, "because I won't be worthy of your vote if I'm not worthy of your trust." He cornered the trust market and he cornered it early, and once he had, though the campaign would have its ups and downs for him, it was never really in doubt, so deep was the country's thirst for someone—anyone—it could trust.

By March, despite the miscalculations in Massachusetts, he had effectively disposed of Wallace in Florida. By the end of April, he had eliminated Jackson in Pennsylvania. By early June, even with Humphrey standing by once again performing his impressive Hamlet, Jimmy Carter had won the Democratic presidential nomination, and he had won it because, as the polls had shown him and as his instincts had told him, there was really only one issue in the 1976 campaign, and no one had approached him in his skillful exploitation of it.

"Without the trust thing, he couldn't have made it," Caddell, his pollster, said after the convention. "But he was the only one who could have used it as the basic thrust of a presidential campaign. Most people would really rather trust other people than distrust them, except in politics; most people have a reason to distrust most candidates. Jimmy was a stranger in town. They had no reason to distrust him and he didn't give them one."

Perhaps not intentionally, but even in his inexorable drive to the nomination, Carter's rhetoric had raised several questions about his credibility. Jordan, in the infant days of the campaign, had stressed to the candidate that his role as governor could become a productive part of his presidential pursuit if he could relate it to the larger responsibilities he was seeking. He had managed a large bureaucratic organization as governor and he could manage a large bureaucratic organization as President; he had brought wholesale reform to Georgia government and he would do the same as the Chief Executive of the Federal apparatus; he had reorganized the state government and he would reorganize the mess in Washington; he had brought order out of chaos and he would do the same in the White House. As governor, he had taken an admirable nonpolitical approach to governmental appointments. The judges he named were chosen on the basis of ability and experience, not connections. He filled his cabinet with both men and women of high competence and integrity—and he would do so as President. It was all fairly innocuous material, but Jordan was right. If handled well, his record as governor could become a valuable part of his campaign. It had just one weakness. Carter was drawn to hyperbole.

He came from a part of Georgia where, as David Nordan, the political editor of the *Atlanta Journal* once explained, the inhabitants are wont to describe a pretty good mule as the "best damn mule in the world." Hence, he would say again and again during his campaign that in reorganizing the Georgia bureaucracy, 278 of 300 agencies were abolished. That was true, technically, and Carter knew it, but the fact of the matter was that only a small percentage of those 278 agencies he eliminated were actually funded by the state government or were functioning. He was prone to do the same thing when he spoke about the welfare reforms the Carter Administration had fostered in the state. They had created hundreds of new jobs for poor mothers who came to work at child-care centers, he said. They were jobs, of course, but they were nonpaying jobs and existed only because many of the mothers, having brought their children to the centers, had no place else to go and simply hung around and helped with the children. He had brought zero-based budgeting to state government and saved millions of dollars in taxpayers' money, he said. That was hard to demonstrate, except through the same sort of fiscal wand-waving that his opponents in the state used to show that it was definitely not true. He had kept the cost of state government down and prevented the bureaucracy from becoming bloated (one of his favorite words), but the actual statistics showed that because of inflation and the addition of several thousand new jobs, the cost and size of Georgia government kept growing during his term—just as it had during Maddox's and Sanders's and every other governor's since Richard Russell had left in the early 1930s and gone to Washington.

The fact of the matter was that Carter had been an effective governor. The problem was that in the context of national politics, in presenting or defending the only record he had, he seemed constantly to enlarge upon it or to enhance it or, at times, deliberately to exaggerate its achievements and its distinctions. Like the *Pomfret,* his government was the best in the country. He had the best damn mule in the country. (Even after he had been President for several months, he could not escape the call. He walked into a room full of visitors to the White House, answered a few questions and then began his next response by saying, "As you know, I'm a nuclear physicist.")

But that weakness for hyperbole had made him vulnerable to a press already cynical of most men who would offer themselves for public office. One afternoon in New Hampshire, for instance, Carter and a reporter sat across from each other at a dingy table in a little restaurant, both fiddling with the cheap, spotted silverware, both playing with the paper napkins that presented Manchester as the veritable hub of the universe. "When you met with Loeb [William Loeb, the right-wing publisher of the *Manchester Union-Leader*], did you make some sort of deal?" the reporter asked, and Carter replied stonily that there had been no deal. "But you did meet with him, didn't you?" the reporter continued, and Carter said yes, there had been such a meeting, but it had not included any discussion of politics. "No politics?" the reporter said. "That's hard to believe." Carter stopped fiddling with the silverware. He stopped playing with the little napkin. He stared at the reporter, his pale eyes unblinking. The vein in his right temple began to pulse. His voice was almost a whisper.

"Listen," he hissed, "I'm not a liar. You get that in your head. I'm not a liar." He stalked away from the table and out of the restaurant, still hungry and mad as hell.

Another reporter sitting nearby asked what had taken place. "He said, and I quote, 'I'm not a liar,'" the first reporter answered.

"Oh, that's not news," his colleague joked. "Everybody knows that. He told us so, didn't he?"

And that, of course, was the problem. By his simple declaration—repeated again and again almost everywhere he went—that he would not lie to reporters, voters or anybody else, Carter had raised the question of his own credibility. It was the lesson of the years just past that American politicians do lie, yet Jimmy Carter was insisting that he did not. It seemed to invite challenge. He and the architects of his campaign had expected the stir and the scrutiny his statement would prompt. He had said he welcomed it. He had said it was good for him and good for the country. He had said the closer the examination of him, the better candidate he would be, and he had said that he would be no better President than he was a candidate. So, come on, boys, he had said, in effect, have at my credibility. I really love it. It's very American. But beneath the invitations for closer scrutiny, he detested the process, positively loathed it—all those questions about his motives and his positions and the mix of his motives with his positions and where was he when the civil rights movement was moving and where was he when the Vietnam War was an issue—and as the weeks dragged on, the vein in his right temple began to throb at every press conference, even before the questions began.

By Monday of the last week of summer in 1977, it had been nearly a month since Carter had conducted a full-scale press conference. The Lance matter had forced him and the White House staff into bunker positions, and Jody Powell had been taking the brunt of the journalists' unceasing questions about the President and Lance, Lance and the banks, Lance and the Senate committee. The pressure had built to a point of real peril, and Powell was thoroughly persuaded that morning that Lance was doomed, one way or another. He suggested as much to the President when he saw him just before the regular Monday morning meeting of the Cabinet, but Carter seemed noncommittal. Instead, he instructed Powell to schedule a press conference for Wednesday afternoon. He had canceled the last one at Powell's suggestion, and he made it clear that, whatever happened with Lance, he wanted his next one to be Wednesday. The press secretary made a note on his yellow legal pad and left. The President picked up his papers and walked through the Oval Office into the Cabinet Room where the men and women he had chosen to help lead the country were waiting. They rose from their large dark leather chairs when he entered.

Given Carter's campaign promises to bring a fresh perspective to Washington as President, it was striking how many members of his Cabinet were not precisely strangers either to the city, to its processes or even to the White House. Cyrus Vance, the Secretary of State, had served under both Kennedy and Johnson, while Harold Brown, the Secretary of Defense, had worked at the Pentagon before, also under Kennedy and Johnson, before becoming president of the California Institute of Technology. W. Michael Blumenthal, Secretary of the Treasury, had served under Johnson before becoming the chief executive officer of the Bendix Co., and Joe Califano, Secretary of Health, Education, and Welfare, had been one of Johnson's most influential domestic aides before joining a prestigious and affluent Washington law firm. Moreover, there were two former Congressmen at the long table as well: Bob Bergland, the Secretary of Agriculture, and Brock Adams, the Secretary of Transportation. Patricia Harris, Secretary of Housing and Urban Development, had become a Washington fixture if not a part of the Washington establishment in several years of activism. She was the only black in the official Cabinet.

There was, of course, some new blood. Ray Marshall, a former university professor from Louisiana by way of Texas, was Secretary of Labor, and Juanita Kreps, the Secretary of Commerce, had been a professor at Duke University before moving to Washington at Carter's invitation. Cecil Andrus, an old friend of the President's from past governors' conferences, was the Secretary of the Interior. For Attorney General—after promising to remove the office from politics and relieve it of the onus of cronyism that had been its longtime burden—Carter had chosen Griffin Bell, an Atlanta attorney, former Federal judge, fellow Sumter Countian, longtime personal friend and one of the people who had sent Carter to Kirbo when he contested the State Senate election in 1962. Also on hand for the meeting were Lance, whose job held a Cabinet-level ranking if not officially in the Cabinet, and Andrew Young, Carter's Ambassador to the United Nations, also a Cabinet-level job.

Carter had envisioned during his campaign a new strength for the Cabinet and when he announced each new nomination at an agricultural extension station just outside of Plains, he had described the individual members of his government team as individually superlative and more than capable of contributing to his basic theory of a robust Cabinet. It had not, however, worked out that way in the first eight months of his Administration. There were certain exceptions, of course. Califano was independent. Brown was aggressive. Vance was adequately resolute. Blumenthal had taken charge of his department. Bell was gradually assuming control at Justice—but as for the rest of them, the President had private doubts. They seemed so deferential to him and that was not what he wanted at all. From their standpoint, however, he had not always seemed receptive to individualistic efforts, prior to White House approval. Carter had come to dread the Cabinet meetings as mere recitations from each department head of past progress or future plans, yet he conducted them in such a manner as to encourage little else. It was, in a sense, a standoff. Carter was unwilling to give more autonomy until the weaker ones were aggressive enough to take it. They were not about to overstep traditional boundaries without the President's encouragement.

For some of the Cabinet, Carter remained an enigma. Cal-

ifano, for instance, was asked to produce a complete welfare-reform package by midsummer, one of Carter's several
rather arbitrary deadlines, all unrelated to the Congressional
calendar or the realistic possibilities of legislative action,
and when the HEW Secretary presented a preliminary draft
of the reform that cost more than the previous welfare program, Carter was not amused. "Hell, if it's going to cost
more we might as well stay with the old one," he snapped at
Califano. His primary aim, it seemed, was to fulfill his promise to balance the budget by 1981—the year he hoped to
begin his second term. Whatever social program did not
contribute to that end would not receive his endorsement.
He wanted programmatic alterations in welfare and housing
policies, not new policies or approaches that would increase
services and costs as well. If he was going to save any
money at all, Carter knew it would have to be in social service areas, for although he had promised again and again to
reduce defense spending by $5 billion to $7 billion annually, he had already given his approval to a Pentagon budget request that would increase spending by that much.

Similarly, his economic package, sent to Congress early in
the year, had included the promise of a $50 tax rebate for
most Americans, but when it had encountered the first sign
of problems in the Senate, he had quickly withdrawn it in
an effort to enhance his standing with the people on Capitol
Hill. So sudden was his reversal, in fact (later defended as
an anti-inflationary, pro-budget balancing decision), that
Blumenthal was out defending the rebate in a speech at almost the very moment Carter was pulling back. When Theo-
dore Sorensen, who had been Kennedy's chief speech-
writer, had run into trouble before the Senate during
confirmation hearings on his nomination by Carter to be director of the Central Intelligence Agency, Carter had
dropped him abruptly; and when Greg Schneiders, his campaign aide-de-camp, became the object of a brief and non-
productive Justice Department inquiry into his unsuccessful
career as a Washington restaurateur, he had been exiled to a

nondescript White House job instead of becoming appointments secretary as Carter had originally wanted.

When the facts about Lance's freewheeling past came to light, though—day after day, edition after edition, all through August and on into September—the President was immovable. He was spending political currency faster than the U.S. Mint could produce legal tender, yet he would not even consider asking Lance to resign. Instead, he interrupted a vacation at Camp David to helicopter back to the White House and tell a nationally televised press conference that he was proud of Lance, despite a most equivocal report by the Comptroller on the Budget Director's banking techniques and ethics. The damned thing would not go away, though, no matter what Carter or anyone else tried, and it hung heavily in the air of the Cabinet meeting on that last Monday of summer, reeking harshly like a harlot's cologne, and as the meeting ended and the leaders of the country filed out to their waiting limousines to be driven back to their respective departments, they left behind them an overlay of melancholia on the White House that no one— not Jordan, not Powell, not Brzezinski, not even the President, apparently—could dispel. The center was not holding. His new code name was "Deacon," and his supermorality had caught up with him.

This supermorality had begun to show a bit in the early days of his campaign. One night in February, up in New Hampshire, he had ended a campaign day with a late-evening speech at a synagogue. He had droned on and on, not a syllable out of place, not an inflection altered from the other speeches he had delivered that day. Finally, it was over and, as usual, he asked if there were questions from the audience. "Governor," called a woman from the back, "we've all read, and may I say with great disappointment, about the— the, uh—the indiscretions in the White House when Jack

Kennedy was, uh, living there. When he was President, you know. You see what I'm talking about?" Carter nodded. "Well," she continued, "I'd just like to ask you what you think about all that. I mean, what are your views on—on, uh—on that sort of stuff?"

Carter smiled down on her, sincerity flowing like a creek down his face. "The Bible says," he began, "that adultery and fornication are wrong. I believe in the Bible. I believe that premarital and extramarital sex are wrong." That was it. There was only a smattering of applause, a suggestion perhaps that there may have been those present who could not bring themselves to endorse with their hands what they had not practiced with other portions of their anatomies. Later, a weary journalist who had spent considerable time with Carter wryly suggested that his answer might have been a mistake.

"What do you mean?" Carter snapped. He was tired and taking it seriously, not at all as the reporter had intended.

"Well, Governor, I think you may have lost the press," the reporter continued. Carter started to smile, but seemed to think better of it and said nothing. "I mean," said the reporter, "coming out against pre- and extramarital sex like that—well, you could hear the notebooks closing and the lens caps clicking shut." Still, Carter said nothing. His face was a blank, but there was something there that suggested to the reporter that he thought it was all reasonably humorous, that he had finally caught on to the joke. "I mean," the reporter pressed on, "here I am, a bachelor out on the road with you, day after day, night after night, and I get laid on the average of maybe once every eleven point five weeks—and now, you want me to give that up, too."

Again, Carter seemed ready to smile, and perhaps even to laugh, but the wheels in his engineer's mind were also spinning at top speed. If he laughed, he presented the possibility that the reporter would write someday that he was amused by off-color humor. He made his choice. "Well," he said, looking stern and unyielding, "I'm sorry, but that's the way I feel."

A few months later, Carter was saying "screw" and "shack up" in an interview with *Playboy* magazine, precipitating a furor that could be measured in points lost in public-opinion polls. The evolution of his appearance in a publication such as *Playboy* was well documented over the next few weeks since it was perceived as a major error in judgment on his part, but the use of the sexual slang provided another insight into the temperament and technique of the Democratic nominee. (Powell had more or less forced the interview on him, saying that *Playboy* readership was large enough to justify his participation; besides, argued Powell, Walter Cronkite and Jerry Brown had also sat down for interviews.)

Just as he seemed to be a hyperbole addict, Carter was prone to try to ingratiate himself with those people he deemed important enough to justify the effort. Around young people, for instance, he spoke of his great interest in and affection for the music of his "good friend," Bob Dylan. Actually, he had met Dylan only once, and the folksinger was genuinely mystified to read during the campaign of their "good" friendship. Similarly, after keeping John Denver, another popular young singer, waiting for nearly four hours on a Georgia-to-California flight (Denver had flown his own jet to Georgia to be able to spend some time with the candidate on the flight to Los Angeles), he finally summoned him to the seat beside him as the plane made its final approach. After ten minutes of conversation, the plane landed, taxied to a stop before a waiting crowd of supporters, and Carter walked to a waiting microphone and told the audience he had just flown out with his "good friend," John Denver.

"Far out," the singer cackled.

Around Dean Rusk, who had become a law professor at the University of Georgia after his eight years as Secretary of State, Carter spoke with sneering disdain for the newspapers that had had the temerity to publish the Pentagon Papers, the purloined secret history of the Vietnam War that rather thoroughly documented various perfidies of the Kennedy and Johnson Administrations, including a few of

Rusk's; but around reporters and their editors, Carter praised the courage of the newspapers that had printed the documents, calling them a "breakthrough in the public's understanding of the war."

It was little wonder then that Carter would talk freely about screwing and shacking up with the interviewers from *Playboy* magazine.

But in addition to the vernacular, the interview provoked yet another example of the candidate's willingness to try, and to try mightily, to avoid admitting a mistake. He had told the magazine that he was fairly certain that he would never lie if he became President, not as Johnson and Nixon had, and when his campaign reached Texas soon after the interview was published, reporters there began asking him about his statement. Well, he groused, it was really quite unfortunate that what he had really said had been "interpreted" that way by the editors of the magazine. Once again, Jimmy Carter had been misunderstood. Once again, the press was misrepresenting him. He was pure and blameless. It was all an "interpretation," and that was the tack he would maintain throughout most of his day in Texas, knowing full well that there had been no "interpretation" at all of his words about Johnson. He had said bluntly that Johnson had lied. Moreover, he knew he had said it.

"There are two things that Jimmy Carter hates," Charles Kirbo drawled one afternoon during the campaign. "He hates making a mistake and he hates admitting it."

But there had been no mistake in Carter's approaches to Mayor Richard Daley, the boss of Chicago and one of the most influential voices in the Democratic party. He had long sought the friendship of other voices in other rooms as well—the Trilateral Commission had been especially helpful to him, as had his stint as the Democratic campaign chairman in 1974—but he had little to show for it until his nomination seemed quite certain. In Georgetown, for instance, that bastion of liberal propriety in Washington, his name had been a joke throughout most of 1975 and early 1976. That was understandable in Georgetown where the parties featured interchangeable guest lists, good wine and good food and a certain sense of political rectitude that issues from being so right so often so long.

One night, Averell Harriman, the doddering patriarch of the community—whose deafness made him as difficult a dinner partner as ever toddled down Q Street—was told by someone just across the table at a candlelit soiree that Carter seemed to be the sort of candidate who just might have a chance for the presidency. Harriman stared incredulously at the bearer of such incredible tidings. "Jimmy Carter," he sniffed. "Jimmy Carter? How can that be? I don't even know Jimmy Carter, and as far as I know, none of my friends knows him either."

But Harriman would eventually get to know Carter and he would ultimately endorse him and would finally say that he was one of "the great leaders of his generation." Harriman would finally come to Carter because there finally seemed no place else to go. That was the thrust of the Carter campaign. He finally left the liberals with no alternative other than Jimmy Carter. They didn't like it, not at all, but they knew they had been had by a master. He just might win, too, they decided, and for once the liberals decided what they really wanted was to win.

But Carter did not focus his attention exclusively on the liberals, the crowd that Jordan had rightly forecast would resent almost any success he enjoyed in the primary campaign. He also went after almost anybody that seemed to be a leader, and he did not ask for ideological credentials. In most cases, they declined to help him. In Texas, he got a cold shoulder from almost every single member of the state's Democratic establishment, all of whom were waiting to back the candidacy of Senator Lloyd Bentsen. Eventually, it appeared that Carter was running as an outsider. He was, of course, but it simply worked out that way. If the Texans had been willing to help him, he would have accepted their aid. What was the purpose of running for President, if not to win? McGovern, whom Carter saw as a suicidal politician, had rejected such a thesis. Carter would not make the same mistake. He would do the best he could with whatever he had or whatever he could get, and if Richard J. Daley, for instance, wanted to help him, why he was most welcome.

Daley did not seem all that interested, however. He had his hands full in the spring of 1976. He was trying to defeat the incumbent Democratic governor, Dan Walker, in the primary with his own machine's candidate, Michael Howlett, the state treasurer. Eventually, Daley and Howlett had won and Walker had become a lame duck. It was Daley's last hurrah in Illinois politics. He would die in December. While he lived, though, he was something to behold in his town. Carter called him a "miracle worker," but if Daley and Howlett had been presented to a casting director for roles in a film about the darker side of American politics, they would have been summarily rejected as caricatures, not characters. They seemed to step full blown from Nast's cartoons: jowly men with pendulum wattles, growly men with thick necks and hammy hands. They might have been born in some smoky back room together, by greed out of avarice, and seen alongside Carter, they presented an almost ludicrous contrast. Still, Carter accepted them both; moreover, like an aristocrat quietly courting a whore, Carter had ardently wooed Daley since the beginning of his campaign. He had gone about it with the same engineer's passion for consistency that had marked his adult life. He had started in 1975 with courtesy telephone calls and casual conversations and, in the long, grinding winter, he had continued to call every few days from wherever he happened to be in the country, just keeping his name there on the mayor's message pad.

When most of Carter's opponents began to roll over on the day after his victory in the Ohio primary, Carter heard an offer from Wallace that was almost too good to refuse. After Carter had narrowly beaten him in Florida, Wallace had wandered off into the wildnerness of national politics, a lost soul searching for a constituency. In a sense, he was like a cuckolded husband. Carter had seduced his people. The wheelchair hadn't helped Wallace, but that had not been the basic problem. He had simply met his match in Carter, a candidate who knew how to say precisely what Wallace himself had been saying for so long in a much more acceptable way—or so everybody seemed to believe, including Wallace. It had hurt Wallace to admit it, but when Carter won in Ohio, Wallace conceded that the Georgian had done what he had never been able to do, though God knows he had tried often enough. He called Carter in Plains that night and told him he would publicly state his own support for him and ask his delegates to do the same. That would have given Carter the nomination, but Carter stepped away from a denouement with a Wallace imprimatur. Instead, he called his "good friend," Daley, and asked instead for the final stroke from him, and he got it. Carter had the prize he had sought, and Daley, once again, had played the role of kingmaker. Nobody was the wiser, everybody was happy and Wallace never really knew what had happened.

Daley must have felt the same sort of satisfaction when Howlett defeated Walker in the spring primary. He had backed him ardently and Walker had fought back just as hard—and in the process, there were hard feelings between Howlett and Walker. They were hurting the Carter campaign in the fall and so, about a week before the election, Carter went there to try to patch things up. He invited Walker, Howlett and Senator Adlai Stevenson 3d to campaign with him across Illinois, but all day long, at rally after rally, Howlett had been booed. They cheered for Stevenson and they cheered for Walker and they cheered for Carter—but for Howlett, they booed.

When the plane finally lifted off for Chicago in the late afternoon, Howlett was in no mood for jokes. Carter was in his private cabin toward the front of the Boeing 727 when the pilot announced the list of guests aboard, starting first with the governor. The reporters aboard, all sitting a few rows behind the politicians, mixed a few cheers with a few good-natured boos, and the governor turned and smiled and waved. "We also have with us today, and we want to welcome him aboard too, Senator Adlai Stevenson," the pilot continued, and once again the reporters responded with another round of applause and hooting. Stevenson turned and waved and smiled. "And we're mighty proud also to welcome the next governor of Illinois, the Honorable Mike Howlett," the pilot concluded. More lustily than before, but with what seemed to be equal good humor, the press corps responded with a rousing chorus of boos, catcalls and a few fragile cheers. Howlett turned slowly in his seat, his face twisted in anger.

"Fuck you!" said the Democratic candidate for governor of the state of Illinois.

A week later, Howlett and Carter lost in Illinois, but Carter's solid base in the South and his victories in New York, Pennsylvania and Ohio were enough for a narrow, electoral college victory over Ford, the incumbent who had never really enjoyed the full advantage of his incumbency, toiling along as a candidate perceived as a bumbler and beneath the considerable weight of his pardon for Nixon. It had been an exhausting campaign for Carter, though not particularly so for Ford, but although it had been occasionally zany and occasionally heated, it had not been especially enlightening for the voters. When it ended, with Ford abed in the White House unaware of the final results and Carter winging home to Plains from his election-night vigil in Atlanta, the soft-spoken man from Georgia was not much better known by the country he would soon govern than when he had begun his pursuit with his speech at the National Press Club nearly nine hundred days before.

He had traveled more than a half-million miles in quest of victory and shaken thousands and thousands of hands in hundreds of communities all across the nation; still, when America awoke on Wednesday morning, there was a prevailing sense that the President-elect was a stranger. He and Ford had engaged each other in three nationally televised debates, though they were something less than classic examples of the form, and all that had emerged was the vague impression that both were probably fairly decent men, that Carter was probably better looking, that Ford was substantially taller than Carter, and that Carter was probably quicker on his feet than the President. There were no real lessons about Carter to be learned from the debate, other than, like other mortals, he could be nervous, his mouth could turn to cotton and his voice could break from the strain.

The campaign itself had produced little more than that. Through it all, Carter had managed to maintain with little deviation the course that he had charted so many months before. He had not spoken of faults but rather of possibilities, and he had constantly laid the burden for American failures not on the American people but on leaders who did not sense and believe in the goodness and the potential of the people. In any other moment in American politics, it might have been a weak thesis on which to build and wage a national campaign, but in 1976, it was precisely the theme required. For any other candidate, perhaps, it might have been a foolish course, but given Carter's flexible credentials, it was ideal. He had finally stretched the process of becoming to its ultimate political limits. He had been right all along. In the twilight gray of a national scandal, he had been perceived as Jimmy Sunshine; in an era of political hackery and chicanery and venality and theft, he had been perceived as Honest Jimmy. Yet, they were only perceptions.

"I guess it's okay now to tell them you're a Marxist, right?" Powell had joked with Carter on the night of his victory—and as in so much of Powell's humor, there were sediments of truth. Like most of those who had known and watched the rising of Jimmy Carter, Powell realized there was more to the man than his candidacy had revealed.

"Or maybe less," Lillian suggested the next day, her face crinkling and cracking with her smile. "Who knows?"

On the night of his victory, however, such questions seemed pointless. He had flown back to Plains from Atlanta after the certainty of his election was known, and he had arrived in the early dawn of a cold November day, wading through a teeming crowd of hundreds who had waited all through the chilly night to greet him. He was fifty-two years old. It had been more than three decades since he had left Plains for Annapolis and more than twenty years since he had come home to watch his father die, sitting there beside his bed, making talk, avoiding real talk, sharing little except his name. It had been sixteen years since his first taste of politics—sixteen years in which he had become a father again and a grandfather for the first time and watched his eldest son go off to war and tried and failed to become governor and been born again and won the governorship and traveled all over the country, napping on planes and writing thank-you notes and speeches on planes and washing his socks and underwear in motel bathrooms and hanging them on the shower-curtain rods to dry—and that night, exhausted with the price of his victory, he had seemed at last at home with his roots.

He stood silently on the platform of the old depot where he had hawked his peanuts as a skinny kid and looked around the little town that would never be the same again, glancing down toward the one block of stores and the railroad tracks stretching east toward Americus and west toward Archery, noticing three old hound dogs loitering and stretching in the early-morning sun. He looked down into the crowd of faces staring as with one eye toward him and he discovered so many that he recognized, that he had known for so many years of his changing life—the faces of people he had liked and disliked, the faces of customers and competitors, the faces of long-ago boys and girls he had gone to school with and fought with and played with—and there beside him, watching him with equal intensity, stood Rosalynn, looking gaunt and haggard despite the plastic surgery she had chosen to have before the campaign, and Billy, pleased with his brother's success but anxious for his own, and Lillian, the strangely perplexing woman James Earl Carter, Sr., had found so fascinating so many years before, her snowy hair mussed from the night's celebration, her wizened countenance glowing with inestimable pride—and Jimmy Carter cried. It was a quick venting of himself and it vanished in a moment, like a man's breath on a cold day, but the tears had been there, nevertheless, in a rush of pleasure and pride and regret he could not stem.

Jimmy Carter had finally come home to Plains with something he and his father might have talked about.

He would not cry again in public until the last Wednesday of the summer of 1977.

It had been a busy, exhausting eight months for the new Administration, and Carter, riding the crest of a new President's natural popularity, had increased his capital considerably by investing skillfully in symbols. Following the general outlines of a memorandum prepared for him by Patrick Caddell, his pollster, he began building an Administration that emphasized style over substance. Carter understood the potential as few men who had held the office ever had. He worked hard at establishing himself in the eyes of the public as a common man, just another American hired to do a particular job. He banned most of the pomp and ceremony traditional in and around the White House. "Ruffles and Flourishes" and "Hail to the Chief" quickly became back numbers. His senior assistants, who had expected to have door-to-door limousine privileges, drove their own cars to work every day instead. He put the mammoth Presidential limousine—purchased during the Nixon Administration—in mothballs and rode in a more modest sedan. He delivered a fireside chat (the fire died as he spoke) wearing a cardigan sweater and an open-necked shirt, and he traveled widely in the country, appearing at town meetings in Massachusetts and Mississippi, tromping down dusty roads in the drought-parched San Joaquin Valley of California, staying overnight with unfamous families in unpretentious homes. He spent an entire Saturday afternoon answering questions from people who phoned the White House, sagaciously choosing Walter Cronkite to answer the phone for him, and he gave picnics for members of Congress on the South Lawn of the mansion grounds, showing up in denims and polo shirts, and the country seemed to love it.

He held two press conferences a month—just as he had promised—and he was as smooth and as apparently candid as he had been in the campaign, getting more comfortable with each appearance before the press corps and beneath the warm lights, making himself sufficiently vulnerable to hang around afterward for a barrage of questions from reporters who had never before experienced such openness. There was much to admire in the new President. He gave himself so thoroughly, so completely to the job, and the White House began spewing out in rapid fire a succession of legislative proposals that dazzled even the most calloused of Congressmen. He wanted a new energy department and he got it, and promptly named another familiar face to head it: James Schlesinger, former CIA chief and former Secretary of Defense. He wanted the same sort of reorganization authority he had enjoyed in Georgia—the reverse-veto arrangement that allowed him to order changes in the bureaucracy that would become permanent if Congress did not officially object—and he got it. He went on television and told the country that his energy program would be the moral equivalent of war. He launched a move to produce legislation for tax reform and he sent his welfare-reform package to Capitol Hill, relenting a bit and asking for more money than required for the old programs.

He seemed to be interested in everything in the country— the preservation of whales, the fate of the American shoe industry, land and water conservation, the nuclear submarine corps that Rickover still led, the plight of the American farmer (he had three or four to lunch at the White House) and the life of the civil servant. He visited every department in the federal government and talked about the partnership he perceived in their work. He would keep some of his promises, too. He declined to allow any further development of the controversial B-1 bomber. He pardoned Vietnam era draft resisters and instituted a Pentagon-managed program for upgrading discharges. Still, as enigmatic as ever, he approved the development of a "neutron" bomb, a weapon that was lethal to animal life, including humans, but only barely destructive to property. Moreover, although he had promised complete and unprecedented financial disclosure for the top-ranking members of his Administration, their official balance sheets as released by the White House were but vague suggestions as to their actual wealth, its sources and their holdings while in office.

It was difficult to pinpoint when the sheen began to fade, but by July, Vernon Jordan of the Urban League and other black leaders around the country had begun to criticize and complain and to accuse him of being insensitive to the needs of American minorities, of not moving with any dispatch or passion to reduce unemployment among young black people, of concentrating his Presidency on foreign affairs, rather than domestic needs. They were right. Like other Presidents before him, Carter found the lure of statecraft difficult to resist. Within a few months of his inauguration, he initiated a phalanx of new policies for Africa, for the Middle East, for the Soviet Union, for the Far East. They had little success. Vance was rebuffed curtly by the Soviets in Geneva and the Strategic Arms Limitation Talks stalled immediately. Vance followed Kissinger and Nixon and Ford to China, and came back with only souvenirs. Carter began stressing "human rights" as an international issue, attracting great attention as a President of the United States who reached beyond its boundaries with his compassion and concern for man's basic obligations to man. For the most part, though, he used "human rights" negatively, criticizing countries already unfriendly to the United States, but remaining mute on the deprivation of the rights of Chileans and Filipinos and South Koreans.

By late summer, Carter was living proof of his thesis that no one in public office can maintain a constant level of public popularity. Then came Lance. As Carter had tried to draw a line through history with his inaugural address and his walk down Pennsylvania Avenue from the Capitol to the White House, so Bert Lance's troubles—and, in turn, Jimmy Carter's troubles—provided a distinctive punctuation mark to the Carter Administration.

On Tuesday afternoon of that last week of summer, Jimmy and Bert played tennis, and then as the sun went down, they sat in wooden chairs beside the White House court and talked about what had happened to them. Lance still seemed undecided about what to do. Carter gently guided him toward resignation. There was no decision. Lance dressed in his offices in the Old Executive Office Building next door to the White House and went home early for a change. Over dinner, LaBelle told him he should not quit. Over dinner at the White House, Rosalynn asked Jimmy when Bert would resign.

Early Wednesday morning, Carter tiptoed from the second-floor bedroom again, already showered, shaved and dressed before the sun rose, and talked again with Lance in the little study next to the Oval Office. Lance had decided to resign; he told the President he thought it was in the best interests of the Administration and the country. "I agree," Carter said. "I'm sorry, but I agree." They knelt together and prayed as they had done so often before. "But first I have to talk to LaBelle again," Lance added as he left.

The President said nothing.

At noon, Lance uncharacteristically went home to his rented town house in Georgetown. Later, he and his wife emerged and drove to the White House together. He was still not telling anyone what he planned to do. "Whatever it is will be God's will," he said. At the White House, Lance and LaBelle and Carter talked again. She left. Lance went to his office. Powell announced that the press conference would be delayed two hours. When it finally began in a crowded auditorium next door to the White House, there were tears in the President's eyes. His friend, his closest friend—his brother, he called him—was quitting.

He answered a few questions, almost perfunctorily, and then without waiting for the traditional "Thank you, Mr. President" from the senior correspondent present, he turned on his heel and left.

The next day, the White House announced an eight-nation, four-continent, ten-day whirlwind foreign trip for the President in the winter. On the first Sunday of autumn, he went to a black church in Washington. The guest preacher was a stocky old black man who shook the rafters with his fire and brimstone. Outside, after the services, the old black man put his arms around the President. "Jimmy Carter's a great man," said Martin Luther King, Sr.